SCANDAL AT THE SAVOY

SCANDAL AT THE SAVOY

The Infamous 1920s Murder Case

ANDREW ROSE

BLOOMSBURY

First published in Great Britain 1991
Bloomsbury Publishing Limited, 2 Soho Square, London W1V 5DE
Copyright © 1991 by Andrew Rose

The moral right of the author has been asserted

A CIP catalogue record for this book
is available from the British Library

ISBN 0-7475-0858-5

10 9 8 7 6 5 4 3 2 1

PICTURE SOURCES
The British Library: pages 2 *top & bottom*, 3, 5, 6 *centre & bottom*, 7 *top*
Popperfoto: pages 1, 8

Photoset by Rowland Phototypesetting Limited
Bury St Edmunds, Suffolk
Printed and bound in Great Britain by
Butler and Tanner Limited, Frome and London

For James

'He was a weak man. She was strong enough.'

Said Enani, private secretary and
confidant, at the inquest on Ali
Fahmy Bey, 12 July 1923.

Contents

Acknowledgements

My thanks are due to the following for their assistance: the British Library; the Public Record Office; the Courts Administrator, Central Criminal Court (Miss M. E. Lightbown, formerly Assistant Courts Administrator); the Chief Registrar and Departmental Record Officer, New Scotland Yard (Mr J. H. S. Hurworth); the Savoy Hotel Archive (Miss Rosemary Ashbee); the School of Infantry and Small Arms Corps Museum, Warminster (Major John Oldfield, retd); Le Chef de Service, Mairie du XIVième Arrondissement, Paris; the British Vintage Wireless Museum, Dulwich (Mr Gerald Wells); the Vintage Motorcycle Club Ltd (Mr P. Heath); the Librarian, English National Opera; the Theatre Museum, Covent Garden; the National Railway Museum, York; the Post Office Archives; and the Wellcome Medical Library. Particular thanks go to James Todd, who has been, as ever, an invaluable source of help and information on a host of matters.

Introduction

On a chilly October afternoon, a young man hurried away from Marischal College and across the centre of Aberdeen to the Joint Station. He was eighteen, a second-year medical student, and this was the first day of the Winter Session, Wednesday 10 October 1923. He arrived just in time to catch the little train, which wheezed a painfully slow progress along the Peterhead line, through Kittybrewster, Dyce and Newmachar, and on to Udny Station, taking three quarters of an hour to travel eleven miles.

Monday's storm had uprooted trees, sent tiles flying and brought down chimneystacks. 'A hurricane in Buchan,' was the local hyperbole, a reference to the bleak, treeless plain that forms much of the north-east shoulder of Scotland. But today, in calmer conditions, the young man had no immediate fear of being blown off his new motorcycle.

He pulled a leather helmet from the pocket of his trenchcoat, much like the headgear worn by the great air aces of the Western Front, and substituted it for his tweed cap. He was already wearing gauntlet gloves, and completed his equipage with a pair of goggles. The machine, a two-and-a-half-horsepower Connaught, was retrieved from the rear of Sandy Mair's grocery shop, which served the little hamlet around the station and the scattered farming community beyond. He turned a tap, flooding the carburettor with petrol, and pedalled the engine into life.

The low-powered motorcycle bore him along at a stately pace, with one interruption, when the belt drive, always an awkward fitment, slipped off and had to be put back on again. Light was beginning to fade as he turned into the driveway of his home, but it was not yet dark enough to

1

require the fiddly task of lighting the acetylene lamps, recently fitted to the machine in anticipation of the long Scottish winter.

With scarcely a nod to his aunts, he was in his bedroom, where all had been made ready for the evening's big event. That night, the Aberdeen broadcasting station of the British Broadcasting Company was due to open at 6.50 p.m., call-sign 2BD, on 493 metres. For weeks, the local press had been full of features about the new studio in Belmont Street, which would give Aberdeen its own transmitter, putting the Granite City on a par with London, Birmingham, Manchester and Glasgow. Monday's storm had brought down the Post Office landline rigged up for the grand opening, and frantic repair work was completed only just in time.

Using the details set out in one of the many magazines devoted to wireless, the young man had built his own crystal receiving set; a simple affair, with a small crystal of mineral ore, about seven millimetres in diameter, held in a metal ring, screwed sideways into a holder and set in a glass tube. At the other end of the tube was a thin coiled wire (the 'cat's whisker') attached to a brass rod and a movable clamp. Prodding about on the rugged surface of the crystal would eventually detect an area receptive to radio signals transmitted up to twenty miles away. The addition of a valve or valves could increase the range – a two-valve set might receive signals within a hundred-mile radius – but such items were expensive and the young man had to be content with the limitations of his crystal set.

The previous day, he had strung an aerial the best part of eighty feet from the bedroom window, attaching it to the gutter of the steading opposite. The set had to be earthed, too, and he had buried the line in a tin outside the conservatory.

When the appointed time arrived, he put on a pair of headphones and poked about the crystal, with its sparkling points on a craggy grey surface. But to no avail. He heard nothing. Nothing at all. Perhaps fortunately, he missed the eldritch skirl of the bagpipes that introduced the broadcast, nor did he hear the rambling address of the Marquess of Aberdeen and Temair, worrying that the Devil might 'get a finger in the pie' of broadcasting. And the young man was deprived of the chance to listen to the band of the 2nd Battalion, Gordon Highlanders, ending the evening with dance tunes, including the season's rage, 'Yes! We Have No Bananas', whose banal chorus was bravely taken up by the crowd who had gathered around Walker's Broad Street showroom in the centre of Aberdeen.

INTRODUCTION

Next morning, a crestfallen visitor, on his way to Udny station and his medical class, called at the house of Dr M'Keggie, the local GP and wireless enthusiast. The problem was soon identified and solved. The earth lead should have been connected to a cold-water pipe. That done, the young man could hear the second night's broadcasting from 2BD with great clarity in those days of uncluttered airwaves. But he was again to be disappointed, for the programme, exceedingly solemn, featured a Verdi opera relayed from Birmingham and a truly awful concert from Glasgow. This was no compensation for missing what, as he knew, was available to London listeners. Between 9.45 and 10.45 p.m., they could hear dance music relayed directly from the ballroom of the Savoy Hotel in London, played by the newly created Savoy Orpheans.

The young man had already heard the 80 rpm gramophone records, recorded by the Savoy Havana Band, at the hotel since late 1921. Now there were to be two resident bands, each playing and broadcasting the latest dance crazes. To someone who had never visited London, let alone the luxurious Savoy, there was an enormous fascination in the hotel's very name, as well as in the promise and excitement of the dance music. And something else had recently brought the great hotel into the headlines, in a welter of sensational and unsought publicity. That summer, at the height of a raging thunderstorm, a twenty-two-year-old Egyptian playboy had been shot dead at the Savoy by his French-born wife, very much a woman of the world in her beautiful gowns and jewels.

Newspaper accounts of her trial for murder revealed a mode of life which, with its luxury and thinly veiled hints of vice, by turns duly horrified and fascinated the good, *couthy*, Calvinist folk of Aberdeenshire. The *Aberdeen Press & Journal* had reported the matter in considerable detail: great notoriety was added to the glamour of the Savoy, a heady mixture for those brought up to draw their blinds on the Sabbath and hearken only unto the Kirk.

On the following Monday night, 15 October 1923, Aberdeen enjoyed a 'Simultaneous Broadcast' relayed by landline from London, and the young man could at last hear the Savoy Orpheans broadcasting loud and clear, direct from the Savoy Hotel. The reception would have been a little mechanical, rather tinny, by modern standards, but one listener, at least, was not disappointed by what he heard.

The young man was my father, who kept the original crystal and cat's whisker used so many years ago. I have them still. Both my parents remembered the trial of Madame Fahmy, the subject of this book, though

3

I doubt if they were aware of the seamier details of a story in which high life and low life were inextricably mixed.

I have long been fascinated by the Twenties, a febrile decade in a Europe still shellshocked from the Great War, and take great delight in the more bizarre manifestations of the period, some of which surfaced in the Fahmy case. Accompanied by outrageous fashions and the staccato rhythm of syncopated dance music, this is a true story every bit as dramatic as anything in the lurid popular fiction of its time, the 'shilling shockers' which exploited the 'East meets West' theme to the full.

A European woman on trial for her life; a bestial Eastern husband; enormous riches; the terrifying dénouement of a tempestuous marriage; shots fired amid thunder and lightning; violent death in one of the world's greatest hotels – all these elements combined to make the trial of Madame Marguerite Fahmy the sensation of the decade.

But accounts of this trial, at the Old Bailey in September 1923, are few and woefully incomplete. This is, I believe, the first full-length study of the case. An early reason for the dearth of such literature probably lay in the allegations which Madame Fahmy had made about her husband's sexual conduct and orientation, matters very much taboo in the 1920s and long after. Furthermore, the case is not in any way a whodunit. Madame Fahmy shot her husband dead with her own gun. Rather, it is a 'how' and a 'whydunit', whose interest lies as much in the awkward questions of sex and race that English society was forced to confront as in the drama of its narrative.

I first became interested in Madame Fahmy when reading the 1929 biography of Marshall Hall, written by Edward Marjoribanks. His account of the trial is fragmentary and very partisan, but enough was revealed to interest me, and when the time came to choose a subject for my second book, Madame Fahmy, with her remarkable story, demanded my attention.

Marguerite Fahmy is inevitably the central character of this story, a woman who started her life at the bottom of the heap and by her toughness and determination became rich, if not always happy. In the autumn of 1923 she faced the prospect of execution by hanging for a *crime passionnel*, an offence unknown to the English penal code, which bleakly charged her with capital murder.

Two men, one a young millionaire, the other a great advocate in his mid-sixties, play the main supporting roles. Rich, handsome, feckless, bisexual Ali Fahmy, a man who could have taken his pick of Egyptian beauty, fell in love and endured a brief tortured relationship with an older woman of volatile temperament. Marshall Hall, at the height of his fame but in poor health, briefed for the defence in this most sensational of murder cases, would fight ferociously for his client, giving one of the finest performances of his long career at the Bar. The barnstorming courtroom tactics of this old pro should raise a smile, but his use of racism and homophobia in his client's cause is a less amusing characteristic, reflecting a stubbornly illiberal streak in English society.

The image of that society is well reflected in contemporary journalism. The 1923 equivalents of today's tabloid press reveal prejudices about sexuality and race which foreshadow those of our time. Not much has changed. We still have newspapers which trumpet a crusading bigotry, just as their predecessors did in the Twenties. I have included a number of examples, from both the press and popular literature, in an attempt to illustrate the public's racial perceptions – of the 'crafty Oriental' in particular – and how newspapers treated the even trickier subject of sex, a subject which the English never quite seem to have taken on board.

Experience in defending and prosecuting criminal cases for nearly twenty years has proved invaluable in assessing the evidence for and against Madame Fahmy. I have tried to avoid the pitfalls that so often beset true crime writers. For example, many lawyer-authors have placed excessive reliance on courtroom dialogue, assuming a knowledge of and interest in forensic procedure which the average reader may well not possess. Other writers hope that scenes in court, easily culled from transcripts (where available) and newspaper reports, make up for the necessary, time-consuming background research.

Though the case was widely reported, few court documents have survived and I was lucky to be the first member of the public allowed to see the Metropolitan Police file, now deposited in the Public Record Office at Kew. These papers contain, among other valuable source material, much previously hidden detail about Madame Fahmy's colourful early life, facts which did not emerge in court.

My research has not been a completely dry-as-dust affair. Many tedious hours were spent poring over old newspapers at the British Library in Colindale, but one highlight was a visit to the School of Infantry and Small Arms School Corps Museum at Warminster, in Wiltshire, where I examined and handled the type of Browning semi-automatic pistol used by Madame Fahmy to shoot her husband; a trip to Paris enabled me to wander around some of her old haunts and visit the site of her birthplace; the British Vintage Wireless Museum laid on a delightful demonstration of a crystal set; and my own collection of battered gramophone records by the Savoy Orpheans and Savoy Havana Band has been pressed into service from time to time by way of glorious inspiration.

1

England 1923

'The 1923 Season has begun,' declared the *Daily Mail* in the middle of a dismally wet April brightened only by the wedding of Lady Elizabeth Bowes-Lyon to the Duke of York. Prince Albert, 'Bertie', was the King's second son and the first of four surviving brothers to get married. On the night of the wedding, the principal chef at the Savoy Hotel, M. François Latry, distinguished successor to the incomparable Escoffier, had prepared such unlikely delights as *Poussin de printemps Glamis Castle* and *Fraises glacées Elizabeth.* The London County Council's Entertainment Licensing Committee graciously allowed the Savoy's patrons to dance until 2.00 a.m. the following morning.

For the new Season, more dances and receptions were planned than in any year since the golden year of 1914 and, if the April newspapers were correct – an unlikely assumption – 130,000 American tourists were expected in London at any minute.

The war, of course, had been the great divide. Britain's various Expeditionary Forces had been literally decimated: one in ten had been killed – some 800,000 young men – and the overall casualty figure was one third of the enlisted total. Though France, Germany and Russia had suffered proportionately worse losses, the psychological impact of the war on British society was immense. If the crass lyrics of 'It's a Long Way to Tipperary' had epitomized the thoughtless mood of 1914, its glum post-war successor was 'I'm Forever Blowing Bubbles', an artless elegy for lost youth and vanished hope.

The brief post-war boom had temporarily shielded demobbed soldiers from the unemployment that would become so persistent a feature of the interwar years. Already in 1923 over a million people were out of work. That August, an unemployed ex-Colour Sergeant of Marines leapt to his death from a road bridge in Kent. A pawn ticket for eight wartime medals was found on his body.

In the early Twenties there was a fierce determination, if not to forget the war, at any rate to try to get back to normal, a pervasive nostalgia for the world before 1914, perhaps prompted by the thought, however absurd, that it was something that the boys who had died in Flanders and Mesopotamia would have wanted. Newspapers and magazines habitually drew comparisons between life pre- and post-war, usually to the detriment of the present, which was depicted as shallow and decadent.

Many saw inspiration in what Signor Mussolini had done for Italy since coming to power the previous October. The podgy dictator had no more fervent admirer than Lord Rothermere, proprietor of the *Daily Mail* group of newspapers. 'This young, vigorous ardent Italian,' wrote the noble lord in 1923, 'did more than save Italy . . . he saved the whole Western world . . . The idea that he is a blustering, flag-waving agitator is foolishly wrong . . .' Lord Rothermere was particularly impressed by the Duce's 'caution . . . skill and . . . gentleness . . .' Throughout the Twenties, articles in the *Daily Mail, Evening News* and *Sunday Pictorial* habitually extolled Mussolini's supposed virtues. Rothermere was not the only fan: Lord Curzon, then British Foreign Secretary, saluted Italy's 'strong man' in February 1923 and a year later Winston Churchill declared himself 'favourably impressed' by the Duce's speech to a Fascist Congress.

More bizarre support came from Sir Gerald du Maurier, the matinée idol, in an address to the Harrow (School) Luncheon Club at the Savoy Hotel on 12 July 1923. He wanted to see the great public schools form 'a freemasonry [sic] which, in these troubled times, will create a sort of Ku-Klux-Klan or Fascisti for public schoolboys to restore England once more to law and order'. And Lord Beaverbrook's *Daily Express* was not far behind its arch-rival in the pro-Mussolini stakes. In what must be one of the earliest references to an enduring myth, a correspondent of that newspaper wrote reverentially of Mussolini as 'a realist who gets things done . . . There is something changed in . . . Italy. One feels it in the very air. Travellers remark on it . . . "Why, have you noticed, the train is on time!"'

In contrast to the machismo of Mussolini's fascism, British youth was seen as decidedly effete. Expressions of concern at this perception were sometimes oddly worded. A clergyman, preaching at Windsor in

September 1923, was worried that many young men were being 'lured by the attraction of the opposite sex to the tennis court and the foxtrot, when they ought to be playing cricket'. At Oxford, the Rector of St Aldate's, later to become well known as Bishop Chavasse, roundly condemned contemporary morals, complaining bitterly that 'girls go about [today] as if to attract men'.

The war had removed thousands of females from domestic labour into an industrial workforce which had been, in the past, a largely male affair. But with the coming of an uneasy peace and chronic unemployment, it was 'last in, first out' and women were expected to return without complaint to household drudgery.

Some people were surprised that women did not want to go back to such elevating work as domestic service. By 1923 there was indeed a shortage of servants. A parlourmaid might, if she was lucky, get £30 a year and her keep, with precious few holidays, while a cook's wages hovered between £40 and £50. The *Daily Mail* was in no doubt about the solution. 'Thousands upon thousands of women are drawing the dole, when they ought to be in domestic service,' it declared, adding that women capable of such work should have their dole money stopped. The dole, in any case, was 'driving a wedge of socialism into the social structure and destroying the foundations of individual effort'.

There was a widespread and persistent feeling that moral standards were in decline. In July 1923, the Bishop of Durham had stated that sexual morality was 'on the brink of complete disintegration'. The same month, the self-appointed inspectorate of the London Council for the Promotion of Public Morality was duly scandalized by what it found going on that summer in London's parks and open spaces. The contemporary equivalents of today's tabloid press played the old English game of prudery and prurience: that year, transvestism seems to have been Grub Street's favourite sin, with lurid reports of cross-dressing in Surrey and Wiltshire. Sensational news of a bank robber in drag filtered across the Atlantic from Chicago.

The President of the Methodist Conference warned that 'the nation's girlhood is exposed to terrible risks of alcoholism, indulgence, midnight follies and . . . licentiousness'. The proprietors of the Metropole Hotel, in London's Northumberland Avenue, would have taken umbrage at one, at least, of these strictures, for 'Midnight Follies' was the name of a cabaret entertainment, of more or less complete propriety, which the hotel had provided with outstanding success since the previous year. On Tuesdays, Thursdays and Fridays, the maximum number of late nights allowed by the LCC under its new powers of regulation, patrons paid thirty shillings to dine, dance and watch two cabaret turns ending at 12.30 a.m.

The war had brought in all manner of restrictions on social life, not least in the retailing of alcoholic drinks. Before the war, public houses in London could stay open till 12.30 a.m. during the week and midnight on Saturdays, but after 1915 opening hours were severely curtailed. The supposedly temporary wartime restrictions were crystallized in 1921 into a Licensing Act born of an unholy alliance in Parliament between total abstainers and the 'beerage', as the brewing lobby had become known. London's weekday closing time became 11.00 p.m., but, as so often in England, a class distinction crept into the draft legislation, and the 'theatre-supper clause' was inserted, providing for a 'Supper Hour Certificate' whereby the well-to-do were granted an hour's extra drinking time by paying for the meal that was a legally required accompaniment to the liquor.

The Metropole had been one of the first hotels to take advantage of the new clause, but others soon followed suit, and in 1923 a majority of the great hotels provided dinner-dance facilities, competing for business with nightclubs proper such as Ciro's, the Embassy, Murray's Club, the Grafton Galleries, the Queen's Hall Roof and, most exclusive of all, the Riviera Club, which overlooked the Thames from its elegant rooms in Grosvenor Road.

During the war, clubs of all kinds, authorized or unlawful, had mushroomed in the West End, catering for the hordes of restless young servicemen on leave in Town. Many of the clubs were simply unlicensed drinking dens or, like 'Ma Meyrick's' notorious '43' club in Gerrard Street, simply flouted the rules. Some were illegal casinos, some were what would today be called clip-joints and a few catered discreetly for homosexual men, a feared and despised minority, which, according to the populist weekly *John Bull*, 'should be hunted out of clean and decorous society'. Some clubs tolerated drug use: cocaine was widely available on the streets and cannabis (or 'hashish', as it was then called) was beginning to catch on, not yet on the list of prohibited substances. The popular press, which regularly ran sensational features alleging a drug menace, almost invariably associated it with black people.

By 1923, London had already a sizeable community of African or Afro-Caribbean origin. The term 'black' at that time was used indiscriminately to embrace virtually anyone with a skin darker than pink. Thus Egyptians were 'coloured' or 'black', as were people from the Indian

Empire. Indeed, almost the entire population south of the Mediterranean and east of Suez, as far as south-east Asia, was liable to be so described. And the references to these 'black' people in the British press make dismal reading. 'BLACK DEVILS AND WHITE GIRLS', headlined *John Bull* that autumn, alleging that 'coloured men are still lurking in our cities, living depraved lives on the immoral earnings of the white girls they have lured to their betrayal'.

In London, these 'degenerate negroes' lived in the streets off Tottenham Court Road and the eastern end of Shaftesbury Avenue, areas 'honeycombed with black men's . . . nightclubs . . . and thieving lodging houses . . . They run gambling houses, they trade in dope, they spread disease . . .' This crude racism was by no means confined to *John Bull*. Many other papers carried regular features which told of 'negro haunts of crime . . . hotbeds of evil', usually linked with drug-taking and prostitution, sometimes adding, for good measure, that an accused black man was 'a member of a jazz band'.

An unmistakable note of sour sexual jealousy can be detected, amid the racial stereotyping and reports of 'flashily-dressed, bejewelled negroes', the men who, as a shocked *Daily Mail* reported in September 1923, were found to be dancing with white women at the ironically named British Colonial Club in Whitfield Street, Soho. These revelations came about during a prosecution for the serious offence of serving liquor after hours: an Old Bailey judge observed that there was nothing unlawful in black men and white women 'congregating' there, but the foreman of the all-white jury was not impressed by this dangerous liberalism. 'These clubs should be abolished,' he said in an uncompromising rider to the jury's verdict.

The principal feature of London life in 1923 that distinguished it from the pre-war world was the extraordinary popularity of dancing. During the war, ragtime rhythm had begun to make way for jazz influences, usually very watered-down versions of what could be heard played so boldly by the Afro-Americans of New Orleans and Chicago. There were 'jazz bands' playing in London during 1919, the year of a successful tour by the all-white Original Dixieland Jazz Band.

In 1920, Bulldog Drummond, the loutish creation of Sapper, could boast that he and a girlfriend had 'jazzed together' but what is now thought of as traditional jazz had little to do with British dance music of the early Twenties. Popular tunes were played in a way which betrayed the influence of homegrown brass and military bands. Contemporary recordings, made by musicians crowding around a large horn in a primitive recording studio, make the music seem as mechanical as the recording technique itself.

The tunes were often catchy and robust, but there seems to have been a brittleness about popular music at this time: certainly, by 1923, people were dancing to a repertoire that consisted almost entirely of the jerky, staccato foxtrot and the very similar rhythm of the onestep. The sentimental waltz, often spelt 'valse', and the tango, by then rather old hat, made up the balance. One bonus was that the inelegant contortions of the shimmy-shake, which had taken New York by storm in 1919 and had dominated the next two or three seasons in Europe, began to give way in 1923 to less anti-social steps: in July, the 'blues', or 'blues trot', made its appearance in London ballrooms, a foxtrot played 'a quarter slower . . . and jazzed up with quaint effect', though this proved to be merely a temporary lull before the arrival of the super-athletic, shin-bruising Charleston some eighteen months later.

The popularity of dancing in this early post-war period has never since been equalled. Early in July 1923, the *Daily Mail*'s editorial noted disapprovingly that 'everyone now dances on almost every possible occasion. Dancing teas, dancing dinners and dancing suppers . . . succeed one another in a giddy whirl . . .' The *Observer* reported that 'almost every West End hotel runs a dinner dance and in many cases a tea dance as well . . .' An 'old-fashioned mother' warned 'our girls are losing that freshness of appearance' by dancing too much. A 'Harley Street woman specialist' was of the opinion that 'a great deal of evil . . . goes on in the modern dance hall' and a psychoanalyst informed readers of *Lloyd's Sunday News* that modern consulting rooms were filled with 'dance-hall wrecks'. Despite this alleged risk to life and limb, as well as the comparatively poor quality of gramophone records, the young loved to dance.

One spur to the new dancing craze was the coming of radio. The London station of the British Broadcasting Company began regular broadcasts on 14 November 1922 from studios in the Strand, on the site now occupied by Bush House. The first dance music was transmitted just before Christmas that year and it soon became a regular broadcast feature. The Savoy Havana Band made its broadcasting debut on 13 April 1923 and a month later the 2 L O Dance Band, an in-house outfit, went on the air from the Savoy Hill studios, to which the BBC had moved in February. The new headquarters was conveniently situated across a narrow street from the Savoy Hotel and even shared the same electrical generator, so it was not surprising that the Savoy's bands were frequently broadcast from October 1923.

ENGLAND 1923

An overhead microphone was fitted to the ceiling of the Savoy's ballroom and a BBC announcer in full evening dress waited backstage to announce the numbers that had been played, poised to operate a cut-out switch if any of the dancing couples misbehaved and tried to shout something undesirable into the microphone. If one early announcer is to be believed, it was not shouted obscenities that were feared, but a much graver possibility, stigmatized, in a very English way, as 'the chance of a possible advertisement'.

2

Imperial Palace

On the morning of Sunday 1 July 1923, a chauffeur-driven limousine turned into Savoy Court, the short street that leads to the Strand entrance of the Savoy Hotel, and drew up underneath a flying stone arch. After the doorman had done his duty, a woman and two men alighted and made their way through the revolving doors. Their stay at the Savoy would prove to be an eventful one.

The trio, who had travelled from Paris overnight, were known to the hotel reception staff as the Prince and Princess Fahmy, accompanied by a Mr Said Enani. The prince was twenty-two, handsome and a reputed millionaire in his native Egypt; his elegantly dressed Parisian wife was all of ten years older. They had been married for six months. Mr Enani was twenty-nine and had already served as the prince's private secretary for some five years.

Reservation of a suite had been made in advance by telegram from Paris and a further wire alerted the General Manager, M. Gelardi, late of Claridge's Hotel, that the princely entourage would be arriving at the Savoy that morning, after the crossing from Le Havre to Southampton, which connected with the Waterloo boat-train.

The prince had stayed at the Savoy early in 1922 and as he was known to be extremely rich it is likely that he and his wife were received by Gelardi himself, whose immaculate appearance included morning coat, wing-collar and cravat. Greeted courteously and appropriately in French (the prince spoke French, English, Turkish and Arabic, Madame Fahmy only French), they were shepherded to a carpeted lift, in which a uniformed attendant escorted them to the fourth floor of Savoy Court.

As they emerged, they could see the door to their suite, number 41, on the opposite side of the corridor, slightly to their right.

Savoy Court had formed part of an ambitious expansion programme in the early years of the century. It was said to have been the first block of service flats in England and was built on a site adjoining the hotel to the east, behind the famous restaurant Simpsons in the Strand, which the hotel had operated since 1904. Some of the suites were leased to tenants on a long-term basis, but others, like number 41, were available for shorter periods. The prince had indicated that he and his wife intended to remain until the end of the month, when the Goodwood races would bring the English Season to a close and Society would emigrate either to the grouse moors or to Continental resorts such as Deauville and Le Touquet.

The Fahmys' suite was decorated in the pastiche of the Adam style then popular. Immediately to their right lay a spacious drawing-room with, in the words of the English popular novelist Arnold Bennett, 'brocaded upholstery everywhere, multiplicity of lamps, multiplicity of cushions, multiplicity of occasional tables; everywhere an exquisite softness . . .' On a desk heavy with gilt and ormolu, lay a three-signal bell plate bearing the legend 'Waiter – Valet – Maid'. The Fahmys, like others of the Twenties rich, had brought their own servants with them. In Paris, the previous October, Madame had engaged her current personal maid, Mlle Aimée Pain. Aimée had a room on the eighth floor of the hotel, sharing accommodation with other guests' servants.

The hotel provided a non-resident valet, Albert Dowding – he lived in Sharratt Street, Bermondsey, five miles and a world away from the Savoy – who had a general responsibility for the fourth floor suites, but the prince was accompanied by his personal valet, an illiterate eighteen-year-old Sudanese youth, quite black and just five feet tall. As was the custom in Egypt, he spent much of his time crouched in the hallway outside his master's door, patiently waiting to be commanded. The couple would be driven about London by Madame's chauffeur, Eugène Barbay, who had charge of her two limousines in Paris and who was also responsible for exercising her dearly loved lapdog, an ugly little beast.

The entrance to the suite was formed by a set of double doors, one of which opened outwards into the hotel corridor. A marbled bathroom stood immediately opposite the entrance, to the left of which lay a short passage, leading to the principal bedroom, its double bed covered in silk sheets, on which in Bennett's description of the hotel, guests sometimes

15

lay 'private embroidered pillows'. It would have been very much her room, for her young husband chose to sleep in the second, slightly smaller bedroom next to the bathroom. From the suite, looking down to Savoy Place, there was a view of the river, which lay beyond the broad sweep of the Victoria Embankment with its continual noisy flow of cars, lorries and trams. Eastwards the elegant but crumbling Georgian structure of Waterloo Bridge spanned the river, on the other side of which stood the new Waterloo Station and, like a lighthouse that had lost its way, the Shot Tower, a stumpy London landmark of the time.

The Savoy Hotel is the creation of Richard D'Oyly Carte – impresario to Gilbert and Sullivan – who, it seems, hit upon the bright idea that the increasing number of American visitors to London, many of whom had enjoyed Gilbert and Sullivan at the Savoy Theatre, would welcome the chance to stay at a luxurious hotel on an adjacent site, which had, moreover, a superb view of the Thames. The new hotel opened for business on 6 August 1889 and soon, assisted by the formidable managerial talents of César Ritz and by the legendary chef Auguste Escoffier, became established as one of London's finest hotels, the equal of any in the world.

The hotel's foyer has witnessed the parade of the royal, the rich and the famous for a century, but, like any other institution, the Savoy has fallen prey to scandal from time to time. Over the years, a highly experienced and discreet management team (including, at least since the 1920s, a house detective) has succeeded in limiting public exposure of the more startling aspects of human frailty to have manifested themselves on the premises.

One early scandal arose from Oscar Wilde's stay, originally in room 361 and later in a suite of rooms, where he entertained a depressing collection of rent-boys, misplaced hospitality which formed a considerable part of the prosecution case against him at his trials in 1895. A later embarrassment for the hotel was the discovery in November 1918 of a young woman's body in the apartment she rented at Savoy Court. Billie Carlton was a twenty-two-year-old actress addicted to cocaine. She had overdosed after a night out at the Victory Ball, held in the Albert Hall to celebrate the Armistice. The inquest revealed just how widespread drug trafficking had become in London, no doubt to the consternation of the Savoy's management.

By 1923, the Wilde case was a distant memory and Billie Carlton all but forgotten. The Savoy's management was in the autocratic but highly efficient hands of George Reeves-Smith, who had become Managing

Director of the Savoy Company at the turn of the century and who would remain firmly in charge for forty years. Under his tutelage, the hotel was considerably enlarged and now boasted the lively Savoy Grill (sharp left at the Strand entrance foyer), which was crowded with business types at lunchtime and with personalities from the media and the theatre at the evening supper table.

The Savoy Grill offered its clientele no background music, but in the restaurant, with its panoramic view of the river, a sedate orchestra played 'Hungarian melodies . . . [of] melancholy sweetness', among other long-standing favourites, for a clientele unkindly described by Arnold Bennett as 'a few truly smart people and a crowd of well-dressed . . . nonentities'. Sparkling or dull as the diners might be, there was a four-course *Dîner du Jour* on offer at 15/6 (*Vin Blanc par Carafe* 3/6) or an elaborate à la carte menu, on which by far and away the most expensive item was chicken, *Poularde de France Dorothy*, at a hefty 30/-. In season, you might toy with half-a-dozen Baltimore oysters at 3/6, followed by a gamy *Râble de Lièvre Polonaise* at 8/-. Today's Savoy would be unlikely to offer diners the choice of four curries then available, but no doubt such *entremets* as crêpes Suzette or a *Coupe Jacques* (3/- each) remain as popular as ever.

The smart set, after the latest dance music, made their way along the broad corridor from the restaurant, downstairs to the magnificent ballroom, decorated in a style that cheerfully commingled Louis Quatorze with Louis Quinze, displaying a wealth of Corinthian capitals and gilded moulding. Here, Bert Ralton's Havana Band held sway, until joined by the Savoy Orpheans in October 1923. 'The monstrous and crushing absurdity of our [liquor] licensing laws' (Arnold Bennett) – Reeves-Smith was an unsuccessful campaigner for reform – and the restrictive hand of the LCC on the separate 'music and dancing' licence meant that the Savoy could offer dancing till 2.00 a.m. on only Monday, Wednesday and Friday, entertainment ceasing at about midnight on other days of the week.

Arnold Bennett came to love the Savoy so much that he wrote at the end of the decade a tribute to the hotel in his novel *Imperial Palace*. Bennett's descriptions of life in this institution of eight floors and 1300 staff are of great documentary value and from amidst the contortions of a laboured plot emerge thinly disguised pen-portraits of the Savoy's staff, many of whom had been serving at the hotel in 1923. Reeves-Smith, for example, became the elegant, world-weary Evelyn Orcham, wistfully searching for romance among the fleshpots of London and Paris; in

Maître Planquet could be seen, just as clearly, the rotund form of the great *cuisinier* François Latry; and possibly, in the guise of Reyer, the fastidious Night Manager and ex-West End actor Arthur Marini.

On the evening of their first day at the Savoy, Ali and Marguerite Fahmy dined in the hotel restaurant. Such a scene was described by Bennett in *Imperial Palace*: 'A thin stream of guests was passing from the great hall, through the foyer and into the restaurant. Other guests were sipping cocktails at small tables in the foyer . . . In the lounge were two cloak-room attendants, knee-breeched and gorgeous, who looked as if they had escaped from the court of the Prince Regent, two cocktail pages in white and gold, a foyer waiter . . . and two head waiters, who stood on the lower stairs to receive diners . . . a crowded confused scene of smart frocks, dowdy frocks, jewels genuine and sham, black coats, white shirts, white table-cloths, silver, steel, glass, coloured chairs, coloured carpets, parquet in the midst, mirrors, melody and light glistening through the crystal of chandeliers.'

Later that evening, as on all the nights she would spend in suite 41, Savoy Court, Madame Fahmy gently placed under her pillow a .32 semi-automatic Browning pistol loaded with six bullets.

3

Maggie Meller

Just before midday on 9 December 1890, a dull and chilly winter's morning on which a bitter easterly wind kept the temperature around freezing-point, a baby girl who would one day marry a millionaire and be styled a princess, was born in a poor quarter of Montparnasse, southern Paris, at 129 boulevard de Port-Royal. The baby was christened Marie Marguerite Alibert. She was the first surviving child of Firmin Alibert, a Parisian cabdriver, and his wife Marie Lauran, who worked as a charwoman, possibly for Madame Langlois, a solicitor's widow, who became the little girl's godmother. (Madame Langlois' late husband had been implicated in the notorious Humbert-Crawford fraud, which had convulsed France in 1902 and 1903.)

The child came to be known as Marguerite, and received her brief education at a Catholic school, the Convent of the Sisters of Mary, at 73 rue des Ternes, some distance from Montparnasse in the more prosperous seventeenth *arrondissement*, not far from the Arc de Triomphe. This religious upbringing suggests that her parents, unlike many others of the Parisian working-class, eschewed the bitter anticlericalism that had manifested itself with such brutality in the 1871 Commune. Indeed, one of Marguerite's aunts was said to have become a nun.

Though she later claimed to have been 'devout . . . in a mystic way, as young sensitive girls sometimes are', Marguerite seems to have fallen from her state of grace rather rapidly. At fifteen, and unmarried, she found herself pregnant. Her only daughter, Raymonde Alibert, was born at 123 boulevard de Port-Royal (possibly the foundling hospital almost next door to the Aliberts' home) on 21 January 1907. By this time Marguerite had two younger brothers and a sister, Yvonne, then about six years old.

In the straitened circumstances of the Alibert family, there were few resources to spare for Marguerite and her child. Raymonde was at first sent to an orphanage and later, when she was seven, her grandmother and aunt adopted her. They lived in Bordeaux, which Marguerite would visit from time to time when money allowed. It seems that Marguerite soon drifted onto the streets, earning her living by prostitution and by singing in cheap cafés and cabarets, much as Edith Piaf would do a generation or so later.

Although Marguerite was described at this time as 'ill-mannered', with 'no accomplishments', she must have possessed a degree of charisma, sufficient at any rate to gain access to the *Folies Bergère*, where she is known to have worked around 1912. Marguerite would have been seen front of house eyeing up likely punters, along with other working girls who walked the floor. Perhaps that was how she made the acquaintance of André Meller, a rich businessman from Bordeaux who was already married, with a child of his own, and fruitlessly asking the Church to annul an unhappy union.

André Meller and Marguerite Alibert became lovers in 1913. He set her up in a flat in the rue Pergolèse, a street in the fashionable sixteenth *arrondissement*, near the northern end of the Bois de Boulogne. Meller's brother owned a racing stable and Marguerite seems to have taken riding lessons there. It was at about this time that she came to the attention of Madame Denart, who ran a high-class brothel, '*une maison de rendezvous*', at 3 rue Galilée, in the same district as the rue Pergolèse and just round the corner from the broad avenue Kléber.

Ten years later, Madame Denart, by then an old woman, told an English private detective how she had transformed Marguerite from a comparative hoyden into a successful Parisian courtesan. 'My poor friend,' she recalled, 'it was I who made her . . . [into] a sort of lady, made her study the piano for three years, so that she could go out with my clients. She's been the mistress of nearly all my best customers, gentlemen of wealth and position in France, England, America, and many other countries as well.'

Madame Denart arranged for Marguerite to have elocution lessons (the younger woman came to speak her French with a slightly old-fashioned formality), teaching her protégée how to dress in style and how to keep her clients entertained in restaurants or at the theatre. In

Paris, unlike strait-laced London, there was no shame in a man appearing in public with his mistress, and Marguerite would have made an attractive companion. Although not a chocolate-box beauty, standing perhaps five feet two, she had a shapely figure, expressive greenish-grey eyes and a large, sensuous mouth. She wore her auburn hair long in those early days with Madame Denart and could be extremely charming if she wished. Nevertheless, she had a fiery spirit and, however rich or well-connected her lovers might be, she was not afraid to show her contempt for them at times. The old lady smiled as she remembered how Marguerite had vigorously slapped one of her rich admirers about the face as they sat in an expensive restaurant, to the great amusement of the Parisian beau monde.

Meller seems to have contemplated marriage and began the necessary civil process in April 1913. That August, however, after he had taken a villa at Deauville for the summer season, there was the last in a series of major quarrels, in which Marguerite's reluctance to give up other wealthy men may have been a powerful and corrosive factor. Meller eventually suffered a nervous breakdown and returned to Bordeaux for good.

Styling herself, without warrant, Madame Meller, Marguerite moved to a spacious apartment at 6 square Thiers, also in the sixteenth *arrondissement*, off the avenue Victor Hugo. Here she kept two servants and again entertained the clients selected for her by the experienced Madame Denart. Her life at this time seems to have resembled that of Marguerite Gautier, the heroine of Alexandre Dumas *fils*' maudlin romance *La Dame aux Camélias*.

Marguerite's persona had been transformed by the practised arts of Madame Denart. The grubby little gamine from Montparnasse was now a well-dressed, elegant young woman, who, if she could not yet hope to gain entry to the more exclusive Paris salons, was often to be found in the more accessible haunts of the rich. One afternoon in 1913, a French journalist met her, for the first time, for tea in the opulent surroundings of the Ritz Hotel in the Place Vendôme.

As a string orchestra essayed sentimental melodies amid a forest of palms, M. Pierre-Plessis made the acquaintance of 'Maggie Meller', introduced by a mutual male friend, perhaps eager to display his new discovery. Like many other men, Pierre-Plessis was captivated by Marguerite's large, deep, rather melancholy eyes ('*les deux grands yeux doux et tristes*'). She was wearing a conspicuously large diamond ring, displaying the first fruits of what would later become a formidable array of jewellery and ornament. Still somewhat gauche, but charmingly so, she spoke of going that evening to the Théâtre-Français and of how much she admired the writings of Pierre Loti, Charles Farrère and Alfred de Musset. It was very much the polite, superficial conversation that her male companions expected to hear.

The Great War began in August 1914. By her own account, Marguerite joined the Red Cross, driving her Renault to aid the war effort. One of her two younger brothers was killed in the sector just north of Reims (her other brother died in an accident). Though she remained in Paris for most of the war, Marguerite made her first journey to Egypt in 1915, braving the Mediterranean sea-crossing with its risk of attack by U-boat. In Cairo she seems to have lived for a few weeks with an Egyptian whose identity is uncertain. On her return to Paris, thronged with service personnel and wealthy foreigners, she found that her absence had not caused her to lose out on business.

It would be a mistake to suppose that Marguerite was operating as a 'prostitute' in the derogatory English sense of the term. She had no need to stand in a darkened doorway of a draughty street in order to drum up trade. Madame Denart's rooms in the rue Galilée would have been comfortably appointed and, although sexual relations might occur on the premises, it was a place where suitable gentlemen could be introduced, for a fee, to eligible ladies. Such introductions might also take place in the lobbies and reception areas of the great hotels and restaurants.

Marguerite would never have thought of herself as a common tart. In the manner of Marguerite Gautier and others of the long line of Parisian *'poules de luxe'*, she succeeded in creating a glamorous, almost wholesome, image for herself, as well as in managing, with considerable professional skill, the simultaneous attentions of a number of men.

Her wartime associates included a 'Belgian landowner', said to be Count von Taltarce*, several Americans, and the millionaire owner of a chain of nitrate mines in Chile, José-Maria d'Astoreca. Jean, as the latter was known to his large and fashionable circle of acquaintances, lived at a splendid address: 23 avenue du Bois de Boulogne. His relationship with Marguerite lasted for many years after the war and, though they often quarrelled, she would go to live with him from time to time as his mistress.

Perhaps Jean d'Astoreca, a bachelor, was too much a man of the world to consider marrying Marguerite, who was anxious to provide some measure of legitimacy for Raymonde, a girl of eleven in 1918. At about

---

* This spelling is probably wrong.

that time, Marguerite later recalled, she had to undergo an operation. In the same hospital was a handsome officer in the French Air Service, Charles Laurent, who had been seconded as interpreter to the Japanese consul in Paris. Charles was then twenty-two, five years younger than Marguerite, and the heir to a considerable estate, derived from his father's interest in the Grands Magasins du Louvre.

Charles fell in love with the charming, attractive Marguerite and proposed marriage. Marguerite accepted, but, according to Madame Denart, privately took a cool, mercenary view of the younger man's infatuation, telling the old madam that she was marrying Laurent only for her daughter's sake and that she would 'kick him out' after six months. She could hardly complain of Charles Laurent's lack of generosity: with his help, she moved from the square Thiers (itself no slum) to a magnificent apartment at 67 avenue Henri-Martin, in the heart of the sixteenth *arrondissement*. He made her an annual allowance of 36,000 francs (£450) and paid the yearly rental of the flat, a substantial 18,000 francs (£225)*.

The Laurent family strongly opposed the match and there is an element of mystery about exactly what occurred. The banns were published for the requisite legal period at the local town hall, but there is no record of a wedding. The couple left Paris for Italy early in 1919, perhaps in a sort of elopement to avoid a confrontation with Charles's family, and the Paris police were satisfied that the pair had been married in Venice in March that year.

Marguerite always claimed that she and Charles had been divorced in 1920 (plaint number 267 at the Paris Tribunal of the Seine), but a British private detective, working three years later, not only doubted the marriage and found no trace of the divorce, but also wrote 'there is no doubt that he [Laurent] was killed in the War'.

Marguerite was adamant that Charles was still alive in 1923 and that the break-up had been caused by his insistence on going to live in Japan. For their part, the Laurent family believed that there had been a valid marriage and Charles may have been simply reluctant to incur further publicity of an embarrassing episode in his life, preferring existence as a 'remittance man' in the Far East. Wherever the truth may lie, 'Maggie Meller' assumed the title 'Madame Laurent' after 1919 and young Raymonde was provided with a more acceptable surname.†

The three years after the war saw Marguerite continue to prosper.

---

* Using as a basis the 1923 exchange rate, which fluctuated around eighty francs to the pound.
 † In France, the birth certificate records details of marriages and divorce occurring within the jurisdiction. In Marguerite's case, no such details are entered.

She could easily afford the apartment in the avenue Henri-Martin and indulged her love of riding (she was an '*amazone accomplie*', an accomplished horsewoman, in the opinion of the Paris police), owning a stable of ten horses and, for more modern travel, two expensive cars and a chauffeur.

In the summer months, after the Paris Season faded at the end of June, Marguerite would take herself to Deauville and Biarritz. She had become a familiar and popular figure in her sector of society. According to Inspector Tabarant of the Paris Prefecture, she was well known among the smart set ('*les milieux où l'on s'amuse*'), even if she was never received in the best Parisian society. Maggie Meller's speciality, he noted, lay in attracting the rich foreigners who passed through Paris.

Marguerite's wartime visit to Egypt had probably been engineered by these means and, using her contacts, she planned another journey there at the end of 1921. Raymonde Laurent, as she was now known, had been sent to a girls' private boarding school in England, The Grange, in Totteridge, north London. Taking Raymonde and another, English, girl along for the trip, Marguerite visited Cairo in December, staying there a month as the mistress of a prominent Jewish businessman named Mossaire.* It was during this stay that Marguerite first set eyes on Ali Kamel Fahmy Bey, a millionaire, a bachelor, and just twenty-one.

---

* Probably the Mosseri given as a founder member of the Egyptian Association of Property Owners in 1911 (Berque).

4

Ali Baba

Even to a sceptic's eye, the brief life of Ali Fahmy cannot be robbed entirely of exoticism and romance. Some hard facts remain, like rocky outcrops piercing a miasma of sensationalism. He was born, probably in the Ismaili-yah district of Cairo, on 10 August 1900, the only son of Ali Fahmy El Mouhandez, a civil engineer and member of the Egyptian upper-middle class, who bore the title '*pasha*'. When Fahmy senior died in 1907, he was already a rich man and his young son was left two-fifths of his father's estate, then worth perhaps £800,000, the other part being divided between his four older sisters, three of whom (Aziza, Fatima and Aicha) were alive in 1923. Ali seems also to have inherited a substantial estate from his mother, Munira Fahmy, who survived her husband by only a few years.

As the only boy, brought up by his mother and sisters, Ali probably had a very spoiled childhood in a society which generally cosseted the young male. He attended the Nasrieh School in Cairo, but was said to have been too delicate to be sent to university. By some quirk of the law, he came into his inheritance at sixteen, two years before the legal majority. Feebleness vanished at once as Ali took enthusiastic possession of his fortune.

And it was some fortune. The Great War had done wonders for the Egyptian cotton industry. The price of Egyptian cotton rocketed, increasing nearly sevenfold as the war progressed, from $29 to $200 per hundredweight. As prices rose, Ali's estate purchased land in Middle and Upper Egypt, amounting in all to some 4500 *feddans* (acres) of best cotton-producing ground. His agents established links with banking and trading organizations in England and France. M. Miriel, a leading banker and long-serving director of the Crédit Foncier, one of the major French banking houses in Egypt, became a personal friend. By the end of the war, Ali's inheritance was producing over £100,000 sterling a year and, even though the post-war slump caused a marked decline in cotton prices, his annual income never fell below £40,000.

It is not surprising that this enormous income should have turned the head of a youth whose earlier life had been so sheltered and indulgent. Possibly on the advice of his elders, in an attempt to prevent this happening, the seventeen-year-old Ali had been provided with a personal secretary. Said Enani was six years older than his employer and had previously worked in the Ministry of the Interior in Cairo. A well-educated man who spoke fluent French and English, he served as a sort of guardian, as well as confidant to a young man who was, in truth, rather unsure of himself.

Ali was five feet nine tall and comparatively light-skinned. He was later described by his secretary as being 'nervous' and of a weak personality. His behaviour certainly had its neurotic side and he appears to have had difficulty in making friendships. Said Enani was generously paid as secretary (£35 per week, nearly twice the salary he had earned at the Interior Ministry) and would remain Ali's closest human contact for the rest of the young millionaire's life.

Like many of the insecure rich, Ali tried to buy friendship and entertained generously. Cairo society came to smile indulgently on his growing extravagance, not only on account of his youth, but also because he had a degree of charm, a ready smile and cut an elegant figure. He loved to dance and was often to be seen at Shepheard's, the Semiramis, the Continental-Savoy and the other smart hotels of Cairo and Alexandria.

Despite allegations of profligacy, Ali showed a sense of social concern unusual among the wealthy. During the war, in his extreme youth, he had given substantial sums of money to the British Red Cross and later set up a fund, administered by the Ministry of Education, to enable poor Egyptian students to visit and study in Europe. He planned to build a new ophthalmic hospital in Magagha, on the west bank of the Nile, ninety miles south of Cairo: the foundation stone was laid by the portly King Fuad I and Ali was honoured with the title 'bey', which was as far up the Egyptian social ladder as he was destined to climb. Although he came to live on a princely scale, he did not warrant the title 'prince' so frequently ascribed to him in foreign countries, a bogus attribution he did nothing to discourage.

Although Ali had no need to work and never gained any professional qualification, his excellent French gained him the honorary post of Press Attaché at the French Legation in Cairo. The French took an active interest in Middle Eastern affairs and had been involved in Egypt at least since the time of Napoleon I. Many of the Egyptian upper class were both francophones and Francophiles, particularly so since Britain had now established an unwanted hegemony over Egyptian affairs.

In 1914, the crumbling Ottoman Empire was finally displaced by a British 'protectorate' and only in 1922 would Egypt be granted a measure of internal self-government, Britain continuing to control its foreign policy and all matters connected with defence and the Suez Canal, the imperial lifeline. There was considerable friction between England and France on Egyptian matters throughout the Twenties: many Egyptian nationalists, including the venerable Said Zaghlul, leader of the *Wafd* party, had found sanctuary in Paris, much to the chagrin of Whitehall.

France was also popular as a playground for the Egyptian rich. As many as 3000 Egyptian families were said to visit it every year. As Berque records, 'Egyptian visitors at [French] watering-places, the Egyptian customers of smart restaurants, fashion houses and gaming tables were prodigal of the wealth they had made from cotton.' Ali happily joined the throng of his high-rolling fellow-countrymen, making extended tours of Europe each year, always taking in Paris, Deauville, Biarritz and Monte Carlo.

Ali also developed a taste for speed, and imported the latest fast cars from France, England and Germany. By 1923 his garage was estimated to contain a ninety-horsepower Mercedes, a Renault coupé and a Buick, together with two Rolls-Royces (one open, with whitewall tyres, the other a more sober saloon), a Berlier, a baby Peugeot, two 'runabouts' and several powerful motor cycles. He would drive at great speed through the narrow, crowded streets of Cairo, indifferent to the confusion and upset that he caused.

This playboy image was seen on the Nile, too. Thorneycrofts of England supplied a 450-horsepower racing motor boat, which, with its aeroplane engine, was reputedly the fastest on the river and capable of crossing the English Channel. This Ali would race along the Nile, its wash disturbing, even capsizing, all manner of craft. Another speedboat was built by Neuilly of Paris at a cost of 440,000 francs (£5500). It was purchased on the recommendation of a member of the French colony in Cairo, one Count Jacques de Lavison, who illustrated the mercenary character of many of Ali's 'friends' by later claiming 55,000 francs (£687)

27

commission from the manufacturers, reduced by the Paris lawcourts to a mere 30,000 francs (£375).

Perhaps it was with this smaller racing boat that Ali won a cup at a regatta in Monte Carlo, but the pride of this little fleet was probably the steam-powered *dahabeeyah*, luxuriously fitted out, in which he could take his secretary, his associates and assorted hangers-on up the Nile to Luxor, which was fashionable between November and May.

Early in 1922, Ali began to refurbish a small palace on the Nile, on the El Gezira side of the Bulaq Bridge at Zamalik, the rich quarter of Cairo. No expense was spared in fitting the place out: a firm of Parisian interior designers was engaged and an 'Italian garden' was planned, at an overall cost of £120,000. Ali also owned a villa, more modestly appointed, on the coast near Alexandria, and a suite of offices in central Cairo.

Life in the fast lane inevitably had a sexual dimension. Ali was handsome as well as extremely rich, and from the day he came into his father's estate he would have been the target of women with matrimony in mind. He seems to have had a number of short affairs with women in Egypt and France. For a while, a Mlle Bosini was his mistress, but behind the façade of conventional high life lay a rogue factor, which would set Cairo buzzing in 1921 and 1922. Said Enani, as befitted the private secretary of a millionaire with so many business and social interests, now had a secretary of his own. The three men began to look like an inseparable trio, always together in public and seemingly in private as well.

The satirical Cairo weekly *Kashkoul* published a cartoon, entitled 'L'AME DAMNÉ DE FAHMI' ('The captive soul of Fahmy'), implying that Ali was under Said Enani's evil influence. The accompanying text referred cryptically to the three men as 'The light, the shadow of the light, and the shadow of the shadow of the light.' However arcane the wording of the inscription might be, many inferred from this that all three men were homosexual.

Homosexuality, though not much spoken of in Egypt, a fact which gave the *Kashkoul*'s squib its cutting edge, was usually regarded as a passing phase in a young man's development or as an adjunct to an otherwise heterosexual life. Most of the male prostitutes in Cairo would have had wives and families of their own. The cartoon suggests that the relationship between Ali Fahmy and his secretary was a particularly close one (Said would call his master 'Baba', after Ali Baba of Forty Thieves fame). Though the suggestion of a physical involvement between the two men was unwarranted, there is evidence to suggest that Ali, rather than his secretary, was bisexual and found difficulty in coping with this orientation, a difficulty which contributed to his early death.

In late 1921, whatever his innermost thoughts, Ali was having to contemplate marriage. There would have been strong family pressure on him, as the sole male heir, to carry on the Fahmy line and in any case he was probably anxious to scotch the rumours about his private life. Around the turn of that year, something of profound significance to him happened at the Semiramis Hotel, in Cairo. Ali saw Madame Marguerite Laurent, as she was now calling herself, for the first time. She was in the company of the rich businessman Mossaire, who was no doubt footing the bill for her visit. At twenty-one, Ali was fascinated by the older woman, undoubtedly a woman of style and fashion, born and bred in Paris, a city he loved and had already visited several times.

Men of weak character, uncertain of important aspects of their personality, are often attracted to older women. Charles Laurent, six years younger than Marguerite, may have also fallen into this category, his substantial wealth forming the other half of the equation as far as Marguerite was concerned.

At the Semiramis, Ali was plainly impressed and whispered to a mutual friend, 'Tell her I will give a *"fête Vénitienne"* on my yacht in her honour.' Marguerite, mindful that a rich businessman in the hand was worth a young millionaire in the bush, politely declined Ali's offer, but must have made a mental note of this most eligible of suitors.

In that spring of 1922, Ali travelled restlessly about Europe, taking in a stay at the Savoy Hotel in London. By the middle of May, he was back in Paris, where he would see Marguerite, among the usual crowd of like-minded women and their admirers, in the smart restaurants and nightclubs. That year, the weather was generally poor, but on the finer days of May society would head for one of the two partly open-air restaurants on the Bois de Boulogne. One, Au Pré Catalan, was situated in the park itself, the other, the Château de Madrid, was on its fringe, near the Porte de Madrid, then one of the gates to the Bois. The building was a pastiche of a château built by François I in 1528 and it was here, according to the *Illustrated London News*, that 'the élite of Parisian society resort to dine and dance on summer evenings'. A dancefloor had been set up under the trees, with space for a large number of tables. Marshal Pétain, hero of Verdun and in 1940 the architect of collaboration with the Nazis, was a frequent visitor, at sixty-six still possessing a lively interest in women.

Marguerite was well aware that Ali Fahmy was attracted to her: she noticed how he would look intently at her on the many occasions their paths crossed, but somehow an introduction eluded him. Marguerite was probably playing hard to get, as well as treading cautiously in a city notorious for gossip. She spent part of July 1922 at Deauville, with a large party of friends, among whom was 'an exceedingly charming woman . . . I felt very sympathetically attracted to her and to her young sister, a remarkably pretty girl, and took them back in my car to Paris.'

Towards the end of the month, Marguerite was telephoned excitedly by her friend, who said that she knew someone who absolutely had to make her acquaintance. 'He says it is his sole ambition while he is in Paris,' she added by way of encouragement, and Marguerite, supposedly mystified, duly arrived at the Hôtel Majestic at noon on 30 July 1922. There she was formally presented to the handsome young man with the dark, intense eyes that she had seen so often in May. 'I felt,' she wrote, 'a curious *"tressaillement"'* (thrill) but, if thrill it was, the sensation was as likely caused by the thought of Fahmy's bank balance and what it might mean for Marguerite and her daughter, as by any truly romantic flutterings of the heart.

Quickly forsaking her friend, Marguerite at once accepted Ali's offer of lunch at the Château de Madrid. As they left the hotel, which stood at the head of the avenue Kléber, a few yards from the Arc de Triomphe, Ali pointed to two cars waiting outside. One was a Rolls-Royce coupé limousine, with attendant burly Sudanese chauffeur, and the other a gaudy sports model in the shape of a torpedo. 'Which do you prefer?' Ali asked casually. Marguerite, no doubt mindful of stories about his crazy driving in Cairo, wisely chose the Rolls.

5

Honey and Roses

The acquaintance was ripening. Two or three days after the rendezvous at the Hôtel Majestic, Marguerite met Said Enani for the first time, and wondered exactly how deep the friendship was between her new friend and his secretary. She was also introduced to the secretary's secretary, and to Ali's peripatetic lawyer, Mahmoud Fahmy. Marguerite later wrote of a whirlwind courtship in which she was pursued by Ali, abrim with '*des avances furieuses*' (madcap advances), for more than a month, to Deauville, to Paris, and back to Deauville again. The truth was more prosaic. Not long after their formal introduction, Marguerite had moved into Ali's suite at the Majestic (which cost 10,000 francs (£125) a week), living with him there for a few days before he left for Deauville.

Ali had taken a suite at the Hôtel Normandy, one of the best hotels in the little town, an unlikely-seeming resort for the smart set, situated as it was on the chilly northern coast of France, opposite Le Havre and the great mouth of the Seine. After the Great War, July and especially August saw its small resident population swamped by the arrival of the migrating rich, who travelled by luxury train, expensive motor car or steam yacht. That season, the Cornelius Vanderbilts were aboard the *Sheelah* (chartered from Admiral Lord Beatty), Earl Fitzwilliam had brought the *Shemara* and Lord Dunraven thrilled onlookers with his speedboat *Sona*, a recent sensation at Cowes.

Weather permitting, there was mixed bathing (still frowned on in some English seaside resorts), the women wearing one-piece costumes that covered them from mid-thigh to short-sleeved arms, perhaps with a V-neck and a daring show of the upper back. Bathing caps in the style of the eighteenth-century mob-cap were popular, as were vertically striped beach robes. The men generally wore more sober one-piece outfits, sleeveless and shorter in the thigh, though some wore trunks and a singlet top. Bare chests were definitely not acceptable.

In the afternoon horse-racing was a popular diversion, the Aga Khan's two-year-old doing particularly well, and it was possible to see King Alfonso of Spain playing a chukker of polo, under the transparent sobriquet 'Duke of Toledo', before returning to his private villa at nearby Hennequeville.

By the early evening, given fine weather, people could be seen strolling along the promenade des Planches, maybe pausing at La Potinière, with its pretty little green tables, for an aperitif or cocktail. Vermouth cassis was popular, though unchauvinistic French nationals might be found sipping a 'Dempsey Cocktail' (one part gin, two parts calvados, two dashes of anise and a teaspoonful of grenadine) introduced the year before, after the gentlemanly Georges Carpentier had been demolished in the boxing ring by the American bruiser Jack Dempsey. And not a few of Deauville's more antique summer visitors might have been tempted by the promise of a 'Monkey's Gland Cocktail', another favourite of the day.

After dinner, the Casino came into its own. During the second week of August 1922, Winston Churchill had been seen there, regularly trying his luck on the tables, in the company of the press baron Lord Beaverbrook and his famous gossip-columnist friend Lord Castlerosse, an Irish peer of enormous girth and zest for life. M. Citroën, the car manufacturer, won 750,000 francs (£9375) on Friday 10 August and lost most of it the following Monday night.

The American Dolly Sisters were a great attraction of the Casino's cabaret, appearing in fantastic costumes, described as 'lacquered silver lace with full skirts gathered on frames extending . . . from their hips, over silver cloth foundations. The bodices, very low at the back, were held on the shoulders by diamond straps . . .' Tall white ostrich plume head-dresses crowned the effect, the creation of the internationally famous couturier Colonel Edward Molyneux, another Deauville visitor at this time.

The inimitable Mistinguette, the Queen of Paris vaudeville, was also in town, wearing what was described by the *Tatler* as 'a very short frock' (at a time when the hem-line still hovered just above the ankle), showing a glimpse of those famous and highly insured legs encased in shiny silk stockings. That autumn, she would play at the Casino for 20,000 francs (£250) a performance, plus a hard-nosed 15 per cent of the box office.

One night in mid-August, when Ali was doing badly at the baccarat table, Marguerite made her entry into the gaming room. She had arrived in Deauville a day or two earlier than expected, a pleasant surprise for Ali, who, immediately he saw her, jumped up from the table and pushed his way through the crowd, genuinely delighted that she had joined him. Marguerite took up residence in Ali's suite, enjoying the pleasures of the resort, bathing and playing tennis and golf. She remained there while he took a short trip to Verona, from which he returned on 21 August. He would call her 'Bella', while Marguerite, taking her cue from Said Enani, referred to her new Egyptian lover rather unoriginally as 'Baba'.

It was about this time that Marguerite received a very special accolade. She was drawn by Georges Goursat, better known as Sem, the most famous French caricaturist of his time. Sem published, for some thirty years after 1900, an annual volume of sketches, invariably in exaggerated profile. He had an often savage insight into the ways of the fashionable world and the caption chosen for Marguerite was no exception. She was titled '*La désenchantée*' ('The disillusioned woman'), a reference to Pierre Loti's highly successful romantic novel, appropriately subtitled '*roman des harems turcs contemporains*' (a novel of present-day Turkish harems).

As autumn approached, the fashionable world drifted down to Biarritz on the Atlantic coast, near the Spanish border. Ali Fahmy and Maggie Meller were now living as man and wife, but Ali never travelled without his entourage, those 'shadows of the light', and Said Enani was always at hand to give advice, even if it was not always heeded. More experienced in the ways of the world than his master, Said viewed Marguerite's patently strategic manoeuvres with suspicion, though a strange intimacy was growing up between them. They had, after all, some coincidence of interests.

From Biarritz, excursions were made to St Jean de Luz, where they dined at the exclusive La Réservée, and to San Sebastián, across the Spanish border. On these trips, Ali would often insist on taking the wheel, fully earning Marguerite's description 'velocimaniac', as he sped recklessly along the narrow, twisting roads in the foothills of the Pyrenees. In 1922, the modern syncromesh gear system had not yet been developed. To change gear, it was normally necessary to slip into neutral before re-engaging, a process which caused a considerable loss of speed. Ali was a proud exponent of the 'racing change', a risky technique calling for deft use of the accelerator and a cavalier disregard for the welfare of the gearbox.

Marguerite particularly like the Biarritz set and, in the first major disagreement of their relationship, declared herself reluctant to break her stay in order to go to Milan, as Ali wanted. Angrily, he set off alone in mid-September, hoping Marguerite would follow, but with her own strong will (and a well-developed sense of strategy) she would not be persuaded to leave. Marguerite nevertheless agreed to Ali's suggestion that she should come to Cairo in the latter part of the year, although just for form's sake she put up a token resistance, saying that she had already planned a winter trip to Cannes.

By 21 September 1922, Ali was back, the quarrel reconciled. Marguerite was spending longer than usual in her preparations for the evening ahead. Her maid would have brought out the costliest items from Marguerite's growing collection of jewellery, recently expanded by the mutual efforts of Messrs Cartier of Paris and her new lover. Wearing the fine bracelet of coral and emeralds which Ali had recently given her, and a plain but impressive pearl necklace, Marguerite was copying the fashion of 1865. Dressed in this way, she would attend the Second Empire Ball, one of two great social events in France that year, the other being the Bal du Grand Prix at the Paris Opera, held earlier in the summer.

The Second Empire Ball, as its name implied, was a re-creation of the court of the Empress Eugénie and her husband, the Emperor Napoleon III, who would spend their hardly modest holidays at the Villa Napoléon in Biarritz. Napoleon III had been toppled after his ignominious defeat by the Prussians at Sedan in 1870 and the villa eventually became the Hôtel du Palais, a luxurious establishment billed in the *New York Herald* as 'The American Headquarters On the Basque Coast'.

That September night, the brashness and vulgarity of 1922 were transformed into the brashness and vulgarity of the 1860s. The front of the hotel was floodlit as 700 guests, including Ali and Marguerite, made their way on a perfect evening, warm, scented and loud with cicadas, through an orangery, which led from the entrance gates to the doors of the hotel. Inside, two large salons had been disguised as a sylvan landscape, leafy arches surrounding the doorways, the marble pillars decorated as full-grown trees.

About 11.30, the Spanish royal anthem crashed out to mark the entrance of King Alfonso XIII, accompanied by his Queen, Victoria Eugénie (better known as 'Ena'), who mounted a dais with the Shah of Persia, the Prince and Princess Sixtus of Bourbon-Parma (the brother and sister-in-law of ex-Empress Zita of Austria-Hungary) and assorted French and Spanish dukes and duchesses.

After the royal party had settled itself, Jean-Gabriel Doumergue, the principal designer, began the first of a number of tableaux. Dressed as the popular idea of the artist, he flicked a paintbrush at a vast canvas which fell away to reveal five aristocratic ladies grouped around the Marquesa de Najera, as the Empress Eugénie, impersonating not only the Imperial court but also a noted painting by Winterhalter, with whom the ambitious Doumergue was no doubt comparing himself.

Then followed a series of entertainments, including 'The Virginians', specially devised for the American colony. The *New York Herald* lovingly described the dresses that had been so expensively commissioned from Worth, who had opened a branch salon in Biarritz specially for the season: 'Mrs Roy McWilliams was in green lamé, bordered with black Chantilly lace, with corsage of pink roses, festooned with bunches of blue grapes and tiny Dresden blue shoulder bows . . .' The men, completely eclipsed, had to be content with the 'spike-tailed coats and tight-fitting trousers of the period'. After their presentation to the royals, the party danced the 'Virginian Reel' to a 'colored orchestra' imported from a local nightclub, who had obediently sung 'plantation songs' at the beginning of the display.

The ball then began and, to the surprise of *Le Figaro*, crinoline and the onestep were found to be compatible. At 2 a.m., '*un souper délicat*' was served, at the end of which King Alfonso joyfully raised his glass to the memory of Empress Eugénie, who had died only two years previously at the age of ninety-four, obligingly leaving her jewellery to Queen Ena, who was seen to be disporting a necklace of 'enormous diamonds', as well as sundry emeralds once worn by the Empress.

Alfonso, a dashing thirty-six, danced with 'many of the débutantes', and it was nearly five in the morning before the royal party joined the waiting cars to begin the journey back across the border to his palace of Miramar at San Sebastián. No one seems to have given much thought to the chronic post-war unrest in Spain, which would lead within twelve months to a *coup d'état* and the establishment of a semi-Fascist dictatorship under General Primo de Rivera, whose incompetent rule would itself lead to the fall of the Spanish monarchy and Alfonso's permanent exile in 1931.

Ali and his new love were probably not among the younger, more energetic dancers who partied on for some time after the royals had left, since Ali, maybe for family reasons, had to return to Egypt. He probably travelled across southern France later that day to take ship from Marseilles. The crossing was evidently a smooth one, but Ali arrived home lovesick and in poor spirits. He had written freely to Marguerite from Milan earlier in September, but even she was unprepared for the long, emotional letter he wrote to her in Cairo on 26 September 1922.

Later described coldly by the English writer Edward Marjoribanks as 'a letter written in abject and sickening terms of flattery', it reads, despite the crudity of the translation from the French, as a courtly statement of love, often quite beautifully phrased. Extracts convey some of the flavour of Ali's passionate, lovelorn style, addressed naïvely to an older woman brought up in a tough school:

My Dear Little Bella

I landed on Monday and my first letter is for you. My first thoughts are for you, who, by your bewitching charm, your exquisite delicacy, the beauty of your heart – in a word, your 'quintessential' feelings – have brought out all that is good and generous in human nature.

The crossing was delightful and more delightful still from that indefinable radiance – that, proceeding from you, invades and envelops me. Your image everywhere incessantly pursues me . . .

. . . Torch of my life, your image appears to me in a still more brilliant light. It appears to me to be surrounded by a halo and your head, so dear, so proud, so majestic, is brightly encircled by a crown, which I reserve for you here. Yes, this crown I reserve for you in the beautiful country of my ancestors . . .

Both unsure of himself and uncertain whether Marguerite would keep her promise to visit Cairo, Ali seems to have been trying, in this revealing passage, to dispel rumours about other affairs, about his own sexual orientation or his unusually close relationship with Said Enani.

. . If, by chance, your journey should be thwarted and if – giving credence to stories, something I would never believe of you – you abandon your planned journey, you will have unwittingly made my life aimless. Envy, jealousy and distraction are common to all times and all countries. They should never have any sway over noble natures like yours . . .

The letter ended with more than a hint of emotional blackmail.

. . . Let me insist . . . with all my force, that you embark so as to arrive here at the beginning of November . . . Come quickly and see the beautiful sun of Egypt . . .

. . . Ill, saved from death in bed, my only consolation is you. My

36

recovery, the regaining of my strength today, I owe largely to your sweet and beneficent vision.

Believe me, I love you very much
From your faithful little BABA
ALI FAHMY

Enclosed with the letter were tickets for the journey, but Marguerite was not yet ready to make the trip. She had other strings to her bow, and back in Paris had resumed her association with Jean d'Astoreca. On her frequent visits to 23 avenue du Bois de Boulogne, she formed a friendship with d'Astoreca's secretary, Miguel-Surgères, who remembered how Marguerite would always sleep with a pistol under her pillow, morbidly fearful that someone would steal her jewellery. When not actually living with d'Astoreca, she would make two sorts of visit. In the mornings, Raymonde came along; the afternoon and evenings were reserved for more adult preoccupations.

But Ali was not to be fobbed off by excuses from Paris and his melancholia may even have brought on some kind of psychosomatic illness, though hardly severe enough to warrant the absurd series of telegrams dispatched on his behalf by Said Enani:

CAIRO: 4 OCT 1922 – NO NEWS FROM YOU. BABA SERIOUSLY ILL SINCE HIS ARRIVAL. HAVE NOT BEEN ABLE TO WRITE TO YOU BEING BUSY WITH HIM BUT HOPE FOR PROMPT RECOVERY. TELEGRAPH FROM TIME TO TIME. SAID.

CAIRO: 7 OCT 1922 – DESPERATE STILL. GRAVE DANGER TODAY. TOMORROW TELEGRAPH HIM HOW YOU ARE – SAID.

CAIRO: 9 OCT 1922 – BABA BETTER TODAY. FIRST WORD YOUR NAME. ALWAYS ASKING FOR YOU. YOUR PRESENCE NECESSARY. TELEGRAPH DAY OF DEPARTURE – SAID.

Marguerite does not seem to have taken this very seriously. 'This is the time o' year,' commented the *Tatler*'s Paris correspondent in late September, '. . . when "*affaires du coeur*" frame up their winter programmes!' Perhaps she was making a final effort to persuade Jean to make an honest woman of her or maybe they had had another quarrel, sufficiently serious to convince Marguerite that her best interests lay in the East.

On 16 November 1922, accompanied by her younger sister Yvonne, now twenty-one, Marguerite boarded the Simplon-Orient Express in Paris and arrived the following day in Trieste. Waiting for them there was the SS *Helouan* (10,000 tons) of the Italian SITMAR line, bound for Alexandria. 'Mrs Laurent' and 'Miss Alibert', as they were listed in the arrivals column of the *Egyptian Gazette*, were to have distinguished company on the voyage. Also aboard ship was Emir Abdulla of Transjordan.

Abdulla was one of the four sons of Sherif Hussein, 'descendant of the Prophet Mahomed, protector of the two holy cities of Mecca and Medina, and ruler of the Hejaz'. With his three brothers, Feisal (at that time King of Iraq), Ali and Zeid, he had taken a leading role during the Great War in the British-backed campaign against Turkish rule. But the British had not kept their promise to their Arab allies and in November 1922 Abdulla was returning, a little sadly, from some disillusioning negotiations in London. At this time, he was described in the *Egyptian Gazette* as being 'a strikingly handsome man of about 40 . . . , of fair complexion and with slender, delicately formed hands . . .'

The voyage would have provided Marguerite and Yvonne with a glimpse of a real Eastern prince, uncompromisingly dressed in the raiment of his ancestors. He wore an 'Arab *kufiya* and *arghai*, with a deep plum-coloured *zabun* and a gold mesh belt, the clasp of which was formed by the highly worked gold and silver scabbard of a large dagger . . .' When reporters pressed him for his impressions of ungrateful England, he had replied with exquisite politeness that everything he had seen had left 'a most favourable impression'. As to the Zionist question, he would only comment wistfully that if the Jews would prove that they did not aim, by immigration or otherwise, at securing control of his country, it would be possible to effect an understanding between them and the Arabs, 'to the advantage of both'.

On Monday 20 November 1922, in brilliant winter sunshine, the SS *Helouan* put into Alexandria. Marguerite recalled how the white mass of buildings on the shoreline was gradually transformed into low houses, overhanging buildings and minarets. As they docked, scores of local porters noisily vied with each other to claim the passengers' luggage. The Emir, formally greeted by the British Consul, was whisked off to Cairo in a special saloon attached to the evening boat-train. The two Frenchwomen, on a very different errand, were met on board by Ali, miraculously restored to ebullient health, whose car was waiting at the quayside, with engine running, to take the party to Ali's private villa overlooking the sea, a few miles out of town.

6

Munira

Ali's seaside villa could not compete for splendour with the mansion at Zamalik, now almost finished, and so the day after disembarkation they took the train to Cairo, a journey of three and a quarter hours. The party was chauffeured across the city in a procession of three cars (the last two of which carried a mass of luggage and assorted servants), over the Nile to the building which Ali unblushingly called his 'palace'. On the steps leading up to the entrance, twelve liveried Nubian footmen, glittering in gold braid, greeted Fahmy and his two guests, who were ushered into salons furnished and decorated in what was supposed to be the style of Fontainebleau. Marble columns, Gobelin tapestries, Aubusson carpets, venerable Persian rugs and eighteenth-century French furniture, carefully selected (on commission, of course) by Fahmy's agents, filled the ground-floor rooms in some of which Ali had attempted to reproduce the design of the parquet floor of the Hall of Mirrors in Versailles.

The Fahmy monogram, a fantastic reproduction of his name in Arabic, designed by Ali himself, was to be seen all round the place, often spelt out in precious stones, on lamps, chairbacks and picture frames, as well as on the surfeit of gold cigarette-boxes strewn throughout the building. As a tribute to his principal guest, Ali had had commissioned a special dressing-table set: four hairbrushes, six perfume dispensers, hand mirrors, powder boxes, a manicure set and scissors, each one wrought in gold and tortoiseshell and adorned with the letter 'M' in small diamonds.

Marguerite's bedroom had been fitted out with items once belonging to King Peter of Serbia, who had died in 1921. The décor was very much in the style of the First Empire, possibly reflecting an admiration

39

for Napoleon on the part of the late king, who had usurped the throne of his country in 1903 by the simple expedient of murdering the previous incumbent.

White marble columns stood out against the blue and gold of the silk hangings. On a dais stood an enormous classically shaped bed, guarded by bronze statues and overhung by a canopy, a silken dome, also in blue and gold. This had been draped with lace and surmounted by large white ostrich plumes. Beyond a marble arch in one wall of the bedroom lay a large solid-silver bath, accompanied by toilette tables of onyx and a divan delicately covered in gold lace.

In those first days as his resident mistress, Marguerite would go horse riding with Ali, early in the Cairo mornings. It was always a delight when, at first, to borrow a description from Lord Edward Cecil's *The Leisure of an Egyptian Official* of 1921, 'there was nothing to be seen but masses of white mist . . . In a minute or two, as the sun strikes over the hills . . . and the mist turns a delicate pink, in the far distance the bright blue hills of the western desert begin to show, and the horizon line is cut by the pyramids, starting out of the sea of blushing cloud. Incredibly quickly, change follows change. The cloud now turns to a liquid translucent gold and through it dimly appear the feathery palms and the graceful sails of passing boats. In a moment more the rising breeze has swept away the cloud . . . and the morning pageant is over.'

Marguerite had come to Egypt, just as she had done in 1915 and 1921, to live as the mistress of a rich Egyptian. Ali Fahmy differed from his predecessors, not merely because he was very young, handsome and super-rich, but because, shortly after Marguerite's installation at Zamalik, he had asked her to marry him. The real reasons behind the proposal will probably never be known, but they appear to have been complex. He certainly considered himself to be in love with her, almost obsessively so, but the very intensity with which he expressed his feelings suggests an inner conflict which could not be resolved by marriage alone, especially marriage to a woman who, despite her air of charm and sophistication, had made her name as a high-class Parisian whore.

Marguerite, for her part, had the simplest of motives for becoming his wife. Though she was already comparatively rich herself, she had an expensive lifestyle to maintain and a daughter, for whom she had an undoubted affection, and the furtherance of whose education and establishment in life was very much Marguerite's ambition. She had no intention of exposing Raymonde to the vagaries and humiliations of her own early years. Moreover, Marguerite was socially ambitious and

Fahmy's wealth, she thought, might open some of the doors of Parisian society currently closed to her. So she accepted, but prudently engaged the services of Maître Assouad, a noted Cairo attorney of considerable guile.

Ali's family were strongly opposed to his marriage to a non-Muslim foreigner of dubious antecedence, an older woman, whom they suspected of being little more than a gold-digging hustler. But Ali would not be deterred, even though the faithful Said Enani did his best to fight a corner for the family. The civil ceremony would take place on 26 December 1922 and a Muslim marriage was planned for a month later.

The Cairo winter season had begun, almost the very day Marguerite arrived with her younger sister. (Yvonne, with whom Ali had been getting a little too friendly for Marguerite's comfort, stayed for a month, before returning, rather precipitately, to Paris.) The active social scene at first masked the deep and irreconcilable differences in temperament between Marguerite and her fiancé. One bond common to both was their love of the bright lights and in the last weeks of 1922 they could be seen dining and dancing in the city's best hotels and restaurants.

There was an added excitement for partygoers that year, an attraction which was drawing more than the usual complement of well-to-do tourists. On 5 November 1922, an archaeological expedition headed by Howard Carter and the Earl of Carnarvon had discovered the entrance of a large and apparently undisturbed ancient royal tomb in the famous Valley of the Kings. The outer part of the tomb was officially opened at the end of the month and there was intense speculation as to what might be revealed at the opening of the inner chamber, an event due to take place early in the New Year. People were already beginning to call this the 'Tut-Ankh-Amun Season'.

The dancing craze had taken hold in Egypt, just as it had in Europe. 'Cairo is not particularly up-to-date; it generally takes Dame Fashion a little while to travel across the Mediterranean,' observed the *Egyptian Gazette*, but the writer conceded that the ballroom of the Semiramis Hotel, where Marguerite had first seen Ali Fahmy the previous December, gave a creditable impression of Paris or the West End of London. Tea-dances were particularly popular with those who sought to show off their dancing skills. 'The fox-trot has changed completely. [In] Cairo . . . it consists of a slow, graceful walk, practically devoid of the chassée, and at the Semiramis one sees it at its best', reported the *Gazette*. The dances were attended by people of all nationalities, but the British, conservative as ever, disliked the stylish, sexually charged exhibitions of dancing at teatime and restricted their appearances on the dancefloor to more sedate occasions after dinner.

Shepheard's was the hotel particularly favoured by Ali, whose fluent English would have enabled him to keep well informed on British attitudes, and it acted as a useful conduit of intelligence during his time as Press Attaché at the French Legation. Built in the 1840s, Shepheard's was very popular with the British and served as a sort of annexe to their headquarters in Cairo. That summer, the hotel's interior had been considerably enlarged, additions being decorated in the Adam style of great hotels everywhere. Old hands, nostalgic for the comparatively cramped hotel lobby of the war years, could console themselves in Gasparini's Bar, before going into the Moorish Restaurant, where diners were serenaded by a French salon orchestra specially engaged from Paris for the season.

The popular RAF Jazz Band played for the foxtrotting young in the ballroom. The *Egyptian Gazette* noted a great influx of 'new men . . . who have arrived in Cairo this trooping season. The majority . . . are dancers and, as most of the ladies present, whether débutantes (it is out of date to use the adjective "shy"), or chaperones, also danced, most of them found partners.' If this style of newspaper copy suggests a peaceful social life, it gives a misleading impression. The British community was decidedly nervous about the rise of militant nationalism in Egypt: a number of British officials and soldiers had been murdered in recent years, and street demonstrations, strikes and riots were a frequent occurrence in Cairo and Alexandria.

Ali and Marguerite, less vulnerable than British expatriates to the prevailing tensions, were determined to make their mark in Cairo society. They were often to be seen at the Royal Opera House, where French influences were still strong, notably among the orchestra and performers, if not so much in the repertoire. Boito's *Mefistofele* opened the season, followed by Bizet's *The Pearl Fishers* on 8 December, and two Italian favourites, *Rigoletto* and *Manon Lescaut*, which took the programme up to Christmas.

In December, Ali persuaded two Italian stars of the Cairo Opera, Nino Piccaluga, the romantic tenor, and his wife, Augusta Concato, to join other friends for a journey by motor boat to the pyramids of Saqqara, where, in a restaurant once the home of Mariette, the nineteenth-century French archaeologist, Ali contrived to impress his guests with an elaborate banquet, complete with orchestra and dancers. Roast sheep were brought to the table whole and carved at each diner's place. Later the party descended into the tombs by candlelight, while Piccaluga and Concato sang *'Mourir si jeune et belle'*, the final aria from *Aida*, which Radames and Aida sing before their entombment.

It was almost as if Ali Fahmy and 'Madame Laurent' were having their honeymoon before the marriage, but living together was already beginning to expose the strains in their relationship, problems that would grow rather than diminish as the months went by. Ali was turning out to be rather possessive of his love, as if to play down the rackety image of his past life. Marguerite was still hedging her bets. She had not lost contact with her old flame Jean d'Astoreca, and an unfortunate incident occurred during mid-December. While out shopping in Cairo, she dropped a telegram and left the premises unaware of the loss. The finder noticed that it was signed 'Jean' and that its message was expressed in a very affectionate way. When it was restored to Marguerite, perhaps on a later visit to the same shop, she was visibly embarrassed by the discovery of what had taken place.

Whether or not Ali found out about this indiscretion, the couple certainly had a major argument three days before the civil wedding, a dispute sufficiently serious for Marguerite to book a passage home on the SS *Sphinx* for herself and her maid. Although she would never specify the cause, the row may have blown up, as a French woman friend recalled, because Marguerite was 'addicted to flirting' and simply expected Ali to put up with her well-practised ways.

The quarrel was patched up in time for a large pre-wedding reception and dinner at Shepheard's Hotel on Christmas Day 1922. Ali indiscreetly confessed to his fiancée that his friends had been betting on whether he would be able to keep her, but, once the capable Maître Assouad was satisfied that the civil contract was in order, there was to be no hesitation on Marguerite's part. She undertook to produce evidence of her divorce from Charles Laurent (this difficulty was overcome by the roundabout expedient of a declaration by the French consul that she was 'free from any bond of marriage'), while Fahmy agreed to pay her a dowry of £E8000 (just over £8000 sterling); £E2000 to be paid on signing the contract, the balance on his death or if he should divorce Marguerite. Ali's lawyer shrewdly insisted on a clause by which Marguerite stood to lose the £E6000 and her right to alimony if she divorced him. Ali would not be 'kicked out' quite as easily as Charles Laurent had been.

Another major provision was that Marguerite should convert to Islam, ostensibly because of a term in the will of Ali's mother excluding Ali from her inheritance if he married a non-Muslim, but it also served to

43

strengthen Marguerite's position if Ali, with his taste for reckless driving and speedboating, should happen to predecease her. Marguerite, a lover of Parisian *haute couture*, was not obliged to wear strict Muslim dress and retained her French nationality. All in all, she had been well advised and, far from being a defenceless woman in a foreign land, she had not only the services of an experienced Cairo advocate, but also the moral support of a former lover from Parisian days (not Jean d'Astoreca), who acted as witness at the civil ceremony, a favour for which Ali may not have been too grateful.

The newly-weds remained in Cairo after the ceremony, giving a number of parties of Zamalik. At one reception, Piccaluga and Concato were joined by the entire Opera House orchestra, who, together with the dancer Maria Bordin, played for their supper, another extravaganza at which the inevitable whole sheep were served up by footmen resplendent in violet-coloured uniforms with Fahmy's monogram stitched in gold broad on the sleeves.

Five nights after the civil marriage, Shepheard's was packed with 1200 diners celebrating a rowdy New Year's Eve. 'One must admit that the native waiters looked somewhat exasperated,' wrote the *Egyptian Gazette*, 'but to have fireworks let off under their noses and paper streamers twisted around their tarboushes at the very moment of serving four plates of hot soup with but one pair of hands was not ... conducive to ... equanimity of temper.' Some young British bucks doused diners unfortunate enough to be sitting near the fountain in the Moorish Restaurant, while bread rolls and cotton-wool pellets were hurled from table to table in the ballroom, which was being used as an overflow dining area.

After supper, once the floor had been cleared, a jazz band belted out the latest favourites, among which were likely to have been 'My Sweet Hortense', 'I'm Just Wild About Harry' and 'Ain't We Got Fun'.

There was barely ankle room for dancing under the great chandelier, which had been decorated in 'magnificent cascades of bougainvillaea [with] a profusion of flowers everywhere'. At midnight the lights were dimmed and two dozen white doves released from a balcony above the hotel foyer, an effect rather spoiled by the wags who lowered a squealing piglet on a rope from an upper fanlight. Bags of red and white confetti were emptied on the heads of the crowd, 'everybody whistled and screeched, cushions were thrown about and a rugger scrum indulged in by the ... men'. In the early hours, a full moon lit the departing *gharries*, as the guests forsook the hotel for Ciro's nightclub or, more romantically, so that their occupants might gaze upon the pyramids by moonlight.

After the civil wedding, the process of conversion to Islam, on the part of a convent-educated woman who had thought of herself as 'devout . . . in a mystic sort of way', proceeded according to the regulations. By these Marguerite was obliged to consult a priest of her own religion, who would be given the opportunity of trying to persuade the intending convert to remain Christian. At the house of the civil governor of Cairo, Father Marshall of St Joseph's Church vainly tried to keep Marguerite within the folds of Mother Church, but to no avail.

On 11 January 1923, after proclaiming in Arabic 'There is one God and Mohammed is His Prophet,' Marguerite added one more to her string of noms de plume. She was now Munira, after her husband's mother, and to mark the occasion had herself photographed demurely wearing the *choudri*.

7

A Punctured Romance

Within a week of Marguerite's conversion to Islam, Ali was writing a revealing letter to Yvonne Alibert, in terms which suggest a reason for the younger sister's rapid departure from Cairo. Ali's emotional immaturity and his wife's unwillingness to change her 'bad habits' were rapidly propelling the marriage towards disaster.

> ... You may rest assured, my little Yvonne, that I have no reproach with regard to you. I would much like you to have spent the winter season with us, but the question of my marriage with Munira – ha, ha, ha – caused a delicate situation which, being considered, perhaps it was in your best interest to return to France.
>
> Just now I am engaged in training her. Yesterday, to begin with, I did not come in to lunch or to dinner and I also left her at the theatre. With women one must act with energy and be severe – no bad habits.
>
> We still lead the same life of which you are aware – the opera, theatre, disputes, high words and perverseness. We leave for Luxor next week.
>
> Accept, my dear child, my affectionate sentiments ...

Ali's attempts to 'train' his new wife were doomed to failure. Five days after he had written to Yvonne, a terrific quarrel erupted, in the course of which each spouse threatened to kill the other. As with so many of their arguments, jealousy was at the root. Marguerite rushed up to her room and, mindful at this early stage of the need to keep a record of events with a view to divorce proceedings, wrote an emotional denunciation of her husband.

> Yesterday, 21 January 1923, at three o'clock in the afternoon, he took his Bible, or Koran, I do not know which, kissed it, put his hand on it and swore to avenge himself on me . . .'

Unconvincingly, she declared that 'this oath was taken without any reason, neither jealousy, bad conduct, nor a scene on my part', adding a postscript which showed where her priorities lay:

> 'PS Today he wanted to take my jewellery from me. I refused, hence a fresh scene.'

Calm had been briefly restored when, at daybreak on 25 January, the steam-powered *dahabeeyah* cast off, on a major voyage up the Nile to Luxor. Ali took command, clad in tarboosh, pyjamas and a pair of red heelless slippers, or babouches, and with evident pleasure successfully negotiated two of Cairo's awkward bridges before going below for breakfast. The pride of Ali's little fleet, the boat was crewed by some twenty-five Nubian sailors, whose complement included a chef, six cooks and two stewards, one of whom was styled Maître d'Hôtel, both in uniforms bearing Ali's self-designed monogram. Fahmy had his valet aboard, Marguerite was accompanied by her maid Aimée, and, unsurprisingly, Said Enani completed the party.

On this leisurely voyage, it was customary each evening to serve elaborate dinners with as many as twenty small courses, starting with a roast meat, followed by various vegetable dishes (aubergines, courgettes and stuffed vine leaves were popular), four or five types of sweet pudding, a rice dish and dessert. A few years earlier, the English novelist Robert Smythe Hichens had written of supper on board a rich man's *dahabeeyah*, describing 'an Egyptian dinner . . . served on a . . . tray of shining gold . . . set out with white silk napkins, with rounds of yellow bread and with limes cut into slices . . .'

The saloon of Ali's boat may have been similarly 'crescent-shaped [containing] a low dais, with curving divans . . . [and] a big balcony that looked out over the Nile . . . protected by an awning. The wooden ceiling was cut up into lozenges of black and gold . . . edged with minute inscriptions from the Koran . . . the windows had lattices of *mashreebeeyah* work fitted to them . . . all over the floor were strewn exquisite rugs. The room was pervaded by a faint but heavy perfume . . .'

Marguerite's bedroom, too, may have resembled the cabin 'evidently furnished from Paris, with bedsteads, mosquito curtains, long mirrors, small armchairs in white, and green, and rose colours; walls painted ivory white; and delicate, pretty . . . curtains and portières, with patterns of flowers tied up with ribbons and flying and perching birds . . .'

At nightfall, when navigation was rendered impossible by the river's treacherous sandbanks, the vessel would put into shore, from which Marguerite would hear the faint, rhythmic throbbing of village drums. Sometimes Ali would persuade the villagers to join his crew and make music. They would sit round, in their flowing white djellabas, while Ali, in princely mood, clapped his hands to the traditional beat.

The journey was slow and daylight did not prevent the boat from running aground from time to time. It might be as much as four hours before it was refloated, using a powerful winch carried for the purpose and with much manoeuvring by the crew, who had to manhandle heavy chains while up to their shoulders in water.

After ten days of such tortuous progress, they drew near their destination and, eager to exchange the comparative loneliness of the *dahabeeyah* for the cosmopolitan society of Luxor, Ali helped Munira into his speedboat, which had been towed up from Cairo, and together they went ahead of the yacht, making for the jetty in front of the Winter Palace Hotel. Here two of Ali's sisters, Madame Said and Madame Roznangi, were waiting with warm greetings for their brother but conspicuously less affection for his bride.

The hotel was fully booked, and many of its two hundred guests were agog to know what discoveries there might be in the boy king Tut-Ankh-Amun's tomb, whose inner chamber was due to be opened in three weeks. In addition, reported the *Egyptian Gazette*, 'tennis, attendance at the Gymkhana meetings and dancing provide amusements for those not interested in tombs and temples'. Accommodation had been reserved for Ali's party and they stayed overnight in the hotel. Typically, Ali rose at the crack of dawn and took his speedboat back downstream to the yacht, in order to be seen making a grand arrival at Luxor later in the day.

Moored opposite the hotel, among the other luxury craft, the *dahabeeyah* boasted an impressive list of guests. Lord Carnarvon accepted an invitation to lunch, and the lavish shipboard parties given by the Fahmys during their two visits to Luxor that February were attended by some of the best-known personalities of the 'Tut-Ankh-Amun Season', including Howard Carter, General Sir John Maxwell, the popular and gregarious

Maharajah of Kapurthala (a great Francophile who, to Marguerite's delight, spoke excellent French), a Greek archaeologist, a distinguished Egyptian poet, various financiers and an assortment of local dignitaries.

In between hosting these entertainments, the Fahmys, gripped by the prevailing Tut-Ankh-Amun fever, hired a pair of donkeys, on which they travelled to Karnak and the Valley of the Kings. En route, they were spotted by an English journalist, H. V. Morton, later to become well known as a travel writer with a gift for the syrupy phrase, already very much a part of his style in 1923. In an article that appeared in the *Sunday Express* on 16 September that year, he described 'one of those crystal-clear mornings which come only in Egypt, bringing with them a sense of indescribable dancing happiness. There was not a ripple on the blue waters of the Nile, the miles of sugar-cane stood motionless and not a breath stirred the tall, feathered palms on the road to Gurnah . . .'

After an hour's ride between the baking-hot rock walls that lead into the famous valley, he saw a little way ahead of him a man and a woman mounted on donkeys. 'At first,' recalled Morton, with sly racism, 'I thought he was a European. He was wearing a grey sun helmet, a well-cut shooting jacket and a pair of Jodhpur riding breeches.'

An hour or so later Morton was sitting outside the entrance to Tut-Ankh-Amun's tomb, when he saw the couple, who had left their mounts at the barrier and were walking towards the crowd. He heard them speaking French and asked an English friend if he knew who they were. 'The Fahmys,' came the reply, delivered patronizingly with 'the peculiar smile with which a white man in the East refers to a mixed marriage'.

Morton asked his friend if they were part of the Egyptian royal family. 'No,' he said. 'Just a bey. Pots of money . . . I'll introduce you.' The prevailing contempt felt by the British for all things Egyptian can be discerned in Morton's thumbnail sketch of Ali:

'[He] impressed me as a very polished upper-class Egyptian, not very dark, clean-shaven and possessing in a marked degree that dangerous magnetism of the eye which attracts more white women than most untravelled people imagine. He was too well dressed to look exactly right. Like most Oriental men, he reeked of scent . . .'

Ali discussed London and Paris, speaking of the journey back to Cairo for the Islamic wedding, now near at hand. No, they were not staying at the Winter Palace, declared Ali with evident pride, as he swished the ever-present flies away with an ivory-handled whisk of white horsehair. 'I have a yacht.' Morton was very suspicious of this glib, disgustingly rich foreigner. 'All the time he talked, he smiled,' and, subtle Easterner that he was, 'had a trick of looking at your mouth when you were speaking to him . . .'

Marguerite was very quiet, possibly because the journey had tired her, but she was a practised rider and may just have been out of sorts, in no mood for polite chatter. Morton spoke to her in English, but in French she replied that she did not understand and, after a few commonplace remarks, settled down to watch the porters removing artefacts from the great royal tomb.

After four or five days of this crowded social programme, a telegram arrived on 9 February stating that preparations for the religious wedding were complete. The couple, leaving their luggage on the *dahabeeyah*, boarded the *train de luxe* for the thirteen-hour journey back to Cairo, arriving at nine o'clock on the evening before the ceremony.

Clothed entirely in black, with only her large, intriguing eyes visible, Munira was driven early the following afternoon to Ali's large suite of offices, in the business quarter of Cairo. The white-bearded *cadi* formally asked her if she had received her dowry. Her answer, duly recorded in a register by the *cadi*'s clerk, was in the affirmative, although she would later claim that she had only been paid the equivalent of £450, instead of the promised £2000. She also alleged that Ali, without warning, had suddenly insisted that she should forgo her right of divorce. There was said to have been a long argument about this, after which, browbeaten, she was cajoled into accepting the provision.

An Islamic marriage contract does not automatically give a wife the right to divorce her husband (who is always permitted to divorce his wife): it is for the woman to claim the insertion of such a clause, which many brides have been reluctant to do. Although it appears that the religious settlement did not give Marguerite the right of divorce, her own account of the episode seems improbable, not only in the light of her assertive nature, but because her lawyer, Maître Assouad, was present throughout the proceedings. Whatever the position might have been in Islamic law, the civil contract, drawn up according to the Egyptian legal code, clearly protected Marguerite's right to divorce her husband.

In the presence of Ali's brother-in-law, Dr Assim Said Bey (a Cairo gynaecologist), lawyers for both parties and the bridegroom's closest friend, Said Enani, marriage documents were signed in front of the *cadi*. Ali and Munira became man and wife, according to Islamic rite. The party made its way to Shepheard's Hotel for the wedding feast, a junket which lasted well into the small hours and at which, in defiance of religious proscription, the 'costliest wines' were served.

Next day, they took the train to Assiout, between Cairo and Luxor, where the *dahabeeyah* was waiting for them. Using the motor boat intermittently for excursions, the honeymoon party reached Luxor with decidedly frayed tempers. This time Ali and Marguerite came to blows. Ali had tried to lock his wife in her cabin during the journey, provoking violent resistance. The arguments continued at Luxor, when he pompously forbade her to leave the ship, posting members of the crew at each end of the gangplank.

With so many Europeans around, including some very distinguished acquaintances, it seems highly improbable that Marguerite was ever a true prisoner. Even by her own account, she was never physically threatened by the servants and, as appears from the divorce-minded letter that she wrote to her lawyer, her main fear appears to have been a public scandal, news of which might trickle back to the gossips of Paris.

'Dear Maître [Assouad]
I have to bring to your notice very grave incidents. For the last three days, I have been a prisoner on board. I am absolutely unable to get out. Threats were made and to avoid a scandal, I had to go inside. This evening I have to go to bed at 7 o'clock. I have on my arms the marks of my husband's gentleness. I ask you to send here one or two persons, who will have this condition established, so as to make use of it . . .'

On 16 February 1923, the inner chamber of the great royal tomb was formally opened, in the presence of a distinguished roll-call which included the Egyptian Crown Prince, the Queen of Belgium and Lord Allenby. Although the greatest artefacts would not be revealed for some months, it was clear that this had been a major archaeological find, though some Egyptian newspapers were tartly critical of Lord Carnarvon's style and motives. *Al Ahram* complained that, by giving the London *Times* a monopoly of access to the team's discoveries (in return for a handsome consideration), Carnarvon had forced them to take the news regarding their national treasures from non-Egyptian sources: 'He [Carnarvon] has come to regard the tomb as his own creation,' was one caustically accurate comment.

British newspaper moguls fell over themselves to get in on the act.

First Lord Beaverbrook, then Lord Rothermere, trumpeted his imminent arrival in the land of the pharaohs. 'Lord Beaverbrook is expected to arrive in Cairo next week . . .', reported the *Egyptian Gazette* on 22 February, later announcing that 'a wireless message has just been received by Shepheard's Hotel that Lord Rothermere is arriving at Port Said . . . in two days' time . . .'

In terms of their private life, the Fahmys' second visit to Luxor was noticeably less successful than the first had been. Marguerite's maid returned to France for a holiday on 10 March, leaving her mistress feeling isolated and without a confidante. There were some lighter moments, as when the pair made a second trip out to the newly opened tomb of Tut-Ankh-Amun: as if to mark the occasion, Marguerite had climbed into a nearby open sarcophagus and lay down inside it. Clad in riding habit and with her arms folded in front of her, she became the subject of a zany snapshot. But the bickering soon began again. Ali wrote to Yvonne Alibert on 16 March, describing the trip, together with a little macho blustering, an evident nostalgia for Paris and a romantic flourish:

> . . . but I quarrelled all the time. I showed her I could act with energy and this is what is needed with women.
>
> I hope you will make a journey with us next year. Give me details about the pretty women in fashion [in Paris]. If you see [. . .], tell her my heart, my soul, my sentiments are at her feet and I am still in love with her. I hope she has not forgotten me . . .

The Luxor season wound down after mid-April, as the heat became steadily less tolerable. The *dahabeeyah* returned to Cairo, a bad-tempered voyage in which the vessel was frequently marooned on sandbanks. Ali, in sulky mood, behaved badly to his wife, his crew, and to any hapless native boatmen or fisherfolk who chanced to get in his way.

Once back in Cairo, their lives started to diverge. Ignoring Said's advice, Ali renewed his acquaintance with the seedier type of dancehall and café, in which women, young men and hashish were freely available. Hashish could be either smoked or chewed and some low dives offered *manzoul*, normally an inoffensive sweet paste, transformed into a kind of 'space-cake' of opium, hashish, even strychnine, taken, reported the *Egyptian Gazette*, 'for its aphrodisiac properties'. The user of hashish, wrote that newspaper, 'sees visions, voluptuous or merely grandiose . . . To promote the hallucinations, the walls of hashish-smoking dens are often covered with pictures of elephants, dancing girls and other imagined accessories of regal pomp . . .' And there were new opportunities for the well-to-do. 'Since the War, the [Egyptian] upper and middle classes . . . have succumbed to the lure of morphine and cocaine . . . [a habit] imported with the French prostitutes who flocked to Cairo in the winter of 1919–20 . . .'

Marguerite, although not fully confined within the traditional boundaries of the Egyptian wife, was getting dangerously bored. Occasional outings to the theatre with one of her sisters-in-law, who had slightly unfrozen from the early days of their acquaintance, were no substitute for the gay life in Paris. By late April, fashionable society had already left Cairo for more temperate climes.

One night, escorted by Ali's diminutive Nubian valet, Marguerite went to the cinema. A man called Mukhta Bey unwisely took her back to Zamalik in a taxi. Ali, who had returned home earlier than expected, was waiting for his wife in the grounds of the mansion. A violent argument took place during which Ali punched his wife on the face, an ugly incident, even if Marguerite's allegation that she had sustained a dislocated jaw may have been a later exaggeration.

At last the day came to set off for summer in Europe. On the morning of their departure, Marguerite's heart missed a beat when Ali capriciously announced that he had decided not to go, but at 7.30 a.m. on 18 May the boat-train pulled out of Cairo on its way to Alexandria, with the Fahmy entourage on board. Just after 1.00 p.m., their ship was making its way out into the Mediterranean, bound for Brindisi, Venice and Trieste, with its rail connection to Paris. The vessel was the SS *Helouan*, on which Marguerite and her sister had travelled to Egypt just six months before. On this voyage, Ali and Marguerite fought so much that they became the talk of the ship and the captain had to be called in to act as umpire.

8

Trench Warfare

The Fahmys argied and bargied, clawed and scratched, bit and kicked
their way from the heat of Egypt to a chilly, wet Paris, where they took
a suite at the Hôtel Majestic, the scene of Ali's first formal introduction
to Marguerite the previous July. Marguerite, delighted to be back in her
home town, exchanged scandal with her women friends, discreetly
renewed some valued male acquaintances, bought another horse for
12,000 francs (£150), ordered several new dresses and, while the going
was still good, expanded her collection of jewellery. Her personal wealth
was now estimated to be in the region of three million francs (£37,500),
a very comfortable sum in 1923.

Despite the ever-present risk of friction, the couple made regular
appearances at the smart nightspots, dancing into the small hours most
mornings, in the swing of the Paris June Season. They would go to
Claridge's, the Carlton, the Club Dannon, Le Perroquet and Ciro's,
from which they emerged early one morning arguing furiously. As
they were motored home by Marguerite's loyal chauffeur, Eugène
Barbay, Ali was heard to shout angrily, 'I've had enough of you,' before
getting out of the car, slamming the door shut, and walking off into the
night.

One of Marguerite's friends later recalled those troubled days in Paris.
'[She] was playing with fire and making the Prince crazy with jealousy . . .
Her marriage to this wild youth of 23 [sic] was a mistake and worse –
a crime. Heedless of everything, she went on in her married life like an
emancipated Parisienne. She received all her admirers with smiles . . .'
Ali felt himself to be humiliated. 'I was a witness to many scenes,'

continued the friend, 'and, though I assured the Prince that his wife was flirting and nothing more . . . his ideas were so narrow that they had no relation to the society life he was leading. One day he insisted that his wife, who was wearing a gown very slightly décolleté, should put a shawl over her shoulders . . .' Marguerite did not easily accept these attempts to restrict her freedom in Egypt, still less so in her native Paris. 'I can't go on living like this,' she confided to her friend at the end of the month, 'We must get a divorce.'

Ali, a strange mixture of martinet and libertine, was himself the butt of his wife's criticism. He had always been generous to the principal members of his all-male entourage, rewarding them with cash and other presents at his whim. Said Enani was the principal beneficiary, but the others, including the boy valet, were not left out. Marguerite grew increasingly resentful of the intimacy between Ali and his staff, which now included a 'minder', one of whose nicknames, '*Le Costaud*', reflected his strapping build.

Ali's fondness for wearing jewellery was a trait common enough in rich Egyptian men, but Marguerite felt that it ought not to be extended to subordinates. Harsh words ensued and Marguerite's will prevailed. 'He had a habit, which I succeeded in breaking,' she said imperiously, 'of letting his suite adorn themselves with some of the contents of his jewel cases.'

Marguerite was particularly suspicious of Said Enani. His friendship with Ali, for the association between the two men went well beyond that of master and servant, predated his acquaintance with Marguerite by several years and, what was more, Said was very close to the surviving members of Ali's family, a rich and powerful lobby not greatly enamoured of the new Madame Fahmy. She resented the way they talked together in Arabic, which she could not understand, as well as Ali's frequent late-night practice of slipping up to Said's room for an hour or so before returning to his wife.

Ali's relationship with his secretary seems to have been platonic, but there is no doubt that he was attracted to young men. From time to time, just as he had done in Cairo, Ali would go out alone, returning in the early hours. Marguerite's lawyer, Maître Assouad, accused him of 'vices so appalling that they can only be hinted at'. Marguerite complained that he was spending time with 'men of bad character'. She had flatly refused his suggestion, made after a visit to the *Folies Bergère* (one of Marguerite's beats in her professional days), that they should go on to what may have been a gay transvestite bar, 'a certain disreputable resort in Paris to which as a rule only men were admitted'.* There were persistent rumours that Ali had been entertaining actors and other male personalities from the world of theatre to 'dinners that became the talk of Paris . . .'

By mid-June 1923, Marguerite's thoughts were moving inexorably in the direction of divorce. She kept in touch with Maître Assouad in Cairo and engaged a French private detective, a M. Gasser, whose instructions, it seems, were to follow Ali and report on his sexual encounters with other men. If it came to a divorce, Marguerite's own past and her present fairly louche behaviour would undoubtedly be a handicap: if, on the other hand, she could show that Ali had been associating with homosexual men, her chances of a substantial pay-off would considerably increase. To avoid scandal, Ali and his family might be willing to settle on terms a good deal more generous than those provided for by the strict wording of the civil marriage contract.

On 17 June, Ali left Paris for a few days in Stuttgart, glad to be away from the domestic maelstrom and able to indulge another of his passions, high-performance cars. He was uneasy at the prospect of what Marguerite might get up to, alone and unchaperoned in Paris, and Said Enani was charged with the unenviable task of trying to secure Marguerite's chastity during her husband's absence.

Ali's obsessive jealousy gnawed at him while they were apart. He wrote her a bitter letter, warning that if she kept on seeing other men, he would publicly call her a very rude name – this was perhaps '*une salope*' (a slag). It was a timely threat: one of the glittering social events so loved by Marguerite was to take place on Saturday 23 June and she would have been anxious not to give the scandalmongers yet more ammunition.

Le Bal du Grand Prix, held amid the splendour of the Paris Opera, was the last great event of the Paris Season, taking place on the eve of the Grand Prix of the Longchamps race meeting, an event at which *Tout Paris* could see and be seen. The Fahmys, despite a marital disharmony that had become common knowledge, seem to have joined the several hundred other guests, who each paid 100 francs (£1.25) for a ticket. The ball was hosted by the Princess Murat, whose husband was the grandson of Napoleon's brother-in-law, who was King of Naples from 1808 to 1815, and the proceeds were devoted to French and White Russian charities.

For the occasion, Jean-Gabriel Doumergue (who, with the artist

---

* 'There was no ban on homosexuality in France and the police were fairly tolerant towards "special" night clubs . . .' (Brassaï, *Secret Paris*; Thames & Hudson 1976).

Georges Scott, had staged the Second Empire Ball at Biarritz in September 1922) employed the exotic theme of the Far East in the Eighteenth Century, enabling the great ladies of France to appear in a series of tableaux which uneasily linked Imperial China to the Court of Versailles. A staircase and walls draped in black velvet symbolized the eastern night, and a procession of rajahs and nautch girls gave way to the France of Louis XV, whose mistress, the notorious Madame de Pompadour, was, reported the *Illustrated London News*, represented by 'none other than Mlle Cecile Sorel [a noted French actress], borne in a palanquin by negroes . . .', amid a painted, powdered and bewigged retinue gorgeously costumed in the fashion of the 1750s.

There were elaborate representations of the treasures brought back from India by Joseph Dupleix, the French adventurer defeated by Clive, and of the court and theatre of China. In one of the latter, the Comte Étienne de Beaumont presented the Marquise de Polignac and other society beauties in costly oriental costume. The final tableau, and the most spectacular, depicted the flowers and birds of the Orient. 'Then appeared floral cascades of lotus, of chrysanthemums, of orchids, [with] pagodas, porcelain bridges, parasols, roses, fountains . . .', reported *Le Gaulois*. Women, gilded eyelids and vermilion-coloured nails aglint, were dressed as subtropical flowers and fantastically coloured birds. Then, at 2.00 a.m., it was time for the company to foxtrot into the dawn on any one of a number of dancefloors, each with its own orchestra.

Convulsions at the ball seem to have been avoided, but two nights later, during a heated argument in their suite at about 2.00 a.m., the Fahmys came to blows. Marguerite pulled her pistol out from under its usual hiding place, the pillow of her bed, pointed it at Ali and threatened to shoot him. Things were getting out of hand. Ali would appear in public with scratches on his face, while Marguerite on occasion sought to disguise bruises with cream and powder. There was a disturbing tendency to wave guns around: Ali also had a pistol, probably a .25 automatic, whose butt was elegantly decorated with mother-of-pearl and gold-leaf chasing.

A violent scene took place in the lobby of the Hôtel Majestic, in front of Ali's sister, Aicha, and his brother-in-law, Dr Said, who were also staying there. People were startled to see a well-dressed couple loudly insulting each other, heedless of passers-by. Ali, carrying out his earlier threat, shouted that she was nothing more than a tart, while she called him '*un maquereau*' (a pimp) and, very likely, '*un pédé*' (a pederast), '*un salaud* (a bastard) or '*un salopard*' (a sodomite). Ali, now furious, grabbed at her left wrist, wrenching off an expensive bracelet – his recent gift to Marguerite – and threw it contemptuously back at her. Dr Said and Said Enani had to separate the pair as they tried to smack each other's face.

Dr Said took the view, supported by the rest of Ali's family, that a separation was desirable. 'The cause seemed to me,' he wrote, 'that being a Christian woman and having taken the Mohammedan vows, she would not fall in with her husband's wishes, as it is generally understood that a wife must strictly obey her husband. He did not like her to go out alone, particularly as he knew of her former conduct and this, I believe, is the cause of the whole trouble. She resented this surveillance upon her and wished to follow her usual bent . . .'

Marguerite's friends and acquaintances in Paris were getting worried. One woman, writing from 3 rue Duphot, a smart address close to the Élysée Palace, sent a letter dated 30 June to Costy Tomvaco, a Greek resident of Alexandria, who was apparently well aware of the Egyptian dimension to the Fahmy marriage. 'You know that my friend [Marguerite] Fahmy is on the worst terms with her husband,' wrote the woman, 'the two don't get on together at all. I fear greatly for her skin. It's got to the point of an armed contest! . . .'

The writer, who signed herself 'Nouile', was corresponding with a close friend, using the diminutives 'Tot', 'Totinet' or 'Totti' for 'Costy', and she had evidently been to the Opera Ball. The letter gives a glimpse of the Parisian beau monde, which Marguerite aspired to join but which would never fully open its doors to her.

I was at the Opera in the dress I'm sending you [? a photograph] and which I had at a gala in the Palace; I have also been much in the house of [the Duke of] Val[l]ombrosa and also, the day before yesterday, was at the house of the Prince d'Esling, [the] Duke of Massena. Do you know him? It was a great and very charming fête at which there was only the nobility and also some common folk like me . . . There were pretty women and all that was lacking was for 'Tot', amidst all these fashionable people, to work up a sweat dancing the Shimmy . . . .

The last few days of June had seen a considerable improvement in the Parisian weather. '*C'est samedi et il fait beau*' ('It's Saturday and the weather's fine'), wrote the Parisian lady, the day Marguerite, Ali and their retinue were seen off at the Gare St Lazare by Dr Said and his wife, Ali's sister. They did not foresee the drama that would take place across the Channel. 'There seemed to be the usual misunderstanding, but nothing unusual,' remembered the doctor.

In London, after a dreary June, 'July made its debut yesterday in half-hearted fashion. For an hour or two in the afternoon, the sun managed to burst through a pall of clouds, but the temperature was below normal, the Kew maximum being 65° . . .', the *Daily Mirror* reported. The Fahmys, not expecting too much of an English summer, sought entertainment in theatres and nightclubs. As if in desperation, they went out, invariably accompanied by Said, on every night of their short stay together.

Likely attractions at the theatre included the revue 'Brighter London' at the Hippodrome, where Paul Whiteman's Orchestra, led by an amiable 280-lb giant from Denver, Colorado, had been playing to packed houses since April, and George Gershwin's 'Stop Flirting!' at the Shaftesbury Theatre, in which London theatregoers could see the young Fred Astaire dance with his sister Adele.

They did the rounds of the nightclubs, which offered a rota of extensions in the face of the LCC's licensing restrictions. That week, nightclub proprietors felt particularly aggrieved: with that breathtaking illogicality which is the hallmark of the English entertainment and liquor licensing system, the Council had allowed them to stay open until 2.00 a.m. from Monday to Saturday of the previous week because of an international horse show, but could not be persuaded to extend the permission, even though Henley Week and Wimbledon were bringing thousands of extra visitors to the metropolis.

The London Ciro's, in Orange Street, off Leicester Square, enjoying a record season that year, was a possible venue early in the week, two of its three late nights being Monday and Tuesday. The Fahmys may also have gone to hear Jack Hylton's Band, recording stars since 1922, play at the Queen's Hall Roof, a very popular rendezvous at the side of the famous concert hall where Sir Henry Wood conducted the Proms each summer. There the cabaret included The Trix Sisters and 'Divina and Charles', who, later that year, earned the peerless accolade 'Banned in Bournemouth', when the local watch committee responded apoplectically to their apache dance, 'Rough Stuff', performed with the help of cracking whips.

On Tuesday 3 July, a letter postmarked Paris arrived for Marguerite at the Savoy. It was written in French and unsigned:

Please permit a friend who has travelled widely among Orientals and who knows the craftiness of their acts to give you some advice. Don't agree to return to Egypt for any object or even Japan. Rather abandon fortune than risk your life. Money can always be recovered by a good lawyer, but think of your life. A journey means a possible accident, a poison in the flower, a subtle weapon that is neither seen nor heard. Remain in Paris with those who love you and will protect you.

Marguerite excitedly showed it to her husband, who cynically replied that she had probably written it herself. The letter has a distinctly bogus air about it and, if not Marguerite's handiwork, may have derived from one of her circle of friends at home in Paris, perhaps a former lover who knew about the marital breakdown.

Towards the end of the first week in London, the Fahmys, still together for the moment, went to the exclusive Riviera Club at 129 Grosvenor Road SW, formerly the home of a brother of Lord Derby. The elegant single-storey house, on the site of some old wharves, faced on to the Thames. The former drawing-room, which became the club's ballroom, enjoyed an excellent view of the river, though not quite 'Venetian in its beauty', as the *Referee* would have its readers believe. In front of the ballroom lay a little formal courtyard, bright with geraniums, where patrons might sit out on warm evenings.

'Barges glide noiselessly down river and occasionally one hears the low siren of a tug. Over the river of black creosote are reflected the lights of the factories on the Surrey side . . . the Riviera has become the refuge . . . of dancers tired of the heat and bustle of the West End night clubs . . .', the *Referee* went on. The Prince of Wales was among those who made the pilgrimage to Pimlico, an open secret to the press ('a very eminent person indeed is to be seen there very often . . .'). It seems that HRH was not present when the club's patrons were treated to the spectacle of a Fahmy row, in the course of which, as the couple stood in the hall overlooking the Thames, Ali shouted, 'I'm tired of you – I've a good mind to throw you in the river.'

Marguerite did not pay much attention to the threat: two or three nights later she went to an out of town nightspot on the banks of the selfsame Thames, The Casino at Molesey. The party included Ali, Said Enani and another Egyptian, Gallini Pasha. On the way, they stopped the car to look at Hampton Court Palace. Here another dispute began, blows were exchanged, and Gallini foolishly tried to separate the warring couple, receiving no thanks for his pains.

The Casino (or, hideously, 'The Karsino', after its creator Fred Karno) was, in fact, a large hotel and restaurant on Tagg's Island, just upstream from Hampton Court. Built in 1912, to the design of the great theatre architect Frank Matcham, its centrepiece was an enormous, baroque-style ballroom, 'large enough to seat some 800 people, with a maple dancing floor under an extensive dome' and a ceiling painted with riverside scenes. The premises were set in extensive landscaped grounds which at night were illuminated by hundreds of coloured lights. Never the success in the 1920s that it had been before the war, Fred Karno's attempt to 'bring the Continental atmosphere up-river' was ultimately a failure and he was declared bankrupt in 1927.

The Fahmys and their party probably enjoyed the novelty of being ferried across to the island on one of the hotel's private punts and this open-air excursion may have been prompted by a change in the weather, the start of a ten-day heatwave.

On the Thursday, further upstream at Henley, as reported by the *Daily Mirror*, '. . . the morning was overcast, but late in the day, the sun came out gloriously, the Americans arrived and the world of fashion seemed assembled on the lawns and in the boats by the riverside . . .' The transatlantic oarsmen were described as 'serious, wide-shouldered young men in low-crowned felt hats and horn spectacles . . . whose accent was a quaint combination of Harvard, Yale, and Oxford or Cambridge'. Those young men either not in training or careless of it might well have slipped up to town that Thursday or Friday, joining the likes of the Fahmys for dancing at the Grafton Galleries or for cabaret at the Metropole Hotel's 'Midnight Follies'.

Friday saw the temperature reach 84°F at Kew and, as ever, London found itself unprepared. '[The] traffic chaos seemed worse than ever, the fumes of the endless motor traffic mingling with the tropic heat . . .', the *Daily Mirror* reported. With no air-conditioning to dispel the sweltering atmosphere, London life grew more than usually sticky. Marguerite, already suffering from a very personal complaint, found that her discomfort had acutely increased.

9

Stormy Weather

Dr Edward Francis Strathearn Gordon was a physician and surgeon with consulting rooms at 26 Southampton Street, on the north side of the Strand, opposite the Savoy Hotel entrance. In 1923, he had the good fortune to be the hotel's doctor, a post which he held for many years afterwards. He was well liked and a practised exponent of the bedside manner demanded by the Savoy's rich and often temperamental clientele.

Marguerite Fahmy summoned Dr Gordon to see her on Wednesday 4 July. It was an afternoon consultation and Ali kept well out of the way elsewhere in the suite. As might be expected, the doctor spoke excellent French, murmuring sympathetically when Marguerite showed him the bruises on her arms, inflicted during some of the more recent matrimonial barneys. No doubt she also gave chapter and verse about Ali's generally disgraceful behaviour. It was unlikely to have been the first time that Dr Gordon had come across this kind of injury, accompanied by complaints about the violent conduct of a husband or lover. But Marguerite's allegations also included a distinctly uncommon element, intimately connected with a painful condition.

Marguerite had developed external haemorrhoids, which were in an inflamed state, as Dr Gordon could plainly see. He examined her again on each of the next two days, telling Marguerite that if no improvement had occurred by the following Monday, 9 July, the advice of a specialist surgeon should be sought. Haemorrhoids, hardly the most fashionable of complaints, are extremely common, come and go rather unpredictably, and often affect women who have given birth. Earlier that summer, in Paris, Marguerite had undergone ultraviolet ray treatment (a medical fad of the day, administered by a special quartz applicator), but it does not appear to have had the desired effect.

At the Savoy, she alleged to Dr Gordon that her husband had 'torn her by unnatural intercourse'. Marguerite said that Ali was 'always pestering her' for this kind of sex, implying that he was not interested in ordinary vaginal penetration. Significantly, in view of the steps Marguerite was already taking with a view to launching divorce proceedings, she repeatedly asked Dr Gordon to provide 'a certificate as to her physical condition to negative the suggestion of her husband that she had made up a story'.

Soothing ointments brought a little relief to Marguerite during that very warm weekend. Friday's heat was such that a train was derailed near Lewes because the rails had buckled in the heat, tar melted in the streets and four ladies playing tennis doubles in Burton-on-Trent were suddenly engulfed in hay, the remains of a haystack which had taken off in a summer whirl-wind. At Wimbledon, women spectators fainted, but, braving the soaring temperatures, the mighty Suzanne Lenglen careered round the court in a calf-length skirt, walloping Kitty MacKane in straight sets, 6–2, 6–2, to win the championship. Across the Channel, there was an unhappy reminder of the war when a buried cache of German high-explosive shells at Domeer on the Somme exploded without warning, scattering shrapnel half a mile and breaking windows within a two-mile radius.

On Saturday, Kew recorded 89°F. Women brought out the parasols, prettily decorated with Japanese paper, which had stood undisturbed in umbrella stands since the blistering summer of 1921. Combining the dictates of fashion with propriety and comfort was not easy, but much could be achieved with lightweight material. 'Diaphanous dresses' made a rapid appearance and the *Daily Mirror*'s Wimbledon reporter could describe 'the pretty girl in gold gossamer, so to say, whose waist was over the hips and skirt touching the ground'. For men, straw hats and panamas came into their own and one exhibitionist was observed strolling along the Strand in full colonial outfit of 'white duck' suit, canvas shoes and sola topi. At Henley, a fairly conservative occasion, 'a few bolder spirits donned tennis shirts open at the neck'.

Sleep did not come easily on these humid nights. In the roof gardens of Kensington, merrymakers in evening dress stayed up till all hours, regularly sending out for new supplies of ice to cool their drinks. One Clapham resident gave up the attempt to sleep and sat, wearing his pyjamas, in a garden chair until daybreak, drinking iced lemonade. For daytime relief, the British Museum was voted a first for coolness, closely followed by the Victoria and Albert Museum.

Sunday's temperatures were a little lower, at 80°, but blue skies had given way to angry masses of cloud: thunderstorms broke out, two people were killed by lightning in the Midlands and a fireball exploded in the clocktower of Dunsford Church, near Exeter. There was a brief electrical storm over London in the early hours of Monday, a day which brought no respite, for the temperature rose again to 84°. Not everybody was behaving decorously; fifteen lads, between sixteen and nineteen, appeared in court charged with 'wilfully trespassing upon the towpath of Regent's Park canal for the purpose of bathing'. They were an unlucky sample of about a hundred youths who had been seen 'bathing with nothing on and using obscene language . . .' The defendants were each fined two shillings and advised to use the public baths, though the chances were that these would all have been full.

Milk was often already sour by the time it was delivered: 'it goes bad when you look at it . . .', reported the *Daily Graphic*. That Monday the Oxford v Cambridge cricket match, a great social occasion, opened at Lord's. 'Summer frocks made a conspicuously cool contrast to the regulation morning dress worn by most men . . . ' Dame Clara Butt (whose junoesque form towered above her husband), Mrs Stanley Baldwin, Field Marshal Lord Plumer and the Duke of Rutland were snapped by the press photographers, as was the Jam of Nawanagar, better known as Ranjitsinhji, the legendary cricketer of the 1890s.

The Fahmys took a cooling drive that morning, returning to the Savoy at 1.00 p.m., in time for lunch in the restaurant with Said Enani. Marguerite's discomfort as she sat at table did nothing for her temper and the customary quarrel broke out. Probably as a diversionary tactic after promptings by the restaurant's head waiter, the orchestra leader came over to the Fahmys' table, bowed low, and asked politely in French whether Madame would care to select a tune for the band to play.

In an act of pure melodrama, Marguerite looked up demurely and said, 'Thank you very much. My husband is going to kill me in twenty-four hours and I am not very anxious for music.' The conductor replied, 'I hope you will be here tomorrow, madame,' a model of hotel diplomacy. Marguerite would not be deflected from her argument and told Ali, 'I'm going to leave you and you'll pay dearly for it.' Her husband, for once, responded half-heartedly and went up to his room for a nap after lunch.

At 3.30, Dr Gordon arrived at suite 41, accompanied by Mr Ivor Back, a consultant surgeon: after a brief examination, Mr Back recommended an operation. Marguerite agreed and Dr Gordon telephoned a London nursing home there and then, arranging for Marguerite to be admitted the next day, to have the necessary minor surgery on the Wednesday. Marguerite asked Mr Back if he would provide her with a certificate as to her physical condition, but it seems that the surgeon politely demurred, just as Dr Gordon had done.

After the consultation was over, Marguerite, with a sudden perversity, decided to use the operation as a pretext to return to Paris. After ordering train tickets for herself and her maid, she took Said Enani with her on a shopping trip to Selfridges, where she bought some new clothes for the trip. They returned for tea at about 5.00, after which Marguerite, as if nothing was the matter, calmly kept an appointment with the hotel's hairdresser.

Shortly before 8.00 that evening, the trio met up in the Fahmys' suite, the men in full evening dress (tailcoat, starched white shirtfront and waistcoat), Marguerite wearing a white satin evening dress, embroidered with small pearls, bought recently from a Paris fashion house for 5000 francs (£62). On an oddly still, humid evening, they were chauffeured to Daly's Theatre, which then stood in Coventry Street, just off the north-east corner of Leicester Square. At 8.15, the curtain rose on a musical comedy which turned out, with grim hindsight, to have been a blackly humorous choice. It was *The Merry Widow*.

This was a popular revival of Lehár's operetta, with Evelyn Laye (a day short of her twenty-third birthday) and the handsome Dane, Carl Brisson, in the leading roles. Even on a Monday night, the house would have been well attended as the three took their seats in the box reserved for them by the ever-efficient Said. The first duet, ironically titled 'A Dutiful Wife', was soon followed by 'Maxim's', a celebration of Parisian nightlife, which must have been a pointed reminder to the couple of the city in which their relationship, now so bitter, had begun only a year before.

In the warm, sticky atmosphere of the crowded theatre, Marguerite would very likely have shuffled uncomfortably on the plush upholstery of her gilt chair. The first act lasted about three quarters of an hour and her irritability surfaced in the first interval. Ali told her how much he wanted her to remain in London, but Marguerite angrily insisted that her mind was made up and that she was going back the next day. She probably asked Said to send a telegram at once to Paris, telling of her impending arrival. In its report of the trial, the *Daily Telegraph* noted that the telegram was dispatched 'at nine p.m. on the evening of July 9th'.

Not to be outdone and with the tit-for-tat attitude characteristic of the Fahmy marriage, Ali immediately ordered three telegrams of his own to be sent to Paris. It seems that the faithful Said either telephoned his employers' instructions to the Savoy or hurried down to the West Strand telegraph office, which was open twenty-four hours a day. Ali's cables were each timed at 9.10 p.m. and contained an identical message, which reveals that relations between the couple were now near to breaking point.

The wording was English and read: 'NOTHING TO BE DELIVERED TO MY WIFE ON MY ACCOUNT DURING MY ABSENCE. FAHMY.' The addressees were Cartier of the rue de la Paix, Van Clef & Arpels of 22 place Vendôme, and Louis Vuitton of 70 avenue des Champs Élysées. The first two firms held substantial quantities of jewellery on Ali's behalf, worth in all around £5000. Vuitton was holding a gold-fitted handbag, valued at 162,000 francs (£2025), and the company had recently been commissioned to prepare a similar bag, bearing Marguerite's monogram, at an estimated cost of 157,000 francs (£1962). It appears that this latter item had been ordered just before Ali's trip to Stuttgart in June. While he was away, Marguerite had called at Vuitton, saying that she wanted it there and then. On being told that it would take another fortnight to complete, Marguerite appeared very annoyed and left the shop.

The last two acts of *The Merry Widow* are set in Paris, a fact which did nothing to calm the growing tension between husband and wife. As they left Daly's, towards 11.00, the distant growling of thunder could be heard above the noise of homeward-bound theatregoers. During a late supper at the hotel Ali's patience snapped and once more a loud argument broke out, worse even than the contretemps at lunch, causing heads to turn at this strictly unofficial cabaret, which had become a twice-daily performance at the Savoy.

Ali roundly told Marguerite that as his legal wife she should not go to Paris on her own. He wanted her to have her operation in London so that they could spend the remainder of the Season in England. Marguerite maintained that she was going to Paris the next day, whereupon the argument degenerated, as so often before, into mutual vituperation. Eventually, Marguerite picked up a wine bottle from the table, shouting in French, 'You shut up or I'll smash this over your head.' 'If you do,' replied Ali, 'I'll do the same to you.'

No doubt to the relief of the restaurant's staff, the Fahmys and the ubiquitous Said then went down to the ballroom, where the Savoy Havana Band was entertaining hotel residents and guests on a 2.00 a.m. extension. The band played from a low dais, in front of the Versailles-like mirrors. It comprised piano, drums and 'high-hat' cymbal, banjo, trumpet, trombone, two saxophones (doubling with clarinets) and the leader's violin. Conspicuous at the rear was an enormous sousaphone of shining brass.

Without doubt, the band would have played (probably several times) the smash hit of the moment, 'Yes! We Have No Bananas'. This utterly banal tune, whose lyric crudely mocked the fumbling attempts at English of an immigrant Greek greengrocer in New York, was an enormous success. Why this should have been so remains a mystery, but by mid-July 1923 sheet-music sales were running at the rate of 37,000 a day. The song was recorded by five British bands between July and September and was a regular feature of dance-music broadcasts until well into the following year.

More discriminating dancers might prefer Gershwin's 'I'll Build a Stairway to Paradise', the bouncy 'Toot-Toot-Tootsie, Goodbye', or, in more reflective vein, 'Three o'clock in the Morning', a slow waltz of enduring popularity. Unfamiliar today, but featured in the summer of 1923, were 'Dancing Honeymoon', 'I Ain't Nobody's Baby', 'Oh Star of Eve' and, most forgettable of all, 'Oogie Oogie Wah Wah'.

A tense and gloomy threesome sat on their white and gold lyre-backed chairs at one of the numerous tables in the ballroom. Ali tried to defuse the situation by asking Marguerite to dance, expressing the vain hope that they could make things up, but she curtly refused. Although she had refused to dance with Ali, she later took the floor with Said. He tried to persuade her to be reasonable and stay on in London. 'Nothing doing!', came the determined response.

Shortly before 1.00 a.m., Marguerite announced that she was going to bed. Said escorted her to the lift and returned to Ali for a brief heart-to-heart. Ali seemed very depressed, concerned that, with Marguerite going back to Paris alone, the marriage was finished. The two men went back to the foyer, from where it was evident that a tremendous thunderstorm was raging outside. When it rains, taxis become a rarity in London and almost an extinct species during a thunderstorm, but the Savoy is a powerful magnet and, even on this wild night, there were one or two cabs hopefully waiting under the entrance canopy. Said Enani went to bed immediately after his chat with Ali, but his young master had other ideas. He was seen by hotel staff, still wearing formal evening dress, standing for a short time in the entrance lobby at 1.00, before the Savoy's doorman ushered him into a cab, whose driver was instructed to take Ali in the direction of Piccadilly.

While Ali was away, Marguerite was putting pen to paper. She was writing to Dr Gordon, as yet unaware that his patient had decided not to go into the London nursing home after all. As the translation reveals, Marguerite was now being a little less than frank about the substance of the disagreement with her husband:

Doctor

> Affairs have come to a crisis. My husband refuses to take the responsibility for my operation. I am therefore returning to my family. That is to say, tomorrow I leave for Paris.
>
> Will you excuse me to the doctor who was kind enough to look after me and, believe me, yours gratefully, M. Fahmy.
>
> Will you please pay the doctor for his trouble? This account is a personal one.

If she was implying that Ali had refused to pay for the operation in London, Marguerite was not telling the truth. While he may have been reluctant to have his wife treated in Paris, away from him, the evidence suggests that he would have been only too pleased for Marguerite to be operated on in London. Marguerite, of course, had to give some excuse to Dr Gordon for her perverse conduct. She enclosed a cheque for £15.

Shortly after 2.00 a.m., with almost continuous thunder and brilliant flashes of lightning all around, Ali returned to the Savoy and went up to their suite. Soon another violent argument broke out between husband and wife, while Ali's black valet crouched in the corridor outside the door, waiting to be discharged from service for the night.

Half an hour later, John Paul Beattie, night porter at the hotel, was taking some luggage to another suite on the fourth floor of Savoy Court, apparently for some late arrivals that stormy morning. As he came out of the lift, almost opposite the Fahmys' suite, the door suddenly opened and Ali, wearing a brightly coloured dressing-gown over a white silk djellaba, came rushing out, closely followed by Marguerite, still in the white satin evening dress she had worn to the theatre. Marguerite's little dog ran about, yapping noisily.

'Look at my face,' cried Ali excitedly to the astonished Beattie. 'Look what she's done.' Ali pointed to his left cheek, on which could be seen a slight red mark, and also to a mark near his right eye. Marguerite interjected in rapid French, which Beattie did not understand, gesturing towards her face, but he could see no sign of any injury.

'Please get back into your room,' asked Beattie, mindful of other guests, despite the storm, 'and don't kick up a disturbance in the corridor.' By now, Marguerite was trying to pull Ali back into the suite, but he was in no mood to return, insisting that Beattie should send for the Night Manager, Arthur Marini.

There were two adjacent lifts on the fourth floor and, as one was descending, Beattie was able to attract the attention of the lift attendant, who was told to pass the message on while the porter continued with his work, wheeling his luggage round the corner, a sharp left turn, then along another short stretch of corridor (with the door to suite 42 and, beyond it, the emergency stairs), and round to the left again on his way to number 50.

As he rounded the second corner, Beattie heard a low whistle and, looking back, saw Ali Fahmy stooping down outside the door of suite 42, apparently whistling to Marguerite's lapdog, which had been following Beattie along the passageway. The porter continued on his way, but after going only about three yards, he heard, above the roar of thunder, the unmistakable sound of three shots, fired in rapid succession.

He ran back in the direction in which he had come and, as he rounded the corner of the short corridor, saw Marguerite throw down a large, black handgun and stumble towards him. On the floor, just by the door to number 42, some twenty-four feet away from his own suite, and with his head towards the direction of the stairs, lay Ali, on his right side, crumpled against the wall. He was unconscious, breathing sterterously, and bleeding profusely from a head wound from which protruded fragments of brain tissue and splintered bone. Alongside him lay a pool of blood in the corridor, about five feet from the door of number 42.

Beattie pushed past Marguerite, who was shouting hysterically in French, picked up the pistol, and put it in one of the two adjacent lifts. Marguerite made as if to follow him, but he caught hold of her arms and led her towards the stairs, where there was a service telephone. Keeping hold of Marguerite with one hand, Beattie told the hotel telephonist to send for a doctor and ambulance. Amid the flood of voluble French, Beattie recognized the English word 'cloak' and took her back to suite 41 so that she could get her wrap.

Arthur Marini was in the night service room when he received a message from the hotel reception that he was urgently wanted at suite 41. Thinking that he was being called in to calm yet another Fahmy altercation, he hurried up the stairs to the fourth floor, where he was horrified to find Ali, terribly injured, lying just to the Night Manager's left as he emerged from the staircase. He looked around and saw Beattie leading Marguerite out from number 41. 'Go and telephone the police at Bow Street,' said Marini crisply, 'and tell the General Manager to come here at once.'

Madame Marie Marguerite Fahmy had some explaining to do.

10

Femme Fatale

Crying out in French, over and over again, 'What shall I do? I've shot him,' Marguerite clutched desperately at Marini's sleeve as he tried to persuade her to return to the drawing-room of the suite. Gelardi, the General Manager, was slow to get to the scene, but his two assistants, Clement Bich and Michael Dreyfus, soon arrived. Dreyfus, in his room at the hotel, unable to sleep because of the heat and the thunder, had himself heard the loud, arguing voices, then three shots. Not able to tell where the sounds had come from, he had taken the lift down to reception: the liftman, warned by Beattie, already knew that there had been trouble outside number 41. Dreyfus, after giving instructions to the reception staff, ran up to the fourth floor in time to find Marguerite, bending over Ali's body, holding his head and repeating *'Qu'est-ce que j'ai fait, mon cher?'* ('What have I done, my dear?').

Beattie was ordered to bathe Ali's face in cold water, upon which it became clear that he was wounded both in the head and in the nape of his neck. Marguerite, grabbing at Clement Bich's arms, again said, 'What have I done?' Bich replied, 'You know that better than I do,' at which Marguerite raised her hands to her face, saying desperately, *'J'avais perdu ma tête. J'ai lui tiré.'* ('I lost my head. I've shot him.') After she had been escorted back into the suite by Marini, Marguerite kept asking to go back into the corridor, but she was prevented from returning to Ali's stricken body. Instead, Marini agreed to telephone Said's room. Said, already in bed, was alarmed to hear a strange man's voice saying an urgent 'hello, hello', seconds before the receiver was seized by Marguerite, who shouted excitedly, *'Venez vite, venez vite. J'ai tiré à Ali'.* ('Come quickly. I've shot Ali.')

70

'We were quarrelling over the divorce,' she unwisely told Marini, before suddenly asking, 'Where is my revolver?' As if in a daze, she hunted through the drawers of the wardrobe and looked under the pillow, saying, 'I kept it there always, as I am so frightened of him.' Her composure was now beginning to return. Marguerite changed out of her evening gown into a jade-green blouse and skirt (bought specially for her return to Paris), put on some lipstick and tidied her hair, to await the arrival of the police.

Ali, his face covered, was being taken away on a stretcher as Said arrived panting outside suite 41, out of breath after running, almost falling, down four flights of stairs. A bystander idiotically told him, 'Everything's all right.' At the same time, Sergeant George Hall, hot foot from Bow Street, was marshalling the gathering in the fourth floor corridor, a small crowd which would have included a number of bemused and horrified guests. Dr Gordon, too, was soon on the scene, where he was surprised to find Fahmy's Nubian valet still waiting, crouched outside the door of the suite. Nobody paid the slightest attention to the silent youth, of whom Ali had once said, 'He is nothing.'

Gordon found Marguerite to be 'excited and dismayed . . .' He recalled that she kept exclaiming, 'Oh, what have I done?', but was evidently not completely out of her wits. She handed her doctor the letter in which earlier that fateful morning she had written of her intention to leave London for Paris. Marguerite was very eager, at this crucial early stage, to get across the story that Ali had refused to allow her to have the operation in London. Madame Fahmy was going to keep her head, whatever happened.

The method of collecting forensic material in 1923 seems a little casual to modern eyes. Almost at the outset of the investigation, Sergeant Hall's function in assembling the first fruits of evidence had been usurped by the hotel's night porter. Beattie handed over the pistol, recovered from the luggage lift, as well as three empty cartridge cases which he had found lying on the floor outside the Fahmys' suite. He also recovered two bullets from the area adjacent to the stairwell, the wooden bannisters of which had been damaged by a shot or shots.

There were ricochet marks on the wall to the left of the door to suite 42, as well as to a set of folding doors immediately to the right of the stairs. Bloodstains could be seen on the carpet in the corridor. After their position had been noted (but not, it seems, photographed), Beattie, by night the hotel's jack-of-all-trades, was ordered to clean them away.

71

His duties were by no means over: he had to wait until 6.00 a.m. to make his first statement to the police.

By the time the exhausted night porter had reached his home in south London, the exceptionally violent weather, which had convulsed southern England for over twelve hours, was almost over. From late the previous afternoon, there had been a series of isolated electrical storms in Surrey and Sussex. At Croydon Aerodrome, an Instone Air Liner from Cologne and a big twin-engined Rolls-Royce Handley Page just managed to land before a thundery squall struck at 7.15 p.m., but soon the really severe storm began to sweep over the Channel from northern France, reaching the coast at about 9.00.

Between midnight and 1.00 a.m., the 'stupendous thunderstorm' reported the next day by the *Star* was at its first great intensity over central London. There was almost continuous lightning and even the most solid buildings vibrated with the thunder. The storm ebbed slightly for a while, before rising to another climax between 4.30 and 5.00. In the six hours from midnight, 2.57 inches of rain – the entire average rainfall for July – was recorded at Hampstead, in north London.

During the downpour, at about 2.30 a.m., a woman was found by police in Parliament Square, screaming hysterically in her nightdress, as Members of Parliament attempted, with varying degrees of success, to get back to their homes. Viscount Curzon was reported by the *Star* as having bravely 'jumped into his swift little 2-seater and careered out of the gates as if it were a lovely moonlight morning', while less adventurous MPs bedded down in the corridors of Westminster, and four representatives of the people were later found asleep in their cars.

Three thousand telephone lines were put out of action, and wireless reception suffered severely. The *Daily News* reported that, 'Broadcatching [sic] in the London area was badly interfered with by atmospheric disturbance . . .' This, at any rate, had the merit of preventing listeners from hearing John Henry, an early radio 'comedian', with lugubrious Yorkshire voice, who seems to have been both very clean and consistently unfunny. Although the newspaper pointed out that 'properly made aerials act as lightning conductors providing they are earthed', a wireless set exploded at Thames Ditton and in nearby Walton a worse fate befell Mr Justice Russell, whose country house was completely burnt out.

The *Times* reported 'one of the most remarkable and spectacular [thunderstorms] seen in London for many years . . . a journey through the streets of London between 1.00 and 5.00 a.m. was a thrilling experience'; to the *Daily Mail*, it was 'the greatest thunderstorm by far in this country that living man can remember.' And at the Star & Garter Home in Richmond, many of the resident ex-servicemen, still traumatized by the horror of the trenches, were reported to have been severely disturbed by the noise of thunder and the brilliant flashes of lightning, a cruel reminder of the Great War.

Ali Fahmy had been removed from the Savoy in an LCC ambulance, as discreetly as circumstances permitted. At 2.55 a.m., Ali, still clinically alive, was seen by Dr Maurice Newfield, the House Physician in the casualty department of Charing Cross Hospital, which then stood two hundred yards from the Savoy, in King William Street. Dr Newfield would have realized at once that there was little to be done for the unconscious man, who was still bleeding profusely, brain tissue bulging from the wound in his left temple. Bandages were applied, and blankets and a hot water bottle put round him, but Ali died at 3.25 that morning.

Fifteen minutes later, Marguerite arrived at Bow Street Police Station by taxi, escorted by Sergeant Hall and Dr Gordon. At Bow Street, the matron, Mrs Greenwood, had been sheltering in the inspector's office, fearful to remain alone in the matron's room during the storm. If Marguerite had been a male prisoner, she would undoubtedly have been incarcerated in one of the evil-smelling cells, lined with glazed brick and devoid of adequate sanitary facilities, which lay beyond the custody area and its 'No Spitting' notice.

Marguerite was more fortunate. She and the matron huddled in a corner of the inspector's office, while Dr Gordon, later to be a vital witness at Marguerite's trial, played the role of detective and tried to find out what had happened. Marguerite was anxious to show her doctor a fresh scratch on her neck which she claimed, had been inflicted by Ali. In her bedroom, she said, he had approached her 'in a threatening manner'. Marguerite had snatched up her pistol, fired a shot out of the window, hoping to frighten him, and, thinking that the gun was now unloaded, pointed it at her husband and pulled the trigger 'several times', after which Ali fell to the ground. At first, she thought he was shamming. When she realized she had shot him, she said, 'I then gave the alarm by telephone.'

For someone who had undergone so shocking an experience, Marguerite was able to give Dr Gordon a surprisingly coherent account of her side of the story, a version, not yet complete, that would later form the germ of her defence. And she needed a good lawyer. Dr Gordon, well versed in the ways of the rich in trouble, suggested that Marguerite should instruct Freke Palmer as her solicitor as soon as possible. At that time, Palmer probably had the largest and certainly the most fashionable criminal practice in London. Luckily for Marguerite, money was no problem, as Palmer's services did not come cheaply. Palmer was no altruist and the Poor Prisoners' Aid Scheme held little attraction for him. His long experience extended back to the 1880s and he had worked on innumerable murder cases with the leading criminal barristers of his time.

Shortly before 4.00 a.m., Dr Gordon broke the news to Marguerite that her young husband had died. She wept. The doctor then wrote out a two-page statement (on the approved police form no. 992) in a fastidious but attractive hand, amazingly legible for a medical man. As the thunder began to die down, Marguerite dozed for a while in her corner of the inspector's room, until the change of shift at 6.00 brought an inevitable disturbance and the offer of a welcome cup of tea. Dr Gordon, who had left the station after writing his statement, probably telephoned the solicitor at his home, before snatching an hour or two's sleep. Freke Palmer was instructed to begin the arduous process of establishing a defence to the capital charge of murder.

That charge was not administered until mid-morning. The officer in the Fahmy case, Divisional Detective Inspector Alfred Grosse, had first gone to the mortuary at Charing Cross Hospital, where he viewed the body of Ali Fahmy at about 5.00 a.m., before examining the scene of the shooting at the Savoy. In Marguerite's bedroom, he took possession of the white evening dress, which she had been wearing when Ali was shot: there was some blood on the hem and beside the bed in Ali's room DDI Grosse found a number of crushed beads (or small pearls) which matched those sewn on to the dress.

When Grosse returned to Bow Street and first saw Marguerite at 7.00 a.m., it was merely to order her removal to the matron's room, above the cells, and to ensure that the prisoner had a cup of coffee. Not until two hours later did the legal formalities begin. Accompanied by Detective Sergeant Stewart Allen, who acted as interpreter, Grosse introduced himself. The bald statement, 'I am a Detective Inspector,' was rather beautifully rendered: '*Je suis le chef inspecteur de la Sûreté ici.*' Grosse, a dapper, clean-shaven man, who sported a bow tie under his wing collar, told Marguerite that she would be charged with Ali's murder and cautioned her in customary fashion: 'Anything you say will be taken down in writing and may be used in evidence.'

The Metropolitan Police files record the following statement. (There are clearly inaccuracies in the police's transcription of the French, below and later in this book.) Marguerite was quite calm by now.

'*Je dis au Police que je le fais. J'ai dit la vérité. Ce ne va rien. Il m'a battue devant tout le monde depuis nous avions été mariés. Il m'a dit plusiers fois, "me tué", et il y a des personnes qui l'ont entendu.*' ('I told the police that I did it. I have told the truth. It doesn't matter. He has assaulted me in front of many people since we have been married. He has told me many times, "kill me", and many people have heard him say so.')

A police telegram was dispatched at 9.40 a.m. informing the Metropolitan Police Commissioner and his senior staff of Ali's death by shooting and of his wife's arrest. In contrast to modern practice, in which lengthy interviews are the norm, Marguerite was not interrogated at any stage by police officers. When she was charged, at 11.00 a.m., Marguerite replied simply '*Je comprends. Je comprends. Je perd la tête.*' ('I understand . . . I lost my head.')

Sometime after noon, Marguerite's fingerprints were taken by an officer who thought her 'a perfect little doll'. Her personal details were recorded, including two beauty spots, one on each cheek. Shortly afterwards, Aimée Pain arrived from the Savoy. She probably brought her mistress scent, soap and towels and took instructions concerning the jewellery that madame would wear at her first appearance in court that afternoon. Marguerite also had the opportunity to speak to her maid about other matters. Aimée had already made her statement to the police, but Marguerite was anxious to talk to her about events on the night of the shooting. Madame Fahmy was beginning to marshal her forces.

After lunch, Freke Palmer walked into the matron's room with his managing clerk Collins. Because of his busy professional schedule and with the clout that comes fromm regular appearances as an advocate, Palmer had persuaded the police, who controlled the list of cases of Bow Street Court, to put Marguerite's appearance at the end of the afternoon, so as to give time for preliminary instructions to be obtained.

The storm and the Savoy shooting had both occurred too late to be included in the daily papers, but by lunchtime the *Evening News*, the *Evening Standard*, the *Pall Mall Gazette* and the *Star* had emblazoned the night's events on their front pages. Already a small crowd was gathering outside Bow Street Court, which forms part of a building also housing the police station, in the hope of securing a place in the limited accommodation available in Number Two Court, on the first floor of the courthouse, up a flight of stone steps and along a narrow corridor.

Bow Street has always had, despite the best efforts of its cleaning staff, a smell of 'old lag' about it and on that broiling July afternoon the heat in the court, which had a glass roof, must have been intense, creating a particularly unpleasant atmosphere. The small dock, with its iron railings, stood a few feet from the door to the custody area, through which, at about 3.30, Marguerite made her entrance, looking pale and tired, escorted by Police Sergeant Claydon of the 'Woman Patrols' (who had relieved the matron two hours before). Necks craned forward to see her, and reporters' pencils scribbled away.

Despite the difficult circumstances, Marguerite had taken some care over her appearance. She was now a widow and the green silk blouse she had put on at the Savoy would have seemed a little too jaunty for so grave a charge as murder. Aimée had access to madame's wardrobe at the hotel and so, despite the intense heat, Marguerite entered court wearing a long, satin '*charmeuse*' coat, suitably black. The softly draped coat, comparatively lightweight, had a smooth, semi-lustrous finish and was trimmed with fur at the neck, sleeves and hem. She wore a small, mushroom-shaped black felt hat, around which lay a lightly patterned strip of silk.

Most eyes, however, were riveted on Marguerite's jewellery, which she could not resist displaying, despite the pressing need for a sober look. Large, pearl-drop earrings matched a plain, but elegant, pearl necklace. Above her gold wedding band, she wore 'a big square marquise diamond ring' and on the third finger of her right hand, an even larger emerald, 'set in quaint oriental style'. On her left wrist she wore a magnificent three-tier diamond and sapphire bracelet, set in turquoise, probably the one that Ali had torn off and thrown at her in the lobby of the Majestic in Paris a fortnight before.

Though these were hardly widow's weeds, the press responded sympathetically to this wan, petite form, described by the *Aberdeen Press & Journal* as 'typically Gallic, [whose] pallor emphasised dark marks under the large and impressive eyes . . .' Those compelling eyes were seen to fill with tears during the brief hearing and from time to time she would dab them dry with a large, green silk handkerchief.

DDI Grosse told of the arrest and gave a short description of the scene of the incident to the Stipendiary Magistrate, Rollo Graham-

Campbell, who agreed to Freke Palmer's request that his client should not be transported to Holloway Prison in a van, like the common run of prisoners, but rather in the comfort of a taxi cab.

11

Inquest

The *Daily Mirror*'s headline of 11 July 1923, 'A PRINCE SHOT IN LONDON', was typical of its contemporaries, accompanied by a report which seized eagerly on the two exotic birds of paradise who had so suddenly found violent notoriety. At first, the references were generally sympathetic to both parties, the affair being seen as a domestic tragedy between two foreigners, a *crime passionnel* worthy of a novel by Zola. For example, the *Sunday Express* referred to 'the painful sensation in those social and Bohemian circles where the "Prince" and his beautiful French wife were very vivid and decorative personalities . . .'

In some early reports, Ali Fahmy was depicted as an ardent young lover, dashingly handsome, regarded by his contemporaries, according to the *Daily Express*, 'with affection, commingled with amusement created by his extravagance . . . His charming manners, happy smile and immaculate appearance placed him in the forefront of Cairo's gaieties, spending lavishly for his own and other people's pleasure . . .' The *Daily Sketch* printed a long article, almost certainly based on an interview with Said Enani ('one who has been the Prince's constant companion for the past five years'), which gave some reasonably correct background material and was headed 'WELL-BELOVED BY ALL HIS PEOPLE'.

Inaccuracies abounded. The *Daily Chronicle* reported that Marguerite was 'a descendant of a noble Turkish family of Alexandria'; according to the *Sunday Illustrated*, she was from 'a good family . . . born just on thirty years ago in the south of France . . . lapped in luxury from earliest hours'. To the *Daily Mirror*, mindful of the year's Tut-Ankh-Amun discoveries, Ali had been a member of 'one of the oldest Egyptian

78

families', a misstatement which paled in comparison with the *People*'s inventive streak, demonstrated on the first Sunday after the shooting. Ali, it declared, had been in London some months ago, helping to revive an ancient Egyptian dance, a visit at which 'a private, but most allegorical [sic], ceremony was performed to celebrate a festival called Amun Toonh (established . . . in 1403 BC . . . to celebrate the goddess of the Sun, Ta Aha) . . . [and] carried on with many mystic movements'.

But there were less favourable references to Ali, a trend to which eventually the entire English press succumbed. The *Daily Mail* was one of the earliest to make use of the 'oily Levantine' approach: 'He was a notorious spendthrift and, being ignorant and vain, had long been the victim of a crowd of sycophants . . . He was very fond of jewellery . . . his glittering diamonds used to attract attention at the [Paris] Opera House . . .' *Lloyd's Sunday News* accused Ali of 'voluptuousness truly Eastern . . . every form of excitement that could appeal to a sensuous nature . . . notorious for the lavish expenditure he incurred in entertaining stage stars of both sexes [in] Paris . . .' This flashy, effeminate foreigner had not so easily impressed the English upper classes as he had their gullible French counterparts: 'From time to time, he was received in good London society, but his vulgarity and extravagant habits caused him to be dropped . . . [He] next drifted into the night clubs and dancing resorts, wearing . . . conspicuous jewellery . . . naturally, he was blackmailed heavily.'

The *Illustrated Sunday Herald* splashed a denunciation of Fahmy across half a page, using information that can only have come from someone close to Marguerite. Headed 'SECRET LIFE OF BOY "PRINCE"', it contrasted 'the beautiful and the bestial . . .' Readers were left in no doubt who was beautiful and who bestial. Marguerite was the 'radiantly beautiful wife', who, before the ill-fated marriage, had 'flitted from capital to capital . . . carrying off in the gay whirlwind of her life a legion of untiring admirers . . .' Although the article hinted at Marguerite's background ('. . . her smart frocks were discussed; her horses and motor-cars were the envy of the grand cocottes . . .'), the fire was reserved for Ali, 'madly jealous', who, 'when she asked him for fidelity . . . pursued the trend of his own devices . . .' Marguerite's alleged imprisonment in the *dahabeeyah* at Luxor became marvellously garbled: 'On one occasion, when Maggie had again gone out at night in Cairo, the Prince had her abducted by his dusky slaves and carried to his yacht . . .'

The first shots of Marguerite's defence came at the inquest on Ali, held at Westminster Coroner's Court, Horseferry Road, on Wednesday 12 July. Public interest in the case was already enormous and, despite a sweltering heat that approached 90°, a crowd had started to form outside the little courthouse at 12.30, an hour and a half before the proceedings were due to begin. 'The house windows looking on to the mortuary,' reported the *Pall Mall Gazette*, 'were crowded with eager spectators.'

The Coroner bore a strange name and possessed an even stranger personality. After just eleven years', mainly prosecution, practice at the Bar, S. Ingleby Oddie had been appointed Westminster Coroner in 1912. He accepted the offer of this gloomy post with wild enthusiasm. 'I had now achieved the object at which I had aimed for so many years,' he wrote, 'and the day I was appointed was perhaps the happiest in my life. I trod on air!' Some of his personal prejudices also verged on the eccentric. 'The average Englishman is a decent sort of fellow, who does not like homicide . . . he hates the use of lethal weapons, always preferring a stand-up fight with his fists. He does not in a quarrel suddenly produce a pistol . . . as is the common practice of certain other nationalities . . .'

Marguerite, of course, was a woman of a certain other nationality who, on any reading, had suddenly produced a pistol during a quarrel and shot her husband dead. Wisely, she did not attend the inquest. Freke Palmer correctly advised his client that she would do herself no good by giving evidence and she remained in Holloway Prison, comfortably accommodated in the hospital wing, well away from less savoury inmates, while her solicitor did battle on her behalf.

In Marguerite's absence, the proceedings were little more than a formality, but there was the chance for her lawyer to put questions to the small band of witnesses and Freke Palmer was anxious to sow some seeds in the public mind. Reporters crammed into the tiny courtroom to hear Said Enani confronted by allegations of Ali's misconduct, with an occasional glimpse of humour:

PALMER: Did he call her in front of other people a prostitute?
ENANI: Yes, they used to exchange names.
PALMER: They exchanged compliments?
ENANI: Yes, she called him a pig.

There was much talk of threats and punch-ups ('they used to exchange hidings,' said Enani, with an incautious smile), before Palmer made some veiled, but potentially explosive, suggestions of homosexuality.

80

PALMER: Did she complain about you and her husband?
ENANI: No.
PALMER: Did she complain that he would go up to your room
and spend an hour with you before he returned to her?
ENANI: Yes . . .
PALMER: Was not one of the complaints she made that he used
to spend the day going out with men of a very bad character?
ENANI: Yes, but he never did.

It was a loyal response, but Marguerite's solicitor went on to suggest that there had been something 'improper' between Said and Ali. He was beginning to forge a dubious link between these innuendos and Dr Gordon's evidence that Marguerite had been suffering from 'external haemorrhoids', a fact which, even in those prudish days, some newspapers reported in full. When his turn came to put questions, Freke Palmer homed in, eliciting from the doctor that 'Madame's complaint was extremely painful . . . [she said] her husband was the cause of it . . .'

In his summing-up, the coroner expressed disgust. 'It was,' he said, 'a sordid, unsavoury and unpleasant story of married life . . .' In the absence of the person accused, 'it would not be proper for a verdict to be returned in this court of anything less than murder'. The jury took their cue and, without retiring, declared a verdict of 'Wilful Murder' against Marie Marguerite Fahmy.

For the authorities, the case of Madame Fahmy had an interest over and above a domestic killing. Marguerite was a Frenchwoman and Ali Fahmy, it was known, had worked as Press Attaché at the French Legation in Cairo. The British were as suspicious of French political activity in Egypt as they were fearful of the ever-stronger Egyptian nationalist movement. An example of British official attitudes arose that year, when an Egyptian civil servant in the Cairo Ministry of Education had the temerity to propose that French should be placed on an equal footing with English in Egyptian schools, also recommending a French company's scheme to take Egyptian students round France at low cost. To the British, this was all 'part of the usual policy of intellectual propaganda . . . the real object . . . is intended to encourage young Egyptians to acquire a knowledge of . . . French life and ways of thought'.

Not surprisingly, Scotland Yard's Special Branch, with its political role, soon came into the picture. A Special Branch detective probably attended the inquest and care was taken to keep the relevant departments of state fully informed. A senior officer's minute in the Metropolitan Police file, dated 13 July 1923, ordered that Grosse's original ten-page police report be sent to 'H[ome] O[ffice] for F[oreign] O[ffice]', adding '[Superintendent] E [Division] to see attached papers from Special Branch.* I understand that – as we expected – the wife is making horrible accusations against the husband.' An additional spur to Special Branch involvement may have been that Ali Fahmy Kamel was the mame of a prominent Egyptian nationalist. Exiled in Paris, Kamel had hurriedly telegraphed home to contradict the rumour that he had been the victim of the 'hotel murder'.

The Assistant Commissioner of the Metropolitan Police, Sir Borlase Elward Wyndham Childs, wrote to the Governor of Holloway Prison on 16 July. Childs had been a Major-General in the British Army, before becoming Assistant Commissioner in 1921 (during his army career, he had worked at the War Office as 'Director of Personal Services'). The seriousness with which the Fahmy case was then being taken can be gauged from Childs's orders, peremptorily given to the prison governor: 'to supply the names and addresses of all persons who have visited Madame Marguerite Fahmy . . . and the names and addresses of all persons to whom she has written and who have written to her'. Childs also wanted to see 'all letters written by her and sent to her from this date'. The governor gently pointed out that two letters 'in a foreign language', sent by Marguerite the previous Saturday, had already been intercepted and sent to the Home Office.

On Thursday 15 July, the temperature peaked at 92°. People were still dancing, despite the heat, according to a correspondent in the *Daily Mirror*, which also reported the sad fate of a carman, found lying beside his horse and van in Kensington. At the West London Hospital, his body temperature was found to be 109°. The unfortunate man had been stripped, bled and put into an ice bath, where a fire hose was placed on him, but he died, still registering 102°. In similar vein, the *Sunday Times* recorded an inquest on a fish-fryer. Thomas Collard had been out of work for three years before getting the job. A week later he collapsed while working during the heatwave. On admission to St Andrew's Hospital, Bow, his temperature was 107°. Medical opinion was that the man had died of sunstroke. His employer disagreed. Death, he thought, was due to the shock of getting work. The steam and heat did not affect the boss. 'Indeed,' he added, 'I have got fat on it.'

---

* The Special Branch papers no longer exist. See Note on Sources (ii), page 194.

An umbrella spontaneously burst into flames in Barrowgate Road, Chiswick. Sixteen deaths were reported by the *Daily Mail* in the first week of hot weather, during which the *Times* had solemnly warned its female readers, 'wise women are buying Harris tweeds for the winter'. Two MPs defied convention and attended the House in shantung suits, but they were to have little opportunity for wearing them. The *Times* had been right. On Monday 16 July, temperatures plummeted, the heavens opened, and 1923's summer was all but over. Four days later, in pouring rain, Folkestone Town Council asserted the Englishman's right to be miserable by voting 6–4 to ban Sunday dancing. 'Praise God from Whom all Blessings flow', sang the crowd of rejoicing, but bedraggled, Wesleyan and Baptist demonstrators outside the town hall.

In the meantime, on 18 July, Marguerite had made her second appearance at Bow Street court. The air in Number Two Court was still as frowsty as ever, but slightly more bearable than it had been in the heat of the previous Tuesday. Shortly after midday, Marguerite again entered the crowded courtroom, very much the grieving widow. Wearing no jewellery and dressed in a black crêpe-de-Chine 'coat frock', she pressed a dark fur to her face, the upper part of which was also obscured by a black waxed straw hat. More fashion-conscious reporters noted that she had cream silk stockings and high-heeled black patent-leather shoes. The *Daily Graphic* was not the only newspaper to buy the image of 'a frail figure . . . [in] deep mourning . . .'

Marguerite's sister, Yvonne, wept quietly, another Frenchwoman murmured '*Bonne chance*', and an interpreter was sworn in to translate Said Enani's evidence, given for a second time and, as at the Coroner's court, laboriously noted down in a longhand deposition. As Said told the now familiar story of marital disharmony, 'tears rolled down [Marguerite's] cheeks and fell on to her hands clasped in her lap'. Beattie's evidence of the happenings that stormy morning caused 'Madame Fahmy's sobs to burst out anew . . . she buried her face in her arms . . .', petulantly shrugging off the hand of a wardress, who had tried to give her prisoner a consoling pat on the arm. From time to time, it was said, Marguerite would look vacantly at the witness-box as the evidence was being given, heaving a long sigh.

Much the same pattern occurred at the adjourned hearing on Saturday morning, when Dr Gordon gave his testimony. As he came to Marguerite's allegations about her husband's sexual behaviour ('certain complaints which she attributed to her husband's practices'), this increasingly important element in Marguerite's defence was duly emphasized. She slumped forward on the wooden bench of the dock, covered her face with her fur and sobbed convulsively. At intervals, a woman prison officer handed her a bottle of smelling salts. When the time came for the Magistrate to commit her to stand trial at the Old Bailey for murder, Marguerite, apparently in a state of collapse, had to be helped from the dock by two wardresses.

12

The Silly Season

The prologue was over. The heart of the drama would be played out at the Old Bailey in the second week of September 1923. In the meantime, reporters, prevented by the *sub judice* rule from making further comment on the Fahmy case, coped as best they could with the news-starved high summer.

Marguerite's committal for trial had coincided with the end of the London Season. Many of the nightclubs closed for redecoration, including the Embassy, at 6 Old Bond Street, which the Fahmys had been planning to visit during the second week of their stay. 'They were not [yet] members,' said the famous Luigi, who had received a letter of recommendation from the Savoy's General Manager on the day after the shooting. 'You will find them very good customers,' M. Gelardi had written.

The Savoy, as was to be expected, took the tragedy in its stride. Among the arrivals from Paris on 1 July, the day the Fahmys came to stay, had been Sir Jagajit Singh, Maharajah of Kapurthala and wife, the former Anita Delgado, described by the *Star* as 'a beautiful Spanish dancer, native of Malaga'. The Maharajah, who had inherited his lands in Oude at the age of three, was a frequent visitor to both Paris and London. Short and fat, he was known as the 'King of Emeralds', loved dancing to the Savoy Havana Band, and was a generous host. The Fahmys had entertained the Maharajah aboard their *dahabeeyah* at Luxor in February.

One event which would surely have attracted Ali and Marguerite, had not fate intervened, was the Air League Ball, held on the night of

Tuesday 17 July. Tickets were two guineas, a fraction short of the week's pension for a war widow and two dependent children. The Duke and Duchess of York, back from their honeymoon and already pitchforked into official duties, were the star attractions at a packed and noisy Albert Hall. When the royal party arrived at 10.30, the Duchess was seen to be wearing a white satin dress, trimmed with diamante, and, noted the *Daily Mirror*, 'a cape of valuable old lace'. Apparently unfazed by some of the more bizarre features of the occasion, her manner was described as 'dignified' at the presentation of Air League worthies, which took place to the lyrical strains of 'Yes! We Have No Bananas'.

The Duke and Duchess danced a foxtrot, 'Romany Love', while those who were temporarily tired of the dancefloor could engage one of a fleet of Daimler cars, equipped with wireless, and 'sit out' while being driven round Hyde Park, listening on headphones to yet more foxtrots, played by the Band of the Grenadier Guards from 2 LO at Savoy Hill. Shortly after midnight, an 'air-raid' took place, in which Major Phillips's wireless-controlled airship buzzed about the hall, spasmodically dropping 'bombs' containing 'valuable presents' on the dancers below – a tasteless entertainment, since over a thousand Londoners had lost their lives in wartime bombing. Later, the airship, hastily converted into a 'Zeppelin', was brought down in flames by the guns of a miniature aeroplane. Overhead, suspended from the roof of the Albert Hall, were two real fighters, Sopwith Camels which had seen action on the Western Front.

But social events were not enough to fill the yawning column inches, so journalists raked around for what they could find in the well-worn grooves of sex, race and drugs, exploiting contemporary fears and prejudices in the perennial circulation war.

From the first few days of press coverage, it was obvious that the Fahmy affair involved topics both sensitive and sensational: a woman 'with a past', a 'mixed' marriage, the spicy revelations of international high life, a perceptible suggestion, despite veiled language, that the dead man had shockingly unusual sexual tastes. Among the readership of the English press would have been most, if not all, the people who would later be sworn in to form the jury in the trial of 'Madame Fahmy', as all the papers now dubbed the defendant.

There has long been a tendency for the English press to exploit, in varying combinations, those three disagreeable elements of the national character: puritanism, prudery and prurience. An ever-popular method has been to give a distorted account of criminal proceedings or in some other way 'expose' socially undesirable activity (a sexual peccadillo perhaps, or illegal drug use), by means of a sensationally worded report. The reader is told as much as is printable of what has allegedly taken place, and the report is accompanied by a rider which shows just how disgraceful, in the newspaper's opinion, is the conduct in question.

In this regard, tabloid newspapers of our time differ little from those of 1923. Seventy years ago, there was more crude racism in the columns of the daily press than is visible today (thanks, in part, to subsequent legislation), but two other old stand-bys can be recognized. Foreigners are quaint, funny folk, when not being downright dangerous and subversive ('ALIEN SOCIALISTS POURING IN' was a typical *Daily Mail* headline in 1924) and homosexual men were to be afforded no place at all in society, except possibly the inside of a prison cell. (In 1921, there had been an unsuccessful attempt in Parliament to criminalize lesbianism, but the subject benefited, or rather suffered, from virtual invisibility until the '*Well of Loneliness*' case several years later.)

As it happened, transvestism, rather than homosexuality, was a major feature of 'silly season' stories in the summer of 1923, stories that in most cases led to consequences not quite so silly for the people involved.

Modern experience suggests that male-to-female cross-dressing is largely a heterosexual phenomenon, but the cases reported in 1923 all appear to have had a gay dimension. Homosexuality and tranvestism are certainly not synonymous, but it suited the bias of the press to report cases where the two elements were present, as a convenient means of expressing disapproval and contempt.

In relation to the Fahmy case, while there is no evidence that Ali Fahmy was himself transvestite (though he may have visited transvestite bars), three criminal cases reported between July and September 1923 illustrate prevailing attitudes to 'deviant' behaviour: a likely guide to the collective outlook of the jury at Marguerite's trial.

An archly worded report from the United States appeared in the *Daily Chronicle* early in July, describing a most unusual crook. 'Stylishly attired, wearing a beaded dress, dainty buckled shoes and a white befeathered hat, [Fred Thompson, aged 34] was identified . . . as the bobbed-haired girl robber with the smiling blue eyes', who, in the course of a raid, had shot an insurance broker. Much was made of his 'sumptuous apartment . . . shared with Frank Garrick, an auto mechanic'. Upon arrest, Thompson was found 'attired in feminine finery and Garrick claimed "her" as his wife . . .'

It was also stated that 'Thompson . . . had long passed as a woman in the Chicago cabarets [he] frequented . . .' and, among the contents of an extensive wardrobe, the astonished policemen discovered a nun's habit. Notwithstanding these successful impersonations, Fred evidently had a few problems with his appearance: although his 'rouged and powdered face' was 'very smooth, his voice soft and his ankles shapely . . . his arms are muscular and hairy and his hands large and powerful . . .'

Nearer home and more overtly linked to a homosexual theme was a short but well-reported trial at Winchester Assizes, presided over by the egregious Mr Justice Darling, one of the least personable of his generation of High Court judges. On the morning of Friday 6 July 1923, the courtroom presented a spectacle that must have been rare even in the judge's quarter-century of criminal trials. 'A pot of rouge, powder puff, eyebrow pencil, a hand-mirror, together with a lady's complete outfit of underclothing, including corsets and silk stockings were spread over the barristers' benches . . .' The owner of the clothing was a private in the RAF, twenty-eight-year-old Albert Davies.

A month before, on 4 June, this young man was standing outside a dancehall in Farnborough, where he was stationed. He was definitely not wearing RAF uniform. *Reynolds's News* reported that 'His face was painted, his lips were coloured and his eyebrows blackened . . .', over an evening dress, in 'the carefully simulated appearance of a fast young woman'. Private John Whyte, of the Royal Scots Regiment, who was twenty, 'had had a drink or two, but was not drunk', and got into conversation with Davies. Exactly what was said was not revealed at the trial, but it is clear that instead of going into the dance they walked off, 'their arms round each other's waists', into a nearby wood.

Unhappily for the pair, they were under official surveillance. It seems that the military police had nursed suspicions about Private Davies for some time. A provost sergeant and an ordinary policeman followed the pair into the darkness of the trees and bushes. 'A remark was overheard which caused the constable to flash his lamp on the couple . . .' The reports do not make it clear how far things had progressed (the corsets suggest a formidable obstacle course), but both servicemen were immediately arrested.

At the police station, Dr Bindloss, a police surgeon, ordered Davies to undress. Davies 'did so with the ease and dexterity of one accustomed to wearing such apparel . . .' He did not strike the doctor as being 'neurasthenic'.

The newspapers could not bring themselves to state the exact nature of the charge against Davies and Whyte, but they were probably arraigned for attempting to commit an act of gross indecency. Davies, after giving evidence in 'a soft well-modulated voice', was convicted. The judge, during the course of the trial, had been horrified to hear that Davies had previously dressed as a woman at camp entertainments. There was some doubt as to whether, so dressed, he would have been allowed out on the street to the knowledge of his C.O.

'I hope,' said Darling, 'that if there is any practice which makes it easy for soldiers to get out of barracks dressed as women it will be put a stop to . . . when a lot of men are got together in barracks such a thing ought to be severely discouraged.' The hapless Davies received the maximum possible sentence, two years' imprisonment, for an attempted fumble in pitch darkness.

Whyte was luckier. Incredible as it may seem today, his claim not to have realized that Davies was a man was accepted by the jury. Discharging him, the judge advised Whyte 'to keep better company in future'.

The populist weekly, *John Bull*, saw wider implications in the 'IMI-TATION WOMAN CASE'. 'Since the War,' it wrote, 'there is a large class of men who devote themselves to this highly undesirable practice of dressing . . . up as women and adopting . . . feminine airs and graces . . . [They] are a menace to decent society.' It could not understand why 'there are men, many . . . well known in society, and some of them the possessors of distinguished titles, who appear to find a depraved pleasure in the society of these dreadful creatures'.

Some of these 'degenerates' appear to have been transvestite male prostitutes ('when money is obtained . . . it is cynically referred to as "rent"'), but other, less mercenary, cross-dressers seem to have regularly partnered soldiers at regimental dances throughout the early Twenties. After approving Mr Justice Darling's call for public female impersonation to be made a criminal offence, *John Bull* launched an uncompromising broadside at the entire homosexual underworld. 'These people ought to be hunted out of clean and decorous society . . .' and should be 'dealt with . . . effectively by the bringing of graver charges, for which the evidence is, unfortunately, far too frequent'.

The third case, and by far the most widely reported, was that of Major Cecil Arthur Hope, fifty-eight, formerly of the Inniskilling Dragoons, and in 1923 a Justice of the Peace, living at the picturesque seventeenth-century Dial House at West Lavington, a pretty Wiltshire village on the edge of Salisbury Plain.

In May 1923, two men, Cyril Benbow and Edward Hyde, were convicted at the Old Bailey of conspiring with one Ricardo Gennert, 'to sell catalogues, pictures and books in violation of [public] morality and good order'. The case, if we read between the coy lines of contemporary newspaper reports, involved the importation and distribution of gay pornography, a subject which has for generations diverted police and customs officials from really serious matters. The process continues to this day.

The material had been imported from Barcelona, where Gennert lived, via Benbow's rented rooms in Exeter. Benbow, who was fifty, had been assisted by Hyde, a young man half his age, who lived in Belgrave Road, Chelsea. Presumably by means of a coded reference, the names and addresses of customers were obtained 'by the insertion of advertisements for the sale of French novels'. 'Benbow,' it was reported in the *News of the World*, 'embarked on the matter from a purely business point of view; Hyde was personally interested in that class of article.'

Unfortunately for Major Hope, his address appeared on the master-list of customers. He was interviewed by police and it turned out that it was he who had introduced Hyde to Benbow. Indeed, letters and drawings from Hope to Hyde formed part of the case against the young man, who was sentenced to nine months' imprisonment, Benbow receiving eighteen months.

It was originally decided not to prosecute the major, who had taken no part in the distribution of material, but the Recorder of London, when passing sentence on the two others, made pointed reference to Hope, who was eventually arrested at Paddington Station and charged with 'publishing obscene libels and sending indecent matter through the post'. The *News of the World* headlines read 'JEKYLL AND HYDE JP – MONSTROUS LETTERS OF A MAJOR – PERVERTED MIND IN NIGHTS OF FRENZY' and its rival, the *People*, came up with 'VILLAGE IDOL'S DOUBLE LIFE OF DEPRAVITY AND DRINK'.

Hope's original meeting with Hyde came about in an extraordinary way, even for those closeted times. An advertisement was inserted in a newspaper, reading 'Corset lovers and tight waisting. Arising from the recent stage search for the smallest waist, correspondence is wanted from ladies and gentlemen on this subject.' The advertising manager thought this an odd topic, but the major replied that his wife had possessed one of the smallest waists in Victorian days and that he, as a cavalry officer, liked to dance with tight-waisted ladies.

Hyde replied, discreetly at first, but the correspondence soon took on a sexual content. Hope, signing himself 'Cissie', sent Hyde a photograph of himself in a dress and on one memorable occasion took Hyde, the latter in women's clothing, to a ball at Devonshire House in Piccadilly.

The major had long had a drink problem, but no one seems to have suspected the cause. 'In moments of abstraction,' declared Dr Stoddart of Cavendish Square, 'he liked to dress in female clothes, with corsets, high-heeled boots and to powder and colour his face.'

All this seems harmless enough, but in 1923 Victorian values still prevailed. The prosecutor, Sir Richard Muir, painted the picture of a nationwide homosexual conspiracy. 'It seems quite clear,' he told the judge, 'that there are a large number of persons in this country who desire to get into correspondence with each other for the purpose of exchanging obscene literature and pictures – or for a more serious purpose . . .' This was, truly, a 'vicious circle' in official opinion and, not to be outdone, *John Bull* had its two-pennyworth, excoriating these 'so-called correspondence clubs', with lurid revelations of 'men-women' at 'orgies' in the West End home of a young peer, who had recently, it was claimed, escaped justice and fled to Paris.

Hope stood in the dock at the Old Bailey on 6 September 1923, four days before the scheduled start of the Fahmy trial. His defender, the advocate also instructed to appear for Marguerite Fahmy, was Sir Edward Marshall Hall KC. It was not to be one of the great advocate's most successful mitigations. Hall did little justice to his client's case by declaring that in his forty years' experience at the Bar he had never come across such appalling letters, photographs and books as those Hope had sent to Hyde. Attempts to blame the problem on drink seem only to have antagonized the judge. The major, described by the *News of the World* as 'a grey-haired and intellectually-looking [sic] man', went down for twelve months.

These three cases, reported in the two months before Marguerite's trial, tend to link homosexuality with other socially unacceptable behaviour: transvestism (then regarded as an almost diabolical manifestation), armed robbery, the 'seduction' of young soldiers, a wholesale conspiracy to corrupt the morals of the nation. Press reports reflected and encouraged a general and widespread condemnation of homosexual men as antinomian creatures: their sexual orientation was 'abnormal', 'perverted', 'contrary to nature'. In this hopeless and degenerate state, they were deemed capable of committing any evil.

To defending lawyers, searching for a way to save Marguerite Fahmy from the gallows, intimations of her husband's deviant sexuality were indeed a prize. Better still, in race-conscious England, the trial jury would regard the late Ali Fahmy not only as a foreigner but as someone distinctly off-white.

13

The Great Defender

Freke Palmer, after taking Marguerite's instructions at Holloway, and with the dry-runs of inquest and committal behind him, knew that this was to be no easy case to defend, despite what he had already gleaned about Ali's background and character. Madame Fahmy was very much a woman with a past and puritanical English juries did not take kindly to such women. She could easily find herself, in effect, on trial for her earlier immorality.

There was no doubt, too, that Marguerite had kept a pistol for some time, well before she came to England. It might be difficult to persuade a jury that a woman of her kind did not know how to use a pistol bought with the express intention of protecting her jewellery. And why had she fired that first shot? Was it, as she said, to discourage Ali from assaulting her, or was it to establish that her gun was in working order before she used it to fatal effect? Moreover, there was the dangerous evidence of John Beattie, apparently supported by the post-mortem report, which suggested that Marguerite had shot her husband from behind, as he was trying to call the lapdog back into their suite.

The state of the criminal law in 1923 also put Marguerite at a disadvantage. The general rule, then as now, was that the prosecution, having brought the case against a prisoner, had to prove that case 'beyond reasonable doubt', so that at the end of a trial the jury would only convict if they were sure that the defendant was guilty. At that time, however, there was a presumption in law that all homicide was murder, 'unless the contrary appears from circumstances of alleviation, excuse or justification', as E. S. Fay notes in *The Life of Mr Justice Rigby Swift.*

In Marguerite's case, there could be no reasonable doubt that (for whatever reason) she had fired the three shots which killed her husband. That being so, the presumption applied and it was then for her to satisfy the jury that, in the circumstances (classically described in 1762 as 'accident, necessity, or infirmity'), she was not guilty of murder.*

With all these considerations in mind, but happily freed from worry about financial constraints, Freke Palmer's first choice as leading counsel had been Sir Henry Curtis-Bennett KC. Marguerite's friends, however, were insistent that the defence team should be headed by an even more famous name. Accordingly, Palmer telephoned Edgar Bowker, head clerk at 3 Temple Gardens, the chambers of Sir Edward Marshall Hall. 'Listen, Bowker,' he said excitedly, 'I've got a very important case for M.H. I want to come along and see you about it right away. I can't say any more about it over the phone, but it is one of the best things I have ever handled . . .'

Negotiations between solicitor and barrister's clerk for the instruction of leading counsel in a serious case resemble a complex mating dance. Fees are the major preoccupation, amid a welter of backstage bargaining in which the barrister plays no overt role. Significantly, Marshall Hall had not accepted a brief in a capital case since 1921. Lucrative civil work had taken up the intervening months and as a result such important murder trials such as those of Herbert Armstrong and Bywaters and Thompson took place without his forceful presence. All three defendants were hanged.

Marshall Hall had several times expressed his reluctance to be instructed in sensational murder cases, but, true to form, the great man soon relented under his clerk's pressure and a fee was agreed. The agreed 'marking' on the brief was 652 guineas, one of the highest fees he ever earned at the Bar. During the negotiations, Freke Palmer had been anxious to impress upon Bowker that the Fahmy affair was no run-of-the-mill murder case, one that might be defended by an Old Bailey hack. Indeed, no less than three counsel were eventually retained in Marguerite's defence. Marshall Hall would have the assistance of Sir Henry Curtis-Bennett, with Roland Oliver (later to be an abrasive High Court judge) as junior counsel.

---

* The law was changed by the decision of the House of Lords in Woolmington v DPP [1935] AC 462, an appeal from the judgment of Mr Justice Rigby Swift, who presided at the trial of Madame Fahmy. There is no longer any evidential burden upon a defendant in a murder trial to prove innocence: the burden of proof remains on the prosecution throughout the case.

Marshall Hall had enjoyed a professional relationship with Freke Palmer for thirty-five years, from the day the solicitor had first seen the young, white-wigged barrister on his feet in the dingy surroundings of Marylebone County Court in 1888. He had then marked Hall down as a 'winner' and, despite the vicissitudes of the other man's tempestuous career, rarely had reason to change his original view.

Nearing sixty-five in the late summer of 1923, Marshall Hall was at the height of his fame and fortune, literally a household name. He looked every inch the great advocate. A handsome, comparatively youthful-looking and well-built six feet three, he had a commanding presence that dominated any courtroom. Yet in many ways his character, 'childlike, uncontrolled and mercurial', according to Marjoribanks, was a far remove from the popular conception of the lean, ascetic lawyer coldly and dispassionately expounding his case.

Perhaps a reason for his great success was this very difference from so many of his contemporaries, a contrast which gave weight to his forensic arguments and enabled him to distance his particular style from that of more conventional opponents. Never an academic lawyer, he was first and foremost an advocate. In his criminal work, he was at his finest as a defender. His attempts at prosecution were half-hearted, when not actually disastrous. Too often, when prosecuting, he would act as a 'supplementary counsel for the defence . . . and once he seems to have suppressed a most damaging piece of evidence against a prisoner . . .'

Edward Marshall Hall was born in Brighton in 1858, the youngest of nine children of a well-known local physician who lived at 30 Old Steyne. His childhood and youth seem to have been restless: he was described as 'sulky, rebellious and disobedient'. Two years at Rugby School, where he would 'barter revolvers and guns and jewellery', were followed by thoughts of the Church, a stint as a clerk in a firm of tea merchants, and matriculation at St John's College, Cambridge.

He took a two-year sabbatical from the university and bummed around Paris, living 'an amusing life with the students and artists of the Quartier Latin' and learning to speak excellent French, before sailing to Australia. En route, he shot an albatross, but luckily did not suffer the awful fate of the Ancient Mariner and was safely back in Brighton by 1880.

During this time, he was developing two talents which would hold him in good stead for the rest of his life. One was a skill at dealing in jewellery and precious stones, a useful supplement to his earnings at the Bar; the other was an almost encyclopedic knowledge of firearms, which he was able to employ to great advantage in a number of criminal trials.

He was a keen shot and in his early days at the Bar most of his winter weekends were spent shooting.

Scraping by with a pass degree in law from Cambridge, Hall was called to the Bar on 6 June 1883. His practice was never exclusively criminal: like many of his contemporaries, he gained experience in the civil courts and even did some divorce work, but his lack of academic ability and his flair for the grand manner drove him inexorably in the direction of crime. His reputation as the 'Great Defender' began with the unpromising Marie Hermann in 1894. This skinny, miserable-looking London prostitute of forty-three had battered one of her few remaining clients over the head with an iron bar and deposited the body in a large trunk. 'Take care of that box,' she had told removal men, 'it contains treasures of mine.'

Marshall Hall found himself defending a woman of bad moral charac-ter who had undoubtedly been in straitened circumstances at the material time: a witness had heard her arguing with the punter over 'my five pounds'. After the killing, she had been flush with money and it was established that the dead man had drawn £50 from the bank shortly before his death. Public indignation against the prisoner was high, whipped up by such exaggerated newspaper headlines as 'THE MOST TERRIBLE MURDER OF THE AGE'.

With considerable skill, Marshall Hall persuasively argued that the fatal blows had been struck in the course of a struggle with her client, a burly, drunken man, and were consistent with Hermann, forced to the ground, having hit the man with a poker in self-defence. The jury evidently accepted the argument in part and brought in a verdict of manslaughter.

Marshall Hall's treatment of the facts of this case was able enough, but it was the emotional force behind his submissions which secured the favourable verdict. Melodramatic as his words and actions seem today, they created a strong emotional atmosphere in court which propelled the jury far beyond a quiet assessment of the issues.

'Remember,' he implored, tears streaming down his cheeks at the end of a three-hour speech, 'that these women are what men make them; even this woman was at one time a beautiful and innocent child.' Right on cue, the prisoner began to sob in her place in the dock as Marshall Hall, with histrionic deliberation, gravely challenged the jury: 'Gentle-men, on the evidence before you, I almost dare you to find a verdict of murder.' Then, pointing to his client's pathetic form, he added the deathless plea, 'Look at her, gentlemen of the jury. Look at her. God never gave her a chance – won't you?', and sat down to tumultuous applause.

To modern eyes, this episode possesses all the risible qualities of the death of Little Nell, but a jury of the 1890s would have been used to such a florid, declamatory style in popular fiction, in the newspapers, and, above all, in the theatre. Anyone who has heard early recordings by turn-of-the-century actors such as Irving and Beerbohm Tree will immediately detect this tone. Such exuberance would become an essential part of the Marshall Hall repertoire, and went on, too long, into the years after the Great War, when juries were less ready than their Victorian counterparts to accept theatrical ham served up before them in court.

'My profession and that of an actor are somewhat akin,' said Marshall Hall, proud of his membership of the Garrick Club. 'There is no backcloth . . . there is no curtain, but out of the vivid dream of somebody else's life, I have to create an atmosphere, for that is advocacy.' He seemed to identify himself with his client, going beyond the strict role of advocate, 'speaking as if the prisoner's thoughts, actions and impulses were his own'.

In 1856, during the trial of Dr Palmer, the Rugeley poisoner, Lord Chief Justice Campbell had given a classic warning to juries: 'When a counsel tells you that he believes his client to be innocent, remember that it is analogous to the mere form by which a prisoner pleads "Not Guilty". It goes for nothing more . . .' Marshall Hall never regarded himself as bound by that judgment: '. . . by the fire of his rhetoric, he threw a cloak of romance and drama around the sorry figure in the dock, convincing the jury that he believed passionately in every word he said . . .'

He would nurse his juries, selecting 'the most intelligent or the most amenable member', addressing himself particularly to this figure until he was satisfied that that person had been won over, before moving on to the next, and so on through the twelve. One of his greatest triumphs was the 1907 case of Robert Wood, known as the 'Camden Town Murder'. Marshall Hall's opening speech for the defence was true to form. 'After twenty minutes of this passionate and pulverising rhetoric . . . the jury were in a state of pulp' Marjoribanks tells us, and, again, during his closing address, 'beads of sweat stood out on [his] face . . . as he wrestled with the one last unresponsive face on the jury . . .'

Wood was acquitted after a defence-minded summing-up from the judge. Another facet of Marshall Hall's character was demonstrated by his petulant aside, 'He's trying to take the credit away from me.' The big man was vain, hot-tempered and indiscreet. He had no scruples about bullying witnesses and cut more than a few ethical corners. Clashes with the judiciary had on occasion brought his practice near to ruin; as a Tory MP (1900–05 and 1910–16), his maiden speech was drowned in derisive laughter when he lost his temper in public.

In addition to these undoubted character defects, his working method was largely intuitive: 'He never had a plan of campaign, or, if he had, he never was faithful to it. So far from preparing his speeches, he scarcely knew what the next sentence was to be himself . . .'

For forty years, Marshall Hall had battled his way through the courts and in the late summer of 1923 he was instructed to appear in possibly the most sensational trial of them all. His reaction, upon reading Freke Palmer's immaculately prepared instructions, was to agree with the solicitor that this was going to be an uphill struggle, yet it was a fight in which the old warrior could identify with his client's predicament. Marshall Hall had his own bitter experience of marriage. His first wife had announced during their honeymoon in Paris that she did not love him: the couple separated in 1888 after five years of constant bickering. A few months later, she died from the effects of an illegal abortion, after an affair with an army officer.

Although he lived happily with his second wife, Henriette Kroeger, Marshall Hall was always prone to recall the misery of earlier years. 'Marriage,' he said late in life, 'can be one of the most immoral relationships in the world.' His impulsive nature immediately sympathized with Marguerite Fahmy, seemingly vulnerable and alone in a foreign country. She needed a champion and Marshall Hall would be her man. Furthermore, they shared another painful experience. For years, Marshall Hall had been a martyr to piles.

14

On Remand

Marguerite had no complaints about her reception at Holloway Prison. After arriving by taxi from Bow Street late in the afternoon of 10 July, she was taken immediately to the hospital wing. Here she was stripped for the compulsory medical examination, which gave her an opportunity to point out the small injury to her neck, which, she said, Ali Fahmy had inflicted on her shortly before the shooting. After the other formalities of admission had been completed, she was put to bed with a sedative and slept soundly until eight the following morning.

She awoke to find five other women prisoners accommodated with her in the dormitory. 'I saw a nurse sitting at the end of my bed,' she recalled. 'She looked young and pretty under her white cap.' The 'nurse' was a prison officer and well disposed to the new arrival. 'Better this morning, Fahmy?', she asked, taking Marguerite's hand.

Marguerite's broad experience of life enabled her to get on well with her fellow-inmates in the prison hospital. 'The other women were mostly there for drunkenness,' she observed, 'or for having tried to commit suicide, which is not, I think, a crime in France.' In the next bed was a girl of eighteen who had killed her baby. She knew a few words of French and Marguerite was able to communicate with her in an Anglo-French patois.

Marguerite was by no means isolated in prison. Though her correspondence was subject to scrutiny and her visitors monitored, she was able to keep in touch with her friends and advisers on both sides of the Channel. As early as 16 July, six days after Ali's death, 'a woman of a very ordinary type' called at 70 avenue des Champs-Élysées in Paris, the

98

premises of Louis Vuitton et Cie. The woman was Marguerite's younger sister, Yvonne, who calmly asked for the two gold-fitted handbags (together worth nearly £4000), 'as they were the property of her sister'. Mindful of Ali's telegram and of possible legal complications, the management refused point-blank to hand over the goods. Marguerite, it will be remembered, had tried to get hold of one of the handbags in June and Yvonne was probably acting on an urgent message from Holloway. Madame Fahmy had regained her cool.

Visitors included Freke Palmer, his managing clerk, Dr Gordon, and, 'frequently before 15 August', a Major Bold*, who, mid-month, had asked the Prison Governor whether Marguerite could be allowed to have English lessons while in prison. It was, said the major, Marguerite's own suggestion, one which found favour with the Prison Commissioners, who minuted their assent to the Governor 'provided . . . that nothing improper passes and that you satisfy yourself as to the character and bona fides of the teacher'.

Bold visited Holloway on 17 August and proposed the name of Mrs M. Barton (otherwise known as Miss Baker) to come three times a week between 4.30 and 5.30 p.m. Investigation proved Miss Baker to be 'highly respectable'. She had been employed at Scotland Yard and, as an official reported, 'Col. Thompson of the NVA tells me that she is an old subscriber . . .'

Back at Scotland Yard, Divisional Detective Inspector Grosse was preparing his case. Eighteen statements had been obtained from possible witnesses and, as in almost all murder cases, cranks tried to make their eccentric contributions. 'Bessie', who wrote from 16 Princes Street, Edinburgh, claimed to possess special powers, 'impressions' from another world. '. . . This morning I have been bothered by some spirit to such an extent that I must write . . .'

More concrete information began to flow in from Egypt. The British Consul-General in Alexandria forwarded a number of letters to Scotland Yard and an unsigned, vituperative attack on Ali and his family, written from Cairo, was sent directly to Grosse. It may have been written by a disaffected ex-employee, who appears not to have been a native English speaker and whose disparaging references to Islam suggest that he was a Coptic Christian:

---

* The 1923 Army List does not contain a Major Bold, though Harold Samuel Bould, born 21 January 1887, who had risen from the ranks to become an officer in 1917, was gazetted Captain in November 1920.

Dear Sir

As you cannot know in London what the world knows about Aly bey Kamel Fahmy & his relations.

. . . Aly Fahmy's father was a peasant of Upper Egypt . . . where by means of robbery he acquired his fortune . . . Aly Fahmy, being the only son, took half the fortune according to Mohammedan law, the other half was divided between his four sisters . . . the sisters should not talk against the wife, as the youngest sister Mdme Said bey is notorious for evil living in Paris & here in Cairo.

Aly Fahmy made the acquaintance of his wife at the Semiramis Hotel . . . where she was staying with her daughter, a very pretty girl of sixteen [sic]. Here is the motive for his death. As a rich Mussulman he would try for the daughter as mistress by the side of the mother. Mahomedan morality.

His as [?so] called secretary, Said Enani eff[endi], was well-known as his master's pimp and very probably worse than that, as morality does not exist in this country.

. . . less is known about [Egypt] in England than the moon, our foul legislators being the most ignorant of anyone, not excepting the daily newspapers.

These rich Mussulmen go to Europe & many ballet girls, shop-girls & prostitutes [sic]. One only has to know the Pashas here and the women they married.

The anonymous letter was ignored and in any case it looks as if Special Branch was dealing with Ali's background and Egyptian connections. For Grosse, the need was to find out as much as possible about Marguerite before the trial started. The Paris Prefecture of Police was contacted late in July and responded with a short background report on Marguerite, dated 7 August, which established that she had no criminal convictions recorded against her in France, though she had earned quite a reputation since her youth. *'De naissance très modeste . . . elle se lança de bonne heure dans la haute galanterie . . .'* ('Of very humble birth . . . she soon joined the ranks of high-class fast women . . .')

Grosse also received information, on 26 August, from Dr Said, Ali's brother-in-law, who had returned to Egypt (probably for the interment of Ali's embalmed body in Cairo), telling of the three telegrams which Ali had dispatched from London to Paris the night before he died. Ali's family were now gearing themselves up for some unwelcome revelations at the trial. Towards the end of August, ex-Chief Inspector Stockley of

Scotland Yard, now retired and operating as a 'private enquiry agent' from offices in John Street, Adelphi, was instructed by Dr Said to make detailed enquiries in Paris about Marguerite's character and background.

On 2 September 1923, after his return, Stockley called on Grosse, telling him of his instructions. He had been able to collect a 'considerable amount of data', contained in a six-page report marked 'CONFIDEN-TIAL', which he passed on to the police. It is not clear whether Dr Said was aware that his private detective was secretly communicating with his old bosses, but Stockley had valid professional reasons for keeping in with the Yard, whatever the ethical niceties of his position may have been.

Stockley had spent four days in France 'with the assistance of an agent of mine, who for many years, in an official and unofficial capacity, has been acquainted with Paris'. The wording of Stockley's report suggests that the former Chief Inspector did not speak French. 'I beg to state,' he began, in wonderful police jargon, 'that on the 27th ultimo [August] I proceeded to Paris . . .' There, with the help of his agent, he secured an interview with Madame Denart, Marguerite's old madam, 'under a certain pretext', which suggests that the old lady was still in business and that her two visitors were posing as clients.

The intrepid detective was told by the manager at Louis Vuitton, Frank Theobald, about the Fahmys' visits to the Château de Madrid, but this reference in Stockley's written report would not have pleased the management: 'I heard that Madame Fahmy was in the habit of encouraging her husband to some place outside Paris, called I think the Château, where she used to introduce him to all sorts of not altogether desirable people and to encourage him to drink.'

At this time, Said Enani was found to be back in Paris, ostensibly waiting for Dr Said, who 'was expected to pass through . . . on his way to London' to attend Marguerite's trial. Said was living it up at the Hôtel Majestic, the scene of much marital strife between his late employer and the accused woman. 'He is staying alone,' revealed Stockley, 'but frequently has various ladies to his apartment. The people at the hotel are rather careful about him and ask him to pay up his account pretty frequently . . .'

There were rumours, too, that Marguerite's husband was not alone in having inclinations towards the same sex. The awkward wording of Stockley's report suggests extreme embarrassment at having to contemplate this subject at all: 'We were informed by one woman and one man . . . that it is well known that Madame Fahmy is addicted, or was addicted, to committing certain offences with other women and it would seem that there is nothing that goes on in such surroundings as she has been moving in in Paris that she would not be quite well acquainted with . . .'

The report provided confirmation that the three telegrams had been sent on 9 July, as alleged by Dr Said. In a last-minute flurry, for the trial was to begin in three days, further information was sought from the Paris police on 7 September. ''Phoning was not satisfactory. Paris could not hear', so a letter was sent by Air Mail from Croydon, as well as a telegram suitably subscribed 'HANDCUFFS . . . LONDON'.*

The time for Marguerite's trial was fast approaching. On Wednesday 5 September, the archaic Grand Jury at the Old Bailey was sworn in to find, as a formality, a 'True Bill' against the prisoner, enabling the indictment to be preferred against her the following Monday. Press interest in the case began to revive and references to Marshall Hall's long and colourful career appeared in the social columns.

The coming of September was a welcome relief to journalists, the summer doldrums being blown away by several international crises. On 1 September, Mussolini's Italian troops invaded Corfu on a thin pretext, subsequently defeating the Greek army. This deliberate affront to the League of Nations sharply divided English opinion. To the *Daily Mail*, of course, 'ITALY IS RIGHT', as its headline proclaimed, and Lord Rothermere's press flagship once again saluted 'the great Italian leader for whom we in this country entertain so well-deserved an admiration'.

Then, on 12 September, a military coup swept democracy from Spain, with the tacit approval of the indolent Alfonso XIII. Germany, too, was in turmoil: claiming unpaid war reparations, France had occupied the industrial lands of the Ruhr in January. By the end of August, a catastrophic inflation, partly engineered by the German government to erode its foreign debt obligations, produced a rate of twenty-three million marks to the pound. And from Germany there appeared in September the first photograph of the man the *Daily Graphic* referred to as the 'Bavarian Mussolini' and the *Daily Mail* called 'Herr Hittler' [sic].

Back in England, the summer ended with the English enjoying yet another of their periodical fits of morality. The Bishop of London had felt impelled to write to the *Times*, which he did on 28 August. 'In broad daylight,' he complained, 'persons are to be seen openly misconducting themselves [in London parks] and committing acts of the grossest

---

* The reply from the Paris police does not appear to have survived.

indecency . . . After nightfall these evils are intensified to an extent that cannot be described in a newspaper . . .'

Hyde Park was, it seemed, the fount of all wickedness, but other popular open spaces, such as Ham Fields, Clapham Common and Hampstead Heath, were targeted by the 'men of great experience', employed as unpaid detectives by the London Council for the Promotion of Public Morality, of which the Bishop was president. 'The observations were made in warm weather between 7 and 11 p.m. in those portions of . . . parks where complaints or previous ordinary patrolling assured us abuses were frequent.'

Instances of deplorable behaviour were categorised as '(1) Immorality or indecency requiring punitive measures; (2) Impropriety . . . such as couples lying on the ground where is reason to fear subsequent moral harm . . .' Additionally, 'unseemly conduct', 'solicitation' and 'known undesirables' found their way into the statistics. In Hyde Park alone, a week's observation by two of the Council's inspectors revealed a total of 1432 shocking incidents observed during six visits.

The Bishop had many supporters, but even in puritan England this was going a bit too far. 'Nosey Parkers' was the robust condemnation of some newspapers: the *Sunday Times*, speaking for the majority of the press, thought it 'a very high pitched indictment'.

Among these preposterous items of newspaper copy which ended 1923's silly season was a report in the *Egyptian Gazette* of an heroic failure, an early experiment in wireless transmission. Late in August, a Mr Syed Ali, an Indian mahout wearing a crimson head-dress, stood in the 'broadcasting room' at London's 2 L O station and solemnly chanted 'words of command in elephant language' into the microphone. At London Zoo, a lady elephant called Indarini, for whose benefit a loud-speaker had been installed, 'showed not the slightest interest . . . [and] went on munching potatoes and locust beans without the flicker of an eyelid'.

15

Curtain Up

People started queuing outside the narrow public entrance to the Central
Criminal Court well before dawn on Monday 10 September 1923.
'Endeavours to be present,' reported the *Daily Sketch*, '[were] as strenu-
ous as in the case of Crippen', thirteen years before. One woman sent
her chauffeur down to Newgate at eight o'clock that morning, armed
with a £10 note and instructions to reserve a place, but he had no takers.

The Old Bailey, as the Court is better known, presents a formidable
appearance to its visitors, a grim and grimy structure, faced with unpol-
ished Cornish granite and the grey Portland stone of the notorious
Newgate gaol, which formerly occupied the site. Number One Court,
home of so many grave criminal trials, stands on the first floor, leading
off the large marble staircase and hall, the latter decorated with coloured
mosaics on suitable juridical themes. By 10.30, when the court day
began, every available seat was taken and many people stood at the sides
and back.

In front of the judge's dais, beyond the seat of the court clerk the
('Clerk of Arraigns' in Old Bailey argot), stood the imposing Treasury
table, designed for the display of exhibits. Nearby sat a number of police
officers, including Divisional Detective Inspector Grosse, the officer in
the case. Behind him, in counsel's row, probably looking through the
notes of his opening speech, sat the principal prosecuting counsel.
Percival Clarke, a tall, thin, colourless man of fifty-one, was a son of
the great Victorian advocate Sir Edward Clarke, who had successfully
defended Adelaide Bartlett (in a classic Victorian poisoning case) and
appeared on behalf of Oscar Wilde in the three trials of 1895.

Percival Clarke's junior was Eustace Fulton, also from a distinguished legal background. Sharing, indeed cramming, into counsel's seats were the defence team (Marshall Hall, the bulky Curtis-Bennett and their junior, Roland Oliver), accompanied by a clutch of lawyers representing the Fahmy family. Cecil Whiteley KC and J. B. Melville sat alongside Dr Abdul Fattah Ragai Bey*, an Egyptian lawyer, for Madame Said. The latter, sombrely dressed, had settled herself quietly at the back of the court. Edward Atkin, described by the *Egyptian Gazette* as 'the well-known ... authority on Egyptian and Eastern affairs', appeared with Dr Abdul Rahman El-Bialy Bey† for another of Ali's sisters, Aziza, now Madame Roznangi.

These family lawyers had no status in the trial and were unable to take any direct part in the proceedings: they merely held a 'watching brief', no doubt with instructions to keep a careful note of the evidence, which might later prove to be relevant to the disposition of Aly's substantial estate in Egypt. Other members of the Bar, wholly unconnected with the proceedings, also squeezed into counsel's seats. Among them were two barristers, Ivy Williams and Helena Normanton, who both caught the eye of the press. Women lawyers were a novelty in 1923.

High above the legal representatives, in the public gallery, could be seen, as reported by the *Daily Express*, an 'Egyptian woman' who had headed the queue of would-be spectators and 'an elegant Frenchman with the mark of Paris stamped on his clothes'. Opposite the lawyers, on the other side of the courtroom, were two empty benches awaiting their complement of twelve jurors.

Elsewhere, reporters balanced their notebooks where they could, while others, who had shamelessly used their influence with well-disposed members of the Bar, quickly secured their places. One high-minded barrister had refused to cooperate with two women friends who begged him for tickets. 'The evidence is likely to be of such a nature,' he told them severely, 'that I am not going to raise a finger to help anyone to listen to it, least of all women.'

Amid the excited buzz of conversation, ushers, policemen, journalists and spotty young solicitors' clerks hurried about on their last-minute errands. At the rear of the court, dressed in morning coat and striped

---

* Dr Abdul Ragai Bey was standing as a candidate in Egypt's first elections as a semi-independent state, scheduled for October 1923.

† Dr Abdul El-Bialy Bey was in London that September to plead for the lives of five Egyptian nationalists sentenced to death for murders and outrages against British officials. They were convicted earlier that summer in the 'Black Arrow' trial and three were hanged.

trousers, stood Edgar Bowker, who would accompany Marshall Hall throughout another celebrated defence, leaving his clerk's duties at Temple Gardens in other hands for the duration of the trial.

Three sharp knocks silenced the company and heralded the arrival of the judge. Everyone stood. In robes of scarlet trimmed with ermine, Mr Justice Rigby Swift entered court with the Sheriff, Alderman Sir John Bell, both carrying the traditional bouquets, a seasonal mélange of red and white roses. 'Oyez, oyez,' cried an usher, making standard, antique reference to the judge's powers of 'Oyer and Terminer and General Gaol Delivery', before the judge, round-faced and rubicund, bowed to counsel and settled himself in the enormous, throne-like chair which stood underneath the great Sword of Justice.

As the Clerk of Arraigns intoned the name 'Marie Marguerite Fahmy', another little procession made its way up the narrow staircase into the dock. Necks craned forward to get a first glimpse of the accused: Marguerite, conscious of the value of first impressions, was dressed as befitted a tragic widow. The *Daily Mirror* reported that 'Madame Fahmy [was] in deep mourning, which emphasised the pallor of her complexion . . .', and she wore a black tailored coat, trimmed with fur, with a small cloche hat, whose wide brim and short veil cast a shadow over the upper part of her face. Her lips appeared pale, pressed tightly together, as she swayed momentarily when approaching the front of the dock. Holding her arm was a wardress, reported by the *Daily Express* as being 'a good looking young women, whose neat and kindly personality suggested a ministering VAD' – a volunteer nurse from the Great War.

Even before the indictment was put to Marguerite, Marshall Hall was on his feet, eager to make his presence and personality felt from the start, knowing that the press would be hanging on his every word. The interpreter, Harry Ashton-Wolfe, was about to be sworn, but Marshall Hall insisted that one interpreter was insufficient in the circumstances and asked for another to be brought in. The idea was that the first should interpret the evidence to Marguerite as she sat in the dock and the other would be used to translate to the court any French oral testimony and documents.

The indictment was simple enough, containing only one count, the particulars of which read 'MARIE MARGUERITE FAHMY on the 10th day of July 1923 in the County of London murdered Ali Kamel Fahmy Bey'. At first, Marguerite appeared not to understand what was being put to her, despite Ashton-Wolfe's translation, so the indictment was read a second time. '*Non coupable*' ('Not Guilty'), she responded, in a loud, clear voice.

A gaggle of people summoned for jury service then made its way into the packed courtroom, each anxious to know whether he or she would be selected to try this sensational case. The jury was made up from their number, the Clerk reading the names aloud from a little piece of card. Margaret Anne Barnwell, George Edmund Galliford, James John Butler, Frederick George Strohmenger, William Cronin, James Atkinson, Ernest William Turner, Arthur Mee, Herbert Horace Holt, Herbert Bracey Eyles, Mary Ann Austin and John Thomas Bailey took their seats in the jury-box. Marshall Hall appears not to have exercised the defence's right to challenge up to seven prospective jurors: perhaps his long experience had led him to believe in taking his jury as he found it.

The two women were described by the *Evening Standard* as 'matronly-looking, wearing gold-rimmed spectacles and dressed in black': both would have had to have been over thirty. The very thought of women jurors remained controversial. In May, the *Daily Express* used the headline 'CAN JURYWOMEN UNDERSTAND?' in reporting a civil case in which Mr Justice Darling, reactionary as ever, had discharged a number of women from jury service. 'It is hardly worthwhile keeping three women on the jury,' said the judge, barely concealing his contempt for the female mind, '[as] the evidence appears to be of a technical character.'

The Clerk of Arraigns read the indictment out to the jury, adding, 'To this indictment she has pleaded "Not Guilty". It is your charge to say whether she be guilty or no.' After a moment's silence, Percival Clarke rose to his feet, waiting for that flicker of the judge's eye which means that prosecuting counsel can embark on his opening statement, a précis of the Crown's case against the prisoner, indicating the principal witnesses and the likely nature of their evidence.

The formidable case against Marguerite was set out by Clarke in a comparatively short speech, lasting under an hour and delivered in a dry monotone. Its character contrasted sharply with the episodes of human rage and passion, the references to high life in Egypt and France and to the violent tragedy that had occurred in London during the great thunderstorm exactly two months before.

Counsel's very first words were prosaic: 'Madame Fahmy was married to her husband in December last. Her husband was in the diplomatic service and was a man of wealth and position...' Clarke went on to chronicle the brief courtship: 'In December she adopted the Mohamme-dan religion. Whether it was necessary or not, I do not know ... Their natures seemed to be entirely unfitted one to the other . . . He is said to have been a quiet, retiring nervous sort of man, twenty-two years old and she a woman rather fond of the gay life . . .'

Reference to events of 9 July, prior to the final scene in and around suite 41 led Clarke to his deadliest evidence, the recollections of John Beattie, the Savoy's night porter. 'Just as the porter was going away,' said Clarke, 'he heard a slight whistle behind him and, looking back, saw the deceased man stooping down, whistling and snapping his fingers at a little dog which had come out of the suite. In that position this man was last seen before he was killed.' Clarke emphasized to the jury that the post-mortem report on Ali was consistent with the Crown's contention that he had been shot from behind.

If this crucial evidence were to be accepted by the jury, it would completely demolish any suggestion of self-defence, or of a provocation so immediate as to reduce the case from one of capital murder to the lesser conviction of manslaughter, punishable not by hanging but by imprisonment.

The defence did not have to indicate the precise nature of their answer to the charge before the trial began. But Clarke had the advantage of knowing, from Dr Gordon's statements in the July proceedings, what Marguerite had said immediately after the shooting. Trying to anticipate the line Marshall Hall would take, Clarke told the jury of Marguerite's assertion that Ali had advanced towards her threateningly in her bedroom (counsel seems to have delicately eschewed any reference to Marguerite's allegations of sodomy). 'She rushed for a revolver and fired it out of the bedroom window. She expected it to frighten him, but he still advanced towards her and [she] . . . pulled the trigger. She was surprised it went off, as having previously fired it from the window, she thought it would be unloaded . . .'

'This statement,' Clarke declared, slowly and with great emphasis, 'would have to be considered to see if the facts proved were consistent with the story she told.' He pointed out that Ali could not have been shot from Marguerite's bedroom: the shooting had, beyond any doubt, occurred in the corridor. Furthermore, the crushed beads, torn from Marguerite's white evening dress, had been found in Ali's room, which suggested that the final quarrel had taken place there, not in her own bedroom, as she had said.

Clarke revealed that a hotel chambermaid had found a spent cartridge underneath the dressing table in Marguerite's room the day after the killing (which suggests a very perfunctory police search of the suite).

Although this tended to confirm Marguerite's account of shooting a first bullet out of the window, Clarke deftly pointed out that 'this night was one of the most serious thunderstorms of the year and the firing of the revolver would have attracted no attention at all'. In other words, Marguerite had ensured that her pistol was in working order before she took it out of her bedroom and into the hotel corridor to shoot her husband.

'Coming to this country,' concluded Clarke in a chilly passage designed to eliminate the possibility of a French-style defence on the grounds of *crime passionnel*, 'persons are bound by the laws which prevail here. Every homicide is presumed to be murder unless the contrary is shown. From her own lips, it is known that she it was who caused the death of her husband. And in the absence of any circumstances to make it some other offence, you must find her guilty of murder.'

Before Clarke could call his first witness, a policeman who would produce a plan of the fourth floor at Savoy Court, Marshall Hall was on his feet again. His intention seems to have been purely tactical, with the aim of securing the jury's attention. Having earlier made a fussy application for two interpreters to be sworn, the great man now declared that he was 'willing to take the responsibility of not having the evidence interpreted to the accused'. The judge agreed, no doubt hoping to save a little public time.

After the plan had been produced and perused, it was the turn of the first important witness to testify. Said Enani came into court, 'a short dapper figure in a well-tailored blue suit', a man whose elegant manner and excellent English could not absolve him from being Egyptian and a non-Christian. To the defence, he was a very dangerous witness indeed: he had known the couple intimately and had been with them up to an hour or so before Ali's death. Unchallenged, he could damn Marguerite in the jury's mind as a hard, ambitious, pistol-packing woman with a violent temper, who had given Said's neurotic young master as good as he gave her and sometimes more into the bargain.

In conference before the trial had started, Marshall Hall had taken a bleak view of Marguerite's chances in the face of the evidence. 'Take any opinion from anyone you like,' he had said, as related in E. Marjoribanks's biography of Marshall Hall, 'this lady's life is in peril. Three shots were fired – three shots, remember that. We are entitled to procure ANY evidence to get at the truth and save her life.' That process had included 'enquiries of the most expensive kind . . . in Paris', and, as a result, sitting in court, presumably as a reminder to Said of his late master's leisure pursuits, were 'two youths who had been associated with [Ali] . . .'

Marshall Hall knew all about Marguerite's allegations of an affair between Ali and Said, as well as the other indications of Ali's bisexuality. But he dared not confront Said directly with the charge that he had been Ali's bedfellow. If Marguerite was to give evidence – and she would have to provide some explanation on oath for what she had done – her own past would not bear close scrutiny. Since 1898, when, for the first time, a prisoner had been allowed to give evidence on his or her own behalf (as opposed to merely making an unsworn statement from the dock, which had little evidential value), an accused had been shielded from questions about character and background. That protection would be lost if imputations of bad character were levelled against prosecution witnesses. Should the defence directly accuse Said Enani of homosexual behaviour, the whole of Marguerite's past life would be laid out for Percival Clarke to explore at his leisure in front of the jury.

The cross-examination of Said Enani was therefore a sensitive matter for the defence: Marshall Hall was tiptoeing across a forensic minefield and his able junior, Roland Oliver, acted 'like a watchdog' to keep his combative leader in check. But luck, as well as good judgment, plays its part in advocacy and, just after Said had begun to give evidence, his credibility began to be undermined by the simplest of tactical ploys.

Said Enani was, of course, a Muslim. Nowadays, a copy of the Koran would be available in court, but in 1923 the Old Bailey did not have one available. So Said was sworn on the New Testament. He had just started to describe Ali's family background, when Marshall Hall stood up and interrupted. Seizing the moment, he asked an innocent-seeming question, knowing full well what the answer was: 'My Lord, I should like to know on which book the witness has been sworn.'

A court usher confirmed that it was the New Testament, whereupon, ignoring Percival Clarke (who was, after all, just beginning to examine his own witness) and looking straight at the jury, Marshall Hall asked Said pointedly: 'Does the oath on the Bible bind you?'

Said replied that it did and the judge expressed himself content, but Marshall Hall had sown a seed in the jury's mind. Perhaps this saturnine Egyptian had something to hide. It was all seeming a bit fishy. Later, during cross-examination, a juryman, taking the bait, stood up and expressed concern. Was an oath taken on the New Testament really binding on a Muslim? Said replied, a shade too glibly: 'We do not swear in our country on books. We swear on the name of Almighty God only.'

Marshall Hall, exploiting the situation to the hilt, boomed out: 'I suggest your oath does not bind you and you know it does not – and

there are Egyptian lawyers here whom you know who will say so.'
Although he was quickly stopped by an irritated Rigby Swift, the tactic
had worked and doubt clearly remained in the ranks of the jury about
Said's credibility.

Marshall Hall had begun his cross-examination with a carefully
worded reference to the relationship between master and secretary:

MARSHALL HALL: How long had you known Ali Fahmy?
SAID ENANI: About seven years.
MARSHALL HALL: Before he came into his money, you lived
together?
SAID ENANI: No.

The phrase 'lived together' was a telling one, despite Said's denial.
The jury could work out for themselves that, seven years ago, Ali had
been only sixteen, Said a man several years older. Marshall Hall pressed
on with his covert suggestion:

MARSHALL HALL: . . . Did you say, he [Ali] was an Oriental
and rather passionate?
SAID ENANI: Yes.
MARSHALL HALL: Did you tell Dr Gordon 'I've lost my job.
I gave up ten years' job with the government to take this. Now I am
a ruined man'?
SAID ENANI: Yes.
MARSHALL HALL: You were very much attached to Fahmy?
SAID ENANI: Yes . . .

Later in the cross-examination, Marshall Hall returned to the same
theme of intimacy between two men:

MARSHALL HALL: Did you address Fahmy as 'Baba'?
SAID ENANI: Mme Fahmy used to call him 'Baba' because
there is a story of Ali Baba . . . I used to refer to him, too, as
'Baba'.*

At the very end of his questioning, Marshall Hall waved a copy of the
cartoon from *Kashkoul*, in which the relationship between Ali, Said Enani
and Said's own secretary had been so cruelly lampooned:

---

* 'Baba' was also Marshall Hall's pet name for his only daughter, Elna.

MARSHALL HALL: Was not the relationship between you and Fahmy Bey notorious in Egypt?

Said, of course, disagreed and this further, blatant innuendo of homosexuality should have been the moment when the judge intervened to warn Marshall Hall that he had gone too far and was putting his client's own character at issue. Percival Clarke, rising to re-examine his witness, complained, rather lamely, that the cartoon seemed to reflect on Said Enani's moral character, but Rigby Swift chose to make light of the situation, employing a poor example of judicial witticism in this capital case, an unpleasant echo of Mr Justice Darling's laboured jokes in murder trials:

JUDGE: It does not reflect on anybody's moral character, except perhaps the artist's. [Laughter]

Although the judge added, obtusely, that the only suggestion of the cartoon had been that the three men were inseparable, the jury had been given the strongest hint, virtually a direct accusation, that Said and Ali had been lovers. Other aspects of Ali's character were more easily exploited by Marshall Hall, who was free from worries about exposing Marguerite to cross-examination because of the simple fact that Ali was dead. Hall mercilessly used Said Enani as a sounding-board for many of Marguerite's accusations of cruelty, compiled since the beginning of the year with a view to an expensive divorce settlement.

Ali's florid appeal, begging Marguerite to join him in Cairo, was read out in full, as was the series of telegrams sent in October 1922, speaking of Ali's supposed grave illness. It all suggested a dark conspiracy between the two men to lure Marguerite to Egypt, though, as sometimes happens to the best advocates, Marshall Hall asked one question too many:

MARSHALL HALL: And the result of that is that this unfortunate lady goes to Cairo?
SAID ENANI: She advanced her date only. She had agreed to go to Egypt [but] he wanted her before the time fixed.

Questions about Fahmy's palace disclosed a local custom, the revelation of which may have startled the more respectable business people on the jury:

MARSHALL HALL: You gave the order for the things in it?

SAID ENANI: No, everything was chosen by Fahmy.
MARSHALL HALL: Didn't you get commission on the orders?
SAID ENANI: Of course I got commission. [Laughter]
MARSHALL HALL: Ten per cent on half a million francs?
SAID ENANI: No, five per cent . . .

But the thrust of Marshall Hall's cross-examination, once the hint about Said's relationship with Ali had been driven home, was to present Marguerite as the abused wife, brought to the East on a false pretext, imprisoned and brutalized by her super-rich husband. A generalized sexual decadence, unquestionably Eastern, was canvassed.

MARSHALL HALL: You have known of Fahmy's intimacies with many women?
SAID ENANI: Yes, sir.
MARSHALL HALL: Do you know he treated them brutally, one and all?
SAID ENANI: No, sir, I cannot say brutally . . .
MARSHALL HALL: He was entitled by law to have four wives, was he not? . . .

It appears that the next part of the cross-examination was not fully reported. Marshall Hall, preparing the ground for Marguerite's evidence, also, writes Marjoribanks, 'put to the witness that Fahmy was a man of vicious and eccentric sexual appetite, but this the secretary loyally denied'.

The following passage, towards the end of the four-hour cross-examination, affords a good example of the way Marshall Hall could get his message across, ending with yet another sideswipe at Said, a venal, corrupt character, too close to his master for the comfort of decent English people.

MARSHALL HALL: Was not the Mme Fahmy of 1923 totally different from the Mme Laurent of 1922?
SAID ENANI: Perhaps.
MARSHALL HALL: Has every bit of life been crushed out of her these six months?
SAID ENANI: I do not know.
MARSHALL HALL: From a quite entertaining and fascinating woman has she become miserable and wretched?
SAID ENANI: They were always quarrelling.

MARSHALL HALL: Did she say you and Fahmy were always against her and it was a case of two to one?

SAID ENANI: Yes.

MARSHALL HALL: Did you say if she would give you £2000 you would clear out of her way?

SAID ENANI: I said if she would discharge me, I should be pleased to go away . . .

The last witness of the day was potentially the most deadly. John Beattie, the night porter, a man with no axe to grind, gave his recollection of the fatal night, perfectly in accord with Percival Clarke's opening statement. Hardened observers wondered how the old pro would deal with the seemingly insurmountable fact that Ali had been whistling for an errant lapdog literally seconds before his wife had shot him dead.

As Bowker writes in *Behind the Bar*, 'The great thing for counsel is to know when NOT to ask questions . . .' Marshall Hall, 'a master of that finesse', barely cross-examined this most dangerous of witnesses, confining himself with the gentle suggestion, itself no more than a polite ridicule, that the man could not possibly have heard someone whistling above the roar of the storm.

Taking a great risk, Marshall Hall did what only the most seasoned criminal advocates dare to do in the face of such damning material. He ignored it.

16

A Browning Version

The second day of Madame Fahmy's trial dawned wet, cold and windy. Only a few of the crowd, several hundred strong, were destined to find seats in the public gallery, spearheaded by an 'elderly, grey-haired woman [who] was the first to dash in . . .', as reported by the *Evening Standard*.

On Monday, the jury had been rewarded with a drive, ordered on their behalf by the judge after the court had risen at 4.15 p.m. Unfortunately, while they were being ferried along Archway Road, the charabanc broke down and they were obliged to spend an hour or two locked up in a hotel billiard-room until a replacement arrived. By court order, the jury was under the care of 'the Sheriffs, Bailiffs Monk & Lake & Mrs Bellini' and that evening spent their first night confined to the Manchester Hotel, Aldgate, their enforced home for the duration of the trial.

Once they had assembled in their jury-box, a few minutes before the court was due to sit, they were treated to the well-rehearsed ritual which now invariably heralded the arrival of the Great Defender. An impression of majesty, with a touch of the valetudinarian (among other ailments, Marshall Hall's haemorrhoids frequently played up), seems to have created a striking and unforgettable effect.

As Marjoribanks wrote, '. . . he would be preceded by a panoply of medical apparatus. First, his clerk [Bowker] would arrange his air-cushion; then there would be a row of bottles to set up on the desk containing smelling-salts and other medicines; there would also be some exquisite little eighteenth century box, containing some invaluable pill; his noting pencils, green, red and blue, would be arranged in a row and, last, but not least, his [throat] spray would be ready to hand, which,

115

according to his opponents, he would be certain to use in order to divert the attention of the jury when the case was going against him. Finally, when all was prepared, and the judge was waiting, the great man himself would come in . . .'

In addition, a footstool would be placed in position, for him to rest his legs, which were severely affected by varicose veins and the phlebitis which made standing for long periods extremely painful. He would manoeuvre the footstool or inflate a pneumatic cushion (very necessary for the great man's comfort) at tactically appropriate moments, just as he would do with the spray, which was, relates Bowker in *Marshall Hall*, 'operated . . . with a disconcerting hissing . . . accompanied by a gargling sound . . . to the distraction of both counsel who was speaking and the jury who were listening . . .'

Marguerite made an affecting entrance. She was seen to walk 'with short steps across the dock, which she entered supported by a wardress and fell listlessly into the chair . . .', frequently making use of smelling salts during the day's proceedings.

The first witness to be called was Arthur Marini, Night Manager at the Savoy, for whom the shooting of Ali Fahmy had become something of a personal nightmare. His account of the scene in and around the corridor outside the Fahmys' suite went smoothly enough, until he testified that he had understood Marguerite to remark that the couple had been quarrelling about a divorce.

Percival Clarke had not mentioned such an argument in his opening speech and Marshall Hall pounced, scenting danger:

MARSHALL HALL: I should like the French of that, because it is quite new.
JUDGE: It is new to me and probably to the prisoner and perhaps you would like it interpreted.
MARSHALL HALL: I would.

Although Marguerite could not understand English and her counsel had waived the need to translate everything to her, she knew that a problem had arisen. 'Madame Fahmy raised her head and listened with an alert air,' reported the *Daily Mail*. Marshall Hall left his place, as if to emphasize the significance of the occasion, went to the dock and spoke to his client in French. The *Daily Telegraph* reported that 'She replied in a few words and then relapsed into her former nonchalant demeanour.'

The little episode indicates how easily a court and jury can be misled. Marshall Hall went on to ask Marini why he had not said anything about the divorce at the committal proceedings in July, in an attempt to weaken the force of a possibly damaging admission by madame, implying that this mention of divorce was a late and unreliable embellishment. Marini replied that he had simply responded to questions put to him in court at the time. 'I had to answer "Yes" or "No",' he said plaintively.

In fact, his original statement to the police (not ordinarily available to the defence, a declaration made less than four hours after the tragedy), quoted Marguerite as saying, 'We were quarrelling over my divorce that was to take place shortly in Paris.' Percival Clarke does not seem to have made any application to the judge, as he could have done in the circumstances, to get the original, damaging statement before the jury. The son had not inherited the forensic talents of his father.

Marshall Hall's fluent French was already standing his client in good stead. After Clement Bich, the hotel's Assistant Manager, had rendered one of Marguerite's despairing statements, '*J'avais perdu ma tête*', as 'I have lost my head', Hall suggested that she could have said '*J'avais perdu la tête*', meaning, 'I was frightened out of my wits.' The witness agreed that this was a possible alternative interpretation.

With the arrival of Police Sergeant George Hall in the witness box, attention shifted to the fatal weapon, a menacingly black, .32 semi-automatic Browning pistol, about six inches by four and weighing some twenty and a half ounces.

George Hall does not seem to have had the sharpest mind. He had been the first police officer to arrive on the scene and must bear responsibility, together with his superior, DDI Grosse, for the exceedingly sloppy detective work. It had been Beattie, the night porter, who had recovered the pistol; a chambermaid had found the cartridge case in Marguerite's bedroom the day after the shooting; and, on 18 July, fully eight days later, a hotel valet had discovered the third of the three bullets which Marguerite had fired at her husband, lying underneath a grating over a radiator opposite the stairs to the fourth floor.

Producing the pistol as an exhibit, Sergeant Hall referred to it quite wrongly as a 'revolver'. He was sternly corrected by Marshall Hall, who knew his weaponry backwards, but the clumsy officer soon afterwards compounded his error in his answer to a pertinent question from the foreman of the jury. The juryman had pointed out that 'certain automatic weapons continued to fire as long as the trigger was depressed' and, therefore, unless the user was remarkably nimble in handling the gun, it would be practically impossible to fire a single shot. According to Sergeant Hall, the pistol would fire as long as the trigger was pulled: the gun definitely did not need pressure on its trigger for each shot.

It was left to the next witness, Robert Churchill, to put matters right. A burly man, Churchill was the country's leading firearms expert and had given evidence in a host of criminal trials. His firm, E. J. Churchill (Gunmakers) Ltd., of 8 Agar Street, Strand (a couple of hundred yards from the Savoy), was renowned world-wide: 'By Special Appointment to HM the King of Spain', read the company's letterhead, 'Contractors to HM War Departments and Gun Experts to HM Home Office and Police'.

He had examined the pistol, manufactured in Herstal, near Liège, by the famous Fabrique Nationale d'Armes de Guerre, and numbered 127303. Its .32 calibre was shared by all the cartridges, cartridge cases and bullets recovered from the scene of the shooting. These latter items were suitable for use in the pistol and were each marked 'SFM', standing for the Société Française des Munitions, in Paris. Churchill told the court that the full capacity of the pistol was eight rounds (seven in the magazine and one in the barrel). He had test-fired the pistol himself and found that it was in perfect working order and not liable to accidental discharge.

Percival Clarke, picking up the foreman's point, asked, 'Is it a weapon that continues to fire when the trigger is pressed or does the trigger require pressure for each shot?' Churchill contradicted Sergeant Hall, giving a reply that seemed ominous for the defence: 'The trigger has to be pulled for each shot. It is automatic loading, but not automatic firing.'

The pistol was loaded by inserting a clip of cartridges in the hand-held butt, a process that did not require much force. With the clip in place, the gun could be primed by pulling back the sliding breach cover (which lay over the barrel) about three quarters of an inch and then releasing it. This was a much more forceful exercise than loading and required some strength and experience of the weapon.

Another dangerous aspect for the defence lay in the degree of effort required to fire the gun. 'The pull of the trigger,' said Churchill, 'is eight and a quarter pounds. It is not a light pull.' Furthermore, the pistol had a threefold safety provision: the magazine had to be in place; the normal safety catch needed to be pressed (usually by the thumb); and the butt safety grip – on the rear of the butt – had to be squeezed by the palm of the firer's hand as the trigger was pulled. Churchill again

Madame Marie Marguerite Fahmy

Marguerite and Ali
Fahmy, probably on the
day of their visit to
Tut-Ankh-Amun's tomb
in February 1923

Madame Fahmy steps gingerly ashore from her husband's
motor-launch during their honeymoon on the Nile at Luxor

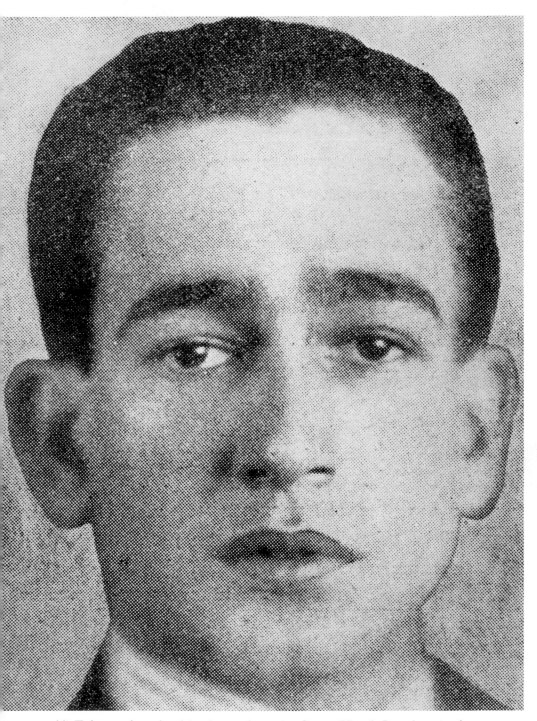

Ali Fahmy, shot dead by his wife at the Savoy Hotel, London, in the early hours of 10 July 1923

The .32 Browning semi-automatic pistol with
which Madame Fahmy killed her husband

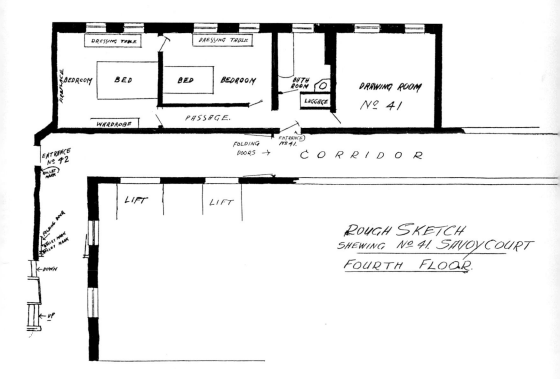

A sketch plan of Savoy Court prepared by the police and used as an
exhibit at Madame Fahmy's trial for murder

ECIAL ST. LEGER NUMBER TO-MORROW : ORDER NOW

DAILY SKETCH.

. 4,517. Telephones {London—Holborn 6510. Manchester—City 6501.   LONDON, TUESDAY, SEPTEMBER 11, 1923.   (Registered as a Newspaper)   ONE PENNY.

KING OF EGYPT'S FRIEND: OLD BAILEY MURDER TRIAL

emal Bey Fahmy, the dead man, is here seen with the King of
at the laying of the foundation-stone of a hospital built at
Fahmy's expense.—(Exclusive).

A studio portrait of Ali Kemal Bey Fahmy. He was 23.

This exclusive portrait of Ali Kemal Bey Fahmy
was taken at his Cairo home.

Mr. Justice Rigby Swift, who is trying the case.

Two portraits of the wife. On the left she is in Egyptian dress. She is French and is 32 years of age.

ies of life in an Eastern Palace, of motor-cars and yachts, were features of the Old Bailey trial when Marie Marguerite Fahmy was brought to trial for the alleged murder
er young Egyptian husband. Ali Kemal Bey Fahmy, the rich friend of the King of Egypt, who was found shot at the Savoy Hotel on July 10, the night of the great London
understorm. She pleaded "Non Coupable" or "Not Guilty." Sir Edward Marshall-Hall took the responsibility of not having the evidence translated for the accused.

The Fahmy trial hits the headlines

'The Captive Soul of Fahmy': cartoon from Cairo's *Kashkoul* magazine, lampooning (from right to left) Ali Fahmy, Said Enani and Enani's secretary, as a gay trio

Said Enani talks to reporters outside the Old Bailey

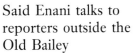

Yvonne Alibert acknowledges the cheers of the crowd on 15 September 1923

Sir Edward Marshall Hall (left), looking tired and drawn, on the last day of the trial with co-defending KC, Sir Henry Curtis-Bennett

The signed photograph that Madame Fahmy gave to Marshall Hall

Madame Fahmy at Princes' Hotel: 'I must pay
my respects to English justice'

affirmed, at the end of Clarke's examination-in-chief, that this was not the sort of weapon to go off accidentally.

Marshall Hall had worried long and hard about this firearms evidence. Churchill was the most important prosecution witness after Said Enani and the tactics that had been successfully employed the previous afternoon to smear Ali's former confidential private secretary were not available to challenge the evidence of a world-renowned gunsmith. Marshall Hall was only too aware that the mere process of getting the pistol into operation suggested that Marguerite knew full well how to use it.

Before the trial started, Marshall Hall had called in to Whistler's, another Strand gun shop, where he enlisted the help of a Mr Stopp, whom he had known for half a century. Together, they minutely examined a similar .32 Browning, which was brought along to court. Years earlier, in a murder trial at Stafford Assizes, Marshall Hall's courtroom demonstration of a revolver had helped secure his client's acquittal. He would keep the idea up his sleeve for possible use on Madame Fahmy's behalf later in the trial.

For the moment, though, the need was to perform a damage-limitation exercise on Robert Churchill. A slice of ham was served up. 'I want you to give me your careful attention,' said Marshall Hall to Churchill, using his most magisterial manner as he rose to cross-examine. He turned solemnly, looking straight at the judge. 'A great deal depends on this witness's evidence and I shall be some time with him.' Rigby Swift, quite used to this sort of technique, blandly assured counsel that there was no time limit, as long as the questions were relevant.

To assist the dramatic effect, the pistol loaned by Messrs Whistler was produced from a box and a second, dismantled one was set out on the exhibit table. Holding the first gun in his hand, Marshall Hall put numerous technical questions to the gun expert. These seem to have been largely irrelevant, designed simply to impress the jury with Marshall Hall's expertise, so that his ultimate submissions, arguments which might not strictly accord with the facts of the .32 pistol's mode of operation, would thereby gain credence.

When the judge asked Marshall Hall if he wanted his pistol made an exhibit, there was a short diversion. Counsel had replied, lightly, that he was afraid it might get lost. Rigby Swift made another little joke, accompanied by a plaint not entirely favourable to the defence:

> You are much safer without it. [Laughter] If there were fewer of these things in the hands of the public, we should not be here so

often and I look forward to the day when it will be a criminal offence to have a revolver [sic] . . . A revolver can be of no legitimate use in this country.'

The crux of Marshall Hall's questioning was the fact that, once the pistol had been primed by pulling back the breach cover and releasing it, and the weapon fired, another bullet would automatically enter the chamber. Churchill agreed that if someone, thinking to clear the barrel of a loaded pistol, discharged a single shot, it would immediately be replaced by another bullet.

The suggestion was then made that, when the pistol was tightly gripped, 'a very small pressure' on the trigger would discharge several shots. This proposition does not accord with the working of this type of pistol and was in manifest contradiction to Churchill's earlier evidence about the substantial eight and a quarter pound pull on the trigger required for each shot. For some reason, Churchill did not robustly disagree with what was being put to him, as surely he should have done. Contemporary reports state simply that 'Mr Churchill hesitated and the pistol was passed round the jury', who tested the mechanism, using a dummy cartridge. Perhaps Marshall Hall's battery of footstool, air cushion and throat spray was being put to use yet again.

Sensing his advantage, Marshall Hall quickly brought the expert back to the loading mechanism, which he had been exploring just a moment before:

MARSHALL HALL: An inexperienced person might easily reload the weapon thinking that, in fact, he was emptying it?
CHURCHILL: Yes.

Marguerite, of course, was that 'inexperienced person'. During Churchill's evidence, she lost her earlier impassivity and showed rather more interest in the proceedings than might have been expected from an *ingénue*. 'Mme Fahmy made notes with a blue pencil on a sheet of paper . . . while her glance travelled continuously from counsel to witness and back again. While her leading counsel was handling the pistol, Mme Fahmy showed great interest . . .', reported the *Evening Standard*.

Towards the end of the gunsmith's evidence, the judge showed that he was still concerned about the evidential conflict with Sergeant Hall. Churchill was able to settle that point, at least, by an analogy that veterans of the Great War, possibly some of the jurymen themselves, would have appreciated. 'A lot of people think these pistols are like Lewis guns. They are not. Each bullet requires separate pressure . . .' His last words also struck a jarring note for the defence: 'It's impossible to load this pistol with the safety catch on.'

If Marshall Hall had won his game with Said Enani hands down, his spar with Churchill failed on points, although some students of the Fahmy case have maintained that this was a great triumph of cross-examination. Marguerite was still extremely vulnerable. She had killed her husband with a large, deadly handgun, indubitably her own property, a lethal pistol far removed from the small revolvers, .22 or less, which were at that time thought of as suitable for ladies to carry in their handbags for self-protection. What was more, to fire the Browning required a considerable degree of skill and application. It was not a weapon designed for pinpoint accuracy, but three of its bullets had struck her husband and one had ploughed its way neatly through his left temple.

The advent of Dr Gordon, whose fleshy face had been snapped outside the Old Bailey that day, beneath a light grey trilby, gave a much-needed tonic to flagging defence morale. In some ways, the doctor was a curious witness for the Crown. He had been the accused's medical adviser, was on friendly terms with her and had visited his patient in Holloway several times while she was on remand. Nevertheless, the prosecution is under a duty to call witnesses 'capable of belief' and, though some of his testimony assisted the defence, Percival Clarke had little option but to call him.

Dr Gordon described how Marguerite had consulted him during the first week of July and made the first clear reference in the trial to those tiresome, painful haemorrhoids, doubtless aggravated by the hot and sticky weather of the brief heatwave. On the fatal morning, he had found Marguerite 'very dazed and frightened' after the shooting, but she had remembered to hand him the letter in which she had set out her reasons for cancelling the booking at the London nursing home and returning to Paris.

Of the greatest importance was what Marguerite had told her doctor in the dawn light of 10 July, while they had sat huddled in the inspector's room at Bow Street with the great storm still rumbling overhead. At the trial, Dr Gordon expanded somewhat on his written statement, composed that same day. In particular, his account of Marguerite's words now included an allegation that 'Fahmy had brutally handled and pestered her' in the suite, before advancing threateningly in her bedroom.

The judge wanted to know whether Madame Fahmy had explained

what she meant by her husband having 'brutally handled' her. 'She told me that Fahmy had taken her by the arms in the bedroom,' said the doctor, adding, 'She showed me a scratch on the back of her neck about one and a half inches long, probably caused by a fingernail. She said it was caused by her husband.'

The doctor was not asked, it appears, whether this injury might just as likely have been self-inflicted, and Marshall Hall, seizing the opportunity, persuaded Gordon to agree that the mark was consistent with 'a hand clutching her throat'.

So far, Dr Gordon seems to have been pussyfooting around the allegations of sodomy. Cross-examination on the point was brief but effective. Bowdlerized reports appeared in the press, the *Daily Telegraph* reporting that 'Madame Fahmy had complained that her husband was very passionate and that his conduct had made her ill. Accused's condition was consistent with the conduct on the part of her husband which she alleged . . .', behaviour described by the *Daily Sketch* as 'violent ill-treatment'.

Another fragment of evidence useful to the defence was Gordon's 'clear understanding', from Marguerite's words, of her belief that the pistol had become unloaded by the single shot she had earlier fired through a window of the hotel suite.

Prosecution evidence also included the post-mortem report of Dr Newfield and the testimony of three witnesses from the Savoy staff. Sharp-eyed valet Albert Dowding had found one of the bullets in the corridor and a chambermaid, Ellen Dryland, had spotted the cartridge case in Marguerite's bedroom. A few days earlier, she had found the Browning pistol under the bolster while she was making the bed. With considerable aplomb, she had put the gun in a drawer of the bedside table. Next morning, she was surprised to find it tucked into the fabric at the back of an armchair. A third witness, Jane Seaman, was possibly night duty telephonist at the Savoy.*

The Crown's case ended with the police evidence, mostly of a formal character, with no significant disputes. DDI Grosse told of seeing Fahmy's body in the mortuary at Charing Cross Hospital (an account which reduced Mme Said to tears in her seat at the rear of the courtroom) and of examining the scene of the fatality, none too carefully it seems, before his first encounter with Madame Fahmy at Bow Street.

---

* Jane Seaman's name appears as a witness on the back of the indictment, so that it is probable she was called to give evidence, but her statement does not appear in the surviving court documents or in the police file.

A BROWNING VERSION

French-speaking Detective Sergeant Allen gave Marguerite's answer to the charge*, though the newspaper copy garbled, 'He has told me many times "kill me" . . .' into 'He has told me many times that he would kill me . . .', just as some reports of Fahmy's impassioned letter to Marguerite in September 1922 turned '*Torche de ma vie*' ('Torch of my life') into the more apt 'Torture of my life'.

---

* See page 75.

17

West Meets East

Marguerite was going to have to go into the witness-box and tell her side of the story. That much was clear. There was no doubt that she had fired the shots which killed her husband and only she could give real force to the gamut of allegations that had been made about Ali in cross-examination and which would be amplified in her counsel's opening speech to the jury. Marshall Hall's invariable practice was to explain carefully to a defendant the pros and cons of giving evidence and secure written authority for the decision.

He began his opening speech for the defence on a low key, pointing out the three possible verdicts of murder, manslaughter or outright acquittal. The kernel of Marguerite's defence would be 'justifiable killing because she was in fear of her life'.

Marshall Hall neatly tackled Percival Clarke's description of Ali as a 'quiet, retiring nervous sort of young man', quoting the physical description set out in the post-mortem report: 'a man of five feet nine or five feet ten, muscular and strong'. This he contrasted with Marguerite's vulnerability. 'Her position is an extraordinarily difficult one,' he argued, 'as she is a stranger in a strange land. She speaks no English and understands practically none and every word that she will give in evidence will have to be . . . translated. The effect . . . will no doubt be seriously lessened before it comes to your ears.' In fact, Marguerite would be greatly assisted by the need for an interpreter. This slows down the pace of questioning (always fairly slow because of the need to make notes of evidence), allowing extra time to deal with awkward questions.

Sensibly, he did not try to whitewash Marguerite's character com-

124

pletely. 'The accused is perhaps a woman of not very strict morality,' he conceded. '. . . She is an extraordinarily attractive woman and when they first met she was as infatuated with [Fahmy] as he was with her.' He moved quickly to the association between Ali and Said Enani. Said, he alleged, 'had been very ungracious to her . . . she was very jealous of his influence over her husband'. Said was a bad lot. 'I am not going to say much about the so-called secretary and great personal friend, Said Enani. You will form your own opinion as to the sort of influence he had over Fahmy.' Together, this odd couple had enticed Marguerite to Egypt by trickery.

Marshall Hall's foray into homophobia was accompanied by a measure of racism. Marguerite, the older woman, had been attracted to the young Ali, who had used his 'Eastern cunning' to make himself agreeable to her. 'You have to consider,' he added, 'the relationship between East and West and the extraordinary pride an Eastern man takes in the possession of a Western woman . . .' Marguerite had been left in Egypt 'absolutely at the mercy of his entourage of black servants'.

Briefly digressing from his theme and plainly to introduce an element of mystery, Marshall Hall made reference to the sealed document Marguerite had written in January 1922. It had been opened by her lawyer, Maître Assouad, in the presence of two barristers. 'Whether or not the contents . . . are evidence depends very much on the line Madame Fahmy takes in the witness-box. I cannot say what the contents are because I am not entitled to at this stage . . .'

Reference to the Muslim marriage brought, in the words of the *Daily Sketch*, 'dramatic gestures and heightened inflection [as] counsel continued to outline the story', using his trump card, the allegations of sodomy:

After the marriage ceremony was over, all sort of restraint on Fahmy's part ceased. He took her away up country. He developed from an attentive, plausible and kind lover into a ferocious brute. That is her own language and I adopt it. She discovered for the first time that he not only had the vilest of vile tempers, but was vile himself, with a filthy perverted taste. From that day onwards down to the very night, within a few moments of the time when a bullet sent that man to eternity, he was pestering her [for unnatural sexual intercourse] . . .

. . . She will tell you that . . . he kept a black valet to watch over this white woman's suite of rooms, conditions that really make me shudder . . . that state of obedience which a black man wants from a woman who is his chattel.

A long catalogue of Marguerite's grievances followed, including an allegation that Fahmy had once refused to let his wife travel in his car, sending her in a tram instead, accompanied by a black servant: 'She could not go anywhere without these black things watching her.' Then, 'to a hushed court', Marshall Hall read out the anonymous letter that Marguerite had received at the Savoy on 3 July, two days after their arrival, with its references to the 'craftiness' of Easterners, poison and possible accidents. Neither the judge nor prosecuting counsel made any attempt to stop Marshall Hall reading out this very dubious document, which, apart from any other defect, was of unknown origin and of little relevance to the direct issue that the jury was trying. But an air of unreality, a touch of hysteria, was beginning to pervade Number One Court.

'Fahmy's threats were not empty threats,' continued Marshall Hall, warming to his subject. 'Orientals have the power of carrying out their threats. Madame Fahmy was guarded by an irresponsible black Sudanese' – in reality, Ali's diminutive valet – 'who was abolutely the creature of his master. Fahmy had said, "You shall not escape me. In 24 hours you will be dead." That threat was made on the night before the tragedy . . .' Marguerite, 'a poor, wretched woman suffering the tortures of the damned' had fired the pistol in desperation as Ali 'crouched for the last time, crouched like an animal, crouched like an Oriental . . .'

He came to his peroration, the usual strong meat of the Marshall Hall style. 'I submit that this woman, driven to exasperation by the brutality and beastliness of this man, whose will she had dared to oppose, thought that he was carrying out the threat he had always made and that, when he seized her by the neck, he was about to kill her.'

That reference to seizure by the neck dovetailed neatly into the evidence of the day's last witness. Although, by the rules, Marguerite should have been the first to be called, Marshall Hall, not for the only time, broke precedent and produced the Medical Officer from Holloway, Dr J. H. Morton. During his speech, Marshall Hall had referred dramatically to 'a new and wonderful piece of evidence' that had emerged 'thanks to His Lordship's intervention'. It was a clever way of exploiting Rigby Swift's concern about Dr Gordon's testimony, which had mentioned a scratch mark at the back of Marguerite's neck.

The judge had asked for a report from the prison and Dr Morton confirmed that Marguerite had been admitted with three abrasions in the same place. It added little to what Dr Gordon had already described. Marshall Hall then asked an outrageously leading question of his own witness:

'Were those marks consistent with having been caused by a man's hand?'

The answer was affirmative, but as in the case of Dr Gordon's evidence, no one seems to have canvassed the possibility of self-infliction. By now it was late in the afternoon and the judge was growing a little worried about the direction the case was taking. When the court adjourned for the day, he warned the jury not to come to a definite conclusion before they had heard all the evidence.

Marshall Hall's opening address resembled the heavy shelling that precedes a battle assault. He was softening up his target, using his dramatic style to the full, appealing to a jury that was likely to have been inimical to homosexuality and suspicious of foreigners, especially 'black' ones. Frequent references to the perceived decadence of the East, to the guile of the 'Oriental', would have struck a chord in an English jury.

In childhood, some of the jury's complement of twelve would have had the *Thousand and One Nights* as nursery reading, with exotic tales of the court of Haroun Al-Raschid, magic carpets, and the journeyings of Sinbad the Sailor. In the expurgated version available to Victorian youngsters, readers would have missed the earthy humour and scatological wit of the complete series, but there would have been much to excite the imagination, even if the stories were a poor guide to contemporary realities in the Near and Middle East.

There was a distinct possibility, too, that one or more of the jurymen had done war service in the eastern Mediterranean. Before the fiasco of the Gallipoli landings in 1915, many British troops had been stationed in Egypt and, further East, the Arabian subcontinent, Mesopotamia and Palestine had all been theatres of war against the Turks. Troopships bound for India would have had to pass through the Suez Canal, putting into Port Said or Ismailia.

Anyone who had spent time in Egypt while serving in the armed forces or who had travelled there as an English civilian would have been exposed to the prevailing prejudice against things Eastern in general and against nearly all things Egyptian in particular. Egyptians were regarded, by and large, as a shifty bunch. The *Daily Mail* lambasted them as 'the most volatile and feather-headed race in the world', a statement that reflected the view that Egyptians were not only incapable of running their own affairs, but were thoroughly ungrateful to Britain into the bargain. Nevertheless, the British in Egypt continued to believe in their mission. That they had never begun to understand, let alone accept, the ways of the native population is evident from contemporary press coverage.

It would be surprising if this pervasive contempt for the Egyptian people had not found its way into the minds of those who comprised the jury in the Fahmy case. Their outlook would have been, in all probability, a hopeless mishmash when it came to anything Middle Eastern.

The recent triumph of Lawrence of Arabia had given substantial, supposedly unwanted publicity to the strange little man who had fought for his beloved Arabs in the Great War. The slick salesmanship of Lowell Thomas, an American journalist, had much to do with the creation of the Lawrence legend in the years after 1918. The image of Lawrence in his spectacular white, flowing Arab costume was striking enough, but this breathlessly romantic impression of 'the East' was by no means the first manifestation of the English public's interest in such things. At least since the turn of the century, there had been a glut of novels written about dusky sheiks, women innocent or 'fast', desert sands, cool oases and searing passion. Stuffy, puritanical England went wild about the desert myth.

One of the most successful exponents of this genre was Robert Smythe Hichens, who had originally made a name for himself in the mid-1890s with *The Green Carnation*, inspired by the world of Oscar Wilde, and written just before his fall. Hichens had travelled extensively in the Arabic-speaking world and was a prolific author. *The Garden of Allah*, set in Morocco, ran to forty-three editions between 1904 and 1929 and was made into a film in 1917. Probably his best known work was *Bella Donna*, published in 1909.

The setting of the novel is Egypt and there are some parallels with the Fahmy story. Ruby Chepstow, at forty-plus 'a great beauty in decline', was 'seen about with young men, almost boys . . .' Marguerite Fahmy, if not yet middle-aged, had been a decade older than her young husband. The hero of *Bella Donna* is Nigel Armine, 'tall, broadchested and fair', who is introduced to Ruby in the Savoy Hotel restaurant. Nigel had 'bought some land . . . in the Fayyüm [of Egypt]'. He falls in love with Ruby, very much a Woman with a Past.

Hopelessly smitten, Nigel marries Ruby Chepstow at a register office. They set out for Egypt and, on board ship, they meet the sinister Mahmoud Baroudi, 'of mixed Greek and Egyptian blood', who embodies a dangerous combination of western manners and eastern deceit. '[Baroudi] was remarkably well-dressed in clothes . . . which he wore with a carelessness almost English, but also with an easy grace that was utterly foreign . . . Probably he was governed by the Oriental's conception of women as an inferior sex and was unable to be quite at home with the complete equality and ease of the English relation with women.' Hichens's description of Baroudi had been read by a wide public for nearly fifteen years by the time H. V. Morton made his slighting reference to Ali Fahmy in 1923.

When the virtuous Nigel is away, tending to the problems of his *felaheen* in Fayyüm, Ruby slips aboard Baroudi's *dahabeeyah* on the Nile, head over heels in love with the brutal easterner, who is attended by 'a huge Nubian'. Wearing 'a suit of white linen, white shoes and the tarbush . . . [Baroudi] acknowledged calmly that he had treated [Ruby] as a chattel. She loved that . . . She felt cruelty in him and it attracted her.' In this regard, *Bella Donna* exemplifies the myth of the potent sheik, an unbridled sexual animal with rape perpetually in mind.

Baroudi's target was the white woman. Marshall Hall's condemnation of Ali Fahmy could have sprung directly from the pages of *Bella Donna*. Baroudi, 'since he had been almost a boy . . . like a good many of his smart, semi-cultured, self-possessed and physically attractive young contemporaries had gloried in his triumph among the Occidental women . . . [striking] a blow at the Western man'. He was 'one of those Egyptians who go mad over the women of Europe . . . their delicate colouring and shining hair'.

Totally vicious, Mahmoud Baroudi one moment would be the 'cosmopolitan millionaire', the next a hashish-smoking decadent. One English character speaks of 'Egyptians he had known intimately, whom he had seen subjected to every kind of European influence, whom he had seen apparently "Europeanized" . . . but who, when a moment came, had shown themselves "native" to the core.' This supposed cultural dichotomy was being applied to Ali Fahmy's character by the defence during his widow's trial.

Baroudi's evil influence prompts Ruby to poison Nigel, but the plot is discovered in time to save his life and, ruined, Ruby wanders off alone into the desert night. *Bella Donna*, forgotten today, was a popular success for some twenty years after its publication. In September 1923, just as Marguerite's trial was starting, news came that Pola Negri, the smouldering Hollywood film star, would be appearing in a film of the novel.

Elinor Glyn had employed a desert theme in *His Hour* (1909) and during the next decade Katherine Rhodes wrote stories of 'the fire and passion of the relentless desert'. Another blockbuster from the mystic East first appeared in 1921, perhaps the greatest (or most notorious) of them all. Promoted by an elaborate hype, *The Sheik* by E. M. Hull (the 'E.M.' stood for Edith Maud) had gone through a hundred editions in English by mid-1923. An accompanying dance tune, also called *The Sheik*, had sold 250,000 copies as sheet music in England alone, where gramophone recordings of it were made by four different bands between March and August 1922.

The movie was a sensation, at any rate in the western world. Starring Rudolph Valentino, *The Sheik*, as the *Evening News* reported in July 1923, 'has been shown in 1260 kinemas in Great Britain', where the Paramount Film Corporation estimated that five million people had paid to see it.

Some authorities have linked the series of desert-based romances that poured out of Hollywood in the early 1920s with the phenomenon of Lawrence of Arabia and Lowell Thomas's publicity machine. Whatever the reason, there was undoubtedly a market in popular western culture for these fantasies, which intermixed racial stereotypes with a strong leavening of sex, a not so soft pornography.

In *The Sheik*, boyish Diana Mayo unwisely contemplates 'an expedition into the desert with no chaperon . . . only native camel drivers and servants'. There she is captured by Sheik Ahmed Ben Hassan, 'the handsomest and cruellest face she had ever seen . . .' Diana succumbs to 'the flaming light of desire burning in his eyes . . . the fierce embrace . . . [of] the man's pulsating body . . . the touch of his scorching lips'. He was an 'Oriental beast . . . in his Oriental disregard of the woman subjugated', presenting 'a hideous exhibition of brute strength and merciless cruelty . . .' The lines might have come from Marshall Hall's opening address to the jury in the Fahmy case.

Having thus far lived their ordinary lives amid this welter of misinformation about Egypt and the Arab world, Marguerite Fahmy's jury were unlikely to have taken a detached, dispassionate view of her relationship with the dead man. For good measure, the Tut-Ankh-Amun discoveries had that very year vividly underlined the widespread perception of Eastern exoticism, at a distant remove from the humdrum world of suburban London, in which most of the jury's membership probably lived.

18

Centre Stage

The knowledge that Madame Fahmy was to go into the witness-box heightened the public's already intense interest (or morbid curiosity). The first would-be spectator to arrive, at 2.00 a.m. on Wednesday morning, was young Mr James Stewart of Lancing, who told the *Pall Mall Gazette*'s reporter that he had been a ship's steward in charge of the Fahmys' suite, when they had travelled aboard the S S *Nile*, possibly before Christmas 1922. Mr Stewart was determined to see the show. At 2.30, he had refused £5 from a 'well-dressed man' for his place and later a woman unsuccessfully offered him '£3 and 50 cigarettes'. The police soon started to break up the queues that were forming in Newgate despite a very chilly wait, but not before another young man received the day's best offer, 'to keep him for a week at one of the best hotels in London', made in vain by a prosperous-looking gentleman.

The *Daily Telegraph* reported that Marguerite seemed 'brighter and more alert' when she entered the dock, which she did for once without the assistance of a prison officer. The start of her evidence was delayed by legal wrangling, during which the jury were sent out of court. Percival Clarke, very properly, had told Marshall Hall that he intended to cross-examine Marguerite 'as to whether or not she had lived an immoral life', to show that she was 'a woman of the world, well able to look after herself'.

Marshall Hall was determined to resist a damaging attack on his client's character. 'The only effect,' he told the judge, '. . . would be to prejudice the jury unfavourably against this woman. I have not opened the case that she is a woman of moral character . . .' Clarke, mindful of

131

the dirt about Marguerite set out in ex-Chief Inspector Stockley's confidential report, said that he wanted to dispel the idea that this was 'a poor child practically domineered over by this man'. He was entitled, he felt, to ask how she treated other men and in any case defence counsel had opened that she was an immoral woman.

The judge decided that the jury would not be told all about Marguerite's eventful past, ruling that prosecuting counsel would have to confine himself to questions about Marguerite's relations with her husband. 'Sir Edward has said that she was a loose woman,' he observed, 'but he said it in such a way that he gave the impression . . . that she was an innocent and most respectable lady. It is a difficult thing to do, but Sir Edward, with all that skill we have admired for so long, has done it . . .' The judge again passed over the accusation of homosexuality that Marshall Hall had put to Said Enani. 'Although I thought there was going to be an attack . . .,' said the judge, flying in the face of plain fact, 'there really was no attack made on his character.'

The jury filed back in, to be told that they were now to be deprived of newspapers for the duration of the trial, since they would report the substance of the legal argument. 'I am sorry to deprive you of them,' said the judge, sympathetically. 'It must be very boring to be shut up all the evening without a newspaper, but I am bound to do it.'

Marie Marguerite Fahmy was then called to give evidence in her own defence. She was seen to falter as she approached the witness-box and required the help of a wardress to complete the short journey. Rigby Swift intimated that Marguerite could give her evidence from a chair and as she took her seat it was possible for most of those in court to see her clearly for the first time. The *Evening Standard* thought that Marguerite 'was not so much beautiful as interesting looking. Small, mobile features; a rather petulant mouth, large expressive eyes – such was the picture framed by a black mushroom hat and flowing black veil'. The *Daily Sketch* saw her as 'dark haired and lustrous eyed', an altogether more flattering description than that afforded readers of the *Daily Mail*, which ungallantly claimed that Marguerite was not 'the handsome woman of the photographs', but rather 'of a pronounced Latin type'.

When Marguerite stood up to take the oath, Marshall Hall, recalling his recent, very effective destabilization of Said Enani, prudently suggested that, as Marguerite was now a Muslim, she should be sworn on the Koran. As before, the judge said the witness could be sworn in any way that was binding in conscience and Marguerite took her oath on the Bible. Unlike in the case of the unfortunate Said, nobody seems to have thought the worse of her for doing so. But then Marguerite was European.

Harry Ashton-Wolfe, the official court interpreter, a stocky man with close-cropped hair and a luxuriant black moustache, stepped forward to translate the oath into French. In barely a whisper, Madame Fahmy declared, '*Je jure*' ('I swear'). Marguerite was again demurely dressed in black: it struck Ashton-Wolfe, he later wrote, as a peculiar thing that a woman should be in mourning for a man she had herself killed.

Marguerite's evidence began with some very brief personal details. She told the court that she had divorced Charles Laurent after his desertion, but the jury were never to be aware of Marguerite's blunt words to old Madame Denart in 1918, that she would 'kick him out' after six months of marriage. She claimed that she had lost an annual allowance of 36,000 francs (£450) from Laurent when she married Ali. Marshall Hall then read out the civil contract of marriage to Fahmy, including the provision that he should pay her a dowry of £2000. Ali had only paid her £450, she said, conveniently forgetting the jewellery and other costly gifts made to her both before and after the wedding, estimated to be worth 200,000 francs (£2500).

The pace began to hot up when Marguerite started to describe her life as a Muslim bride. The *Evening Standard* reported that 'Her low, musical voice carried well as she answered in rapid French the questions put to her. Now and then there was just the ghost of a shrug of the shoulders. Occasionally, the black-gloved hands toyed with a grey silk handkerchief . . . sometimes pressed to eyes or mouth.'

After her sister Yvonne had returned to Paris (possibly because she and Ali had been getting on rather too well), Marguerite was left alone with Fahmy Bey. 'There were twelve black men as servants in the house,' she said, 'but no other white women apart from my maid and I.' After a quarrel, Ali had sworn on the Koran to kill her, an allegation which enabled Marshall Hall to make a second dramatic reference to the document Marguerite had composed on 22 January 1923.

Rigby Swift tetchily intervened to express disapproval of mysterious documents that did not form part of the evidence. 'This court,' he said portentously, 'is not a receptacle for waste paper . . .' Marshall Hall responded by claiming that he had simply wanted to show that 'on a particular day this woman wrote a particular document and I wanted her to identify it'. 'Quite irrelevant,' declared the judge. 'You might as well say that on Christmas Day 1920 she sent a Christmas card to her lawyer.' On that abrasive note, the matter ended, at least for the moment.

Wisely avoiding further contact with this judicial hornets' nest, Marshall Hall shifted attention to the scenes on the Nile en route for Luxor. 'The first day,' said Marguerite, '[Ali] tried to frighten me and fired a revolver several times above my head. He had three revolvers.' She had often tried to leave him, but each time she did so, he would cry and beg her to stay, promising to reform. Once he had got her aboard the *dahabeeyah*, however, Ali's attitude had changed. He had frequently struck her, saying, 'You can never leave me any more', eventually locking her into her cabin, evidence which Marguerite gave 'in a choking voice', noted the *Evening Standard*.

Marguerite's letter to Maître Assouad was read out, providing an opportunity for more racial mileage. 'I was terrified,' Marguerite claimed, 'I was alone on board and surrounded by black men.' She described her 'horror' of the 'black valet', who was 'always following her', even to the extent of coming into her room while she was dressing. Her complaints to Ali had met with a dismissive response, distinctly resembling dialogue from *The Sheik*: 'He has the right. He does not count. He is nothing.'

She claimed that she had been forced to take the tram to visit a Cairo cinema, because Ali had denied her the use of a car. In the presence of 'Said Enani and four black men', Fahmy had delivered an unprovoked blow to her chin on her return to the mansion with Mukhta Bey. 'I fell against the door, suffering excruciating pain . . . next day I was treated for a dislocated jaw.'

All this neatly led to revelations of the sexual decadence of non-white society. 'Madame Fahmy proceeded in a faltering and hesitating voice to describe her relations with her husband . . .', reported the *Daily Telegraph*. The press drew a veil over these intimate details, though it was noted by the *Evening Standard* that 'only three women got up and left [the public gallery] when Madame Fahmy was being asked questions of such a nature that she finally buried her face in her hands'. After she had endured this sexual abuse, said Marguerite, Fahmy had again threatened to kill her with a pistol in Cairo, crying, 'I am all powerful; I shall be acquitted.'

In Paris, Ali had refused to pay her dress bill of 18,000 francs (£225). 'He told me to get a lover to pay for them,' she sobbed, 'he said he would call me the worst name in the French language – and it hurt.' After a visit to the *Folies Bergère* (where, unknown to the jury, Marguerite had once solicited for custom), her decadent husband had proposed to visit a 'notorious place'. Taking a higher moral stance than circumstances justified, 'she refused as it was not a fit place for her and her sister', the *Star* reported.

Marguerite recounted further argy-bargy, including an absurdly melodramatic incident during which, she alleged, Ali had seized her by the throat and threatened to horsewhip her. Yvonne Alibert had come to her elder sister's rescue, brandishing a pistol in her hand.

At this point, the fatal Browning was passed to Marguerite by the interpreter, Harry Ashton-Wolfe, who 'fully expected that she would shrink and hesitate. Nothing of the sort! As unconcernedly as if it had been a toy, she took the deadly, blue [sic] weapon in her hand . . .' The *Daily Telegraph*, however, reported a 'strained face' as she briefly let it slip onto the ledge of the witness-box: '. . . in the tense silence it seemed that some great weight had crashed on the wood', in the words of the *Daily Express*.

Marshall Hall, the great opportunist, took his cue. 'Come, Madame Fahmy,' he said softly, 'take hold of the pistol. It is harmless now.' Marguerite 'attempted to pull open the [sliding cover of the] magazine, but without success and, rising to her feet, said she was unable to open it'.

This was a delicate moment for Marguerite. She had admittedly been in possession of a lethal firearm, apparently for some time (though Marshall Hall was keeping this aspect deliberately vague). Did she know how to use it? There had to be an explanation of why, in the early hours of 10 July 1923, Marguerite's pistol was loaded and capable of being fired. Marguerite's story was that Ali had himself cleaned and loaded his wife's gun in Paris, saying that she ought to have something with which to protect her jewellery. 'It's all ready to fire,' he had told her, before leaving for his short visit to Stuttgart in mid-June. Marguerite maintained that she had never known how the pistol worked: 'I know nothing of the mechanism.'

MARSHALL HALL: Had you ever fired a pistol in your life before 9 July?
MARGUERITE: No.

Probably mindful of the inherent improbability of this evidence, Marshall Hall quickly changed tack to resume allegations about Ali's sexual habits: 'Several times . . . she put her hand to her forehead and once she almost broke down and applied her handkerchief to her eyes . . .' She could not escape Fahmy, she said, even in Paris.

Marguerite spoke emotionally of the man 'Costa', otherwise '*Le Costaud*' or 'Hercules', who 'owed his life and his liberty' to Ali and 'would carry out any orders given him', including, it was said, Fahmy's threat to disfigure Marguerite with 'sand in a bottle and acid from accumulators'. 'Costa' was an Algerian who had been expelled from Egypt and a 'horrible man'. At this point, 'Madame Fahmy rested her head on the front of the witness-box and sobbed loudly. Counsel paused for some moments until she had composed herself . . .', reported the *Daily Telegraph*.

Yet another strange document was read out to the court by Marshall Hall. Written in Marguerite's hand, over Ali's signature, it purported to be an agreement between herself and her husband that provided that she could live as she pleased, even commit adultery, without fear of divorce, but that, if she did so, Ali would feel himself free to call her a 'filthy name', which the newspaper reports did not reveal. However, the *Daily Express* reported that when Marshall Hall read certain 'improper phrases . . . Madame Fahmy covered her face with her black gloved hands'.

Marguerite had consulted a private detective in Paris because of Ali's behaviour, though not, it seems, the police, even though one day, as she was being driven with Said Enani and 'Hercules' to Neuilly, a western suburb of Paris, Fahmy had said that he was looking for a house in which to imprison her. She had agreed to come to London only because her daughter, Raymonde, was at school there. Marguerite had not seen her for nine months. Tears welled up.

MARSHALL HALL: Did you think you would be safe in London?
MARGUERITE: I passed from despair to hope and from hope to despair.

Rigby Swift asked if she would like to pause, but Marguerite dried her eyes and went on to describe the incidents at the Riviera Club and the Molesey Casino. Appearing to speak of the Sunday night before the shooting, she told how 'Fahmy came to her room . . .' (the *Daily Telegraph*'s cryptic report breaks off here), where, it seems, he sodomized her yet again. 'I told him that I preferred to die rather than go on living in the way I was doing. He said, "You have a revolver", and pointed to the open window [of the suite], saying, "It's quite easy. There are four floors."'

It was now one o'clock and, as Marguerite left the witness-box at the start of the lunchtime adjournment, reported the *Daily Telegraph*, 'she almost swooned and a second wardress ran to her assistance and, with the marks of tears on her face, the prisoner was half carried into the dock'. There would be a good deal more swooning before Marguerite had finished her lengthy testimony.

19

A Frail Hand

A glance at the public gallery, where all the seats were filled, would have revealed a substantial majority of women, among whom were 'girls who did not appear to have been more than 18 . . . Some seemed to have come with their mothers . . .', the *Daily Express* noted, each agog to hear these unsavoury tales of Franco-Egyptian married life. After lunch, the first three rows, it seems, were filled with 'shop assistants released from their counters for the weekly half-holiday . . .'

The jury was clearly unhappy that witnesses such as Said Enani, John Beattie, and other members of the Savoy staff had remained in court to hear this sordid material and, after lunch, they sent a note up to the judge, who ordered 'non-professional witnesses' to withdraw.

The problem of Marguerite's haemorrhoids began the afternoon's evidence. Ali had told her to 'go to the devil' and 'take a lover' when she had asked him for money to pay for the operation in London. That was why, she said, she had decided to return to Paris, but Ali had furiously told her, 'You will not escape me. I swear to you that in twenty-four hours you will be dead.'

The angry exchanges in the Savoy Restaurant, both at lunchtime and at supper on the day before the shooting, were recalled. When Marguerite pointed out that the Head Waiter had heard Ali's threats, he had replied, 'For £10 the Head Waiter will say what I want him to say and will be against you.' Said Enani, too, was venal: he had told Marguerite that he would go away only if she paid him £2000.

These uncorroborated assertions paved the way for the pivotal evidence – the shooting itself. 'I took the pistol from the drawer,'

Marguerite told a hushed, expectant court. 'I knew that it was loaded. He had told me so and I had not touched it since the day he went away [to Stuttgart]. I tried to look into it to see if there was a bullet . . . I tried to do as I had seen him do to get the cartridge out of it . . . I had not the strength to pull sufficiently to make the cartridge fall out.'

MARSHALL HALL: Why did you want to get the cartridge out of the barrel?
MARGUERITE: Because he said he was going to kill me and I thought I would frighten him with it . . . I was shaking it in front of the window when the shot went off.
MARSHALL HALL: What did you think was the condition of the pistol after it had been fired?
MARGUERITE: The cartridge having been fired, I thought the pistol was not dangerous.

Marguerite was now claiming that the pistol had been fired out of the window, not during the thunderstorm, immediately before killing her husband (as she had told Dr Gordon at Bow Street police station), but earlier the previous evening, before the party had left to see *The Merry Widow* at Daly's Theatre.

She had been alarmed by Fahmy's threats, made at about 7.30 p.m., after he had seen her luggage packed up and ready for her return to Paris. He had taken his photograph from her dressing-table, torn it up and flung the pieces at her. 'Pale and aggressive', he handed back a tie-pin she had given him before their marriage. 'As you are going away,' he had said, contemptuously, 'do not forget your presents to me,' adding, 'You will see; you will see.'

At the theatre, Ali had said, 'Even if you manage to escape from London and get to Paris, Costa will be waiting for you,' and at supper had again threatened to disfigure her. In a disturbed state of mind, and frightened of the storm, Marguerite had not gone to bed, but had written 'a letter or two' (including the one discharging Dr Gordon), when there was a loud knock at her bedroom door. 'Sobbing and occasionally throwing back her head and shutting her eyes, [Madame Fahmy] described the tragedy', reported the *Evening Standard*.

The *Daily Mail* noted that Fahmy had banged on the door, shouting, 'You are not alone, then. Open. Open.' She let him in and saw that he was wearing a djellaba and dressing-gown, his night clothes. Ali asked her what she was doing. 'I said I had sent a cheque to the doctor and asked him, "Are you going to give me any money to leave tomorrow?" He said, "Come into my room and see if I have any money there for you."'

In terms which resembled the more purple moments of Robert Smythe Hichens and E. M. Hull, Marguerite described the drama that took place in her Egyptian husband's bedroom. He had produced some pound notes and about 2000 francs, which he held sneeringly before her. The *Times* reported that when Marguerite asked him for the French money to cover her travelling expenses, Fahmy said, 'I will give it to you if you earn it', and started to tear off her dress. The unreported suggestion was that, unless Marguerite submitted yet again to his unorthodox sexual demands, despite her painfully inflamed condition, she had no hope of escaping to Paris.

'He struggled with me. I ran to the telephone, but he tore it out of my hand and twisted my arm. I hit him and ran towards the door. He struck me and spat in my face. I rushed to the corridor, where there were several people . . .'

It had, of course, been Ali who had first emerged from the suite, closely followed by his wife and both had accosted the long-suffering night porter, showering him with mutual recriminations. Beattie's evidence suggested that it had been Ali who was more frightened of Marguerite's temper, rather than the other way round, but that was not what Marguerite was saying from the witness-box.

She had been ordered back to her room. There she saw the pistol on top of a suitcase, where she had left it some hours before. Ali banged on the door again: 'I was very frightened and felt weak,' she recalled. She was now sobbing convulsively, tears running down her cheeks, as she told how Ali had come towards her, saying, 'I will revenge myself.' Marguerite picked up the pistol. Ali shouted, 'I'll say that you threatened me,' and by some unexplained means Marguerite managed to slip out from her room, through the lobby of the suite, and into the hotel corridor.

'He seized me suddenly and brutally by the throat. His thumb was on my windpipe and his fingers were pressing in my neck. I pushed him away and he crouched to spring at me, saying, "I will kill you."'

At this point, noted the *Daily Telegraph*, 'her voice broke into a moan, and between her sobs she lifted her left hand and tapped excitedly on her black hat, as if this movement helped her to get through this ordeal. She stretched a frail hand across the witness-box and, closing her eyes, sobbed out, "I now lifted my arm in front of me and without looking, pulled the trigger. The next moment, I saw him on the ground before me . . . I do not know how many times the pistol went off."'

Marguerite's examination-in-chief ended on an impressive note:

MARSHALL HALL: When you threw your arm out when the pistol was fired, what were you afraid of?
MARGUERITE: That he was going to jump on me. It was terrible. I had escaped once. He said, 'I will kill you. I will kill you.' It was so terrible.

Marguerite had already spent some four hours in the witness-box before Percival Clarke rose to cross-examine. Experienced counsel can often sense the unspoken mood of a court and it is likely that Clarke was aware of a distinct change in the atmosphere since his opening speech on Monday morning. The case was beginning to develop a momentum of its own; a mist of unreality was gradually befogging the courtroom.

Much of Marguerite's testimony had in all likelihood derived from exaggerated accounts of incidents stored away in the memory for use in divorce proceedings. There were a number of improbabilities and inconsistencies in her story. She had, for example, just given a very wobbly account of escaping into the hotel corridor from a murder-bent Ali. Could he really have been about to jump on her in so public a place? Clarke had the material for some very awkward questions, but his was to be a lacklustre cross-examination. Indeed his first question could only have served to strengthen the defence case:

CLARKE: Were you afraid he was going to kill you on that night?
MARGUERITE: Yes, I was very afraid.

Yet a little later it seemed that Clarke was beginning to make progress:

CLARKE: How long have you possessed a pistol?
MARGUERITE: I had a pistol during the War in 1914. A second one was given me two years ago . . .

CLARKE: What did you have a pistol for if you did not know how it worked?
MARGUERITE: It is the usual thing in France to have a pistol.

Clarke then made a major tactical blunder. Going against the judge's ruling, he started to ask personal questions about Marguerite's back-ground. Marguerite proudly told the court that Raymonde, her only and much loved daughter, had been legitimized by her marriage to Charles Laurent. Her defiant answers to this insensitive probing probably enlisted the jury's sympathy, as did this foolish, unanswered question:

CLARKE: Was your father a cabdriver in Paris?

Rigby Swift was very angry. 'Does it matter whether he was a cabdriver or a millionaire? I do not want a long inquiry into the lady's ancestry . . .', but Clarke failed to take the hint. After Marguerite had told him, a little riskily, that she had a number of friends in Paris of 'wealth and position', he asked:

CLARKE: Can I correctly describe you as a woman of the world?
INTERPRETER: The meaning is not the same in French.
CLARKE: A woman with experience of the world?
MARGUERITE: I have had experience of life.

This world-weary answer did much for Marguerite and probably impressed the jury, who might have been surprised to know just how extensive Marguerite's experience of life had been. Clarke's cross-examination was foundering, but before the court rose for the day, he managed to score a rare success:

CLARKE: Would it be right to say that this black valet my friend has spoken of is a boy of eighteen?
MARGUERITE: Yes, he was fairly young.
CLARKE: Is he only five feet high?
MARGUERITE: Yes, he is very small.

And she agreed that it was customary for wives of Egyptians to be attended by servants. The long day was near its end. Clarke tried a last attempt to impress the jury, asking sternly:

CLARKE: Madame, were you not very ambitious to become his wife?
MARGUERITE: Ambitious, no. [Here she wiped her cheek] I loved him so very much and wished to be with him.
CLARKE: . . . What did you do while he was being so cruel? Sit down quietly?

MARGUERITE: Only once I boxed his ears when he had beaten me very much . . . He beat me so much when I did so that I never dared do it again. I never boxed his ears in public.

Clarke's last question of the day was callously worded and Marguerite's answer, in contrast, seems the poignant response of an abused widow. In keeping with her role, she again appeared to faint before leaving the witness-box and had to be almost carried down the stairs to the cells by a wardress and a male prison officer.

Barely three hours after Number One Court had adjourned for the day at 4.30 p.m. on Wednesday 12 September, figures again began to congregate around the public entrance to the Old Bailey. By 11.00 p.m. there were about fifty, and an hour later that number had doubled. By 2.00 a.m., several hundred people had gathered in Newgate Street, defying the persistent attempts of police to move them on. In one of the side streets, pretty girls, smartly dressed, were seen sitting on rubber cushions, 'bivouacking' on sandwiches and oranges. One man, asked by the *Pall Mall Gazette* why he had come, responded, 'Well mister, it's life ain't it?' The trial of Madame Fahmy was now the acknowledged sensation of the year.

When the case resumed on Thursday morning, Marshall Hall used another diversionary tactic, aiming a blow at Clarke's faltering cross-examination. Madame Fahmy, he told the judge, found it very difficult to understand Ashton-Wolfe's French, as he spoke in a low voice. Counsel asked if Maître Odette Simon, a twenty-four-year-old French barrister, might be allowed to sit near the witness-box and 'hear if the questions were translated properly'.

The judge agreed, but before Percival Clarke had posed more than a question or two to Marguerite, Marshall Hall was again on his feet, this time objecting to Ashton-Wolfe's translation. 'I very much deprecate these difficulties about the interpreter,' said Rigby Swift testily. 'He seems to me to have been performing his difficult duties very well . . .'

Ashton-Wolfe was discharged with thanks and Mlle Simon took the interpreter's oath. She was staying with relatives in England after the French courts had adjourned for their vacation at the end of July and had been eager to see an English trial. Odette, one of eighty women barristers in France, had practised law for some four years. Wearing, noted the *Evening Standard*, 'a navy blue costume with a white collar and a large-brimmed dark hat, trimmed with bluish-green brocade', she gave her translation from the well of the court, standing between the judge and the witness-box.

There had been a tactical dimension to Marshall Hall's request. The previous day, Helena Normanton, Mlle Simon's English barrister colleague, had sent counsel a note in which she wrote that Mlle Simon was anxious to 'offer you her aid as witness or otherwise, if you care to avail yourself of it . . .' Marshall Hall realized the advantage that would accrue to the defence by presenting 'the romantic situation . . . of one young Frenchwoman helping another in her hour of extreme peril in a foreign country . . .'

Marguerite was reported by the *Daily Telegraph* to be 'more composed than she had been the previous day' and was able to step into the witness-box unaided. At first, during Clarke's resumed cross-examination, she sat very still in her black marocain dress and hat, which, the *Evening Standard* reported, accentuated 'the olive tints of throat and face', delivering answers almost too calmly, as Clarke investigated how far her complaints about Ali derived from the compilations of a divorce dossier. Rightly, prosecuting counsel was concerned to know why Marguerite had stayed with so brutal a husband, regularly appearing with him in public places.

CLARKE: While you were in Paris before he went to Germany, were you leading a very gay life – I do not mean immorally gay – but going to the theatres, dining etc?
MARGUERITE: Yes, we were going out every evening.
CLARKE: When your husband went to Stuttgart on 17 or 18 June, why did you not leave him while he was away?
MARGUERITE: [Giving a slight shrug] Where could I have gone to? If I had gone to my flat, Said Enani would have come to fetch me back the next day.
CLARKE: But you had lived in Paris all your life and had many friends there of influence and wealth?
MARGUERITE: I did not want my friends to know all about my sorrow, because I thought they would laugh at me. Except for two or three intimate women friends, I have always tried to save appearances.

Marguerite's stated reasons for not leaving Fahmy were manifestly weak and Clarke pressed home his advantage by putting questions about the document, containing 'improper phrases' and supposedly giving

Marguerite the right to commit adultery. Fahmy, she said, had dictated it, 'because he was always so brutal when he wanted a thing to be done . . .'

CLARKE: Did you write that letter in order to assist in your divorce?
MARGUERITE: I never produced it. It was so degrading.

Her voice began to quaver and she gesticulated wildly as she related the unconvincing story that Ali, unable to form the French characters, had been in the habit of dictating letters to Said Enani, who wrote them out for Ali to copy.

CLARKE: If this were a genuine document, why did he not write it himself?
MARGUERITE: It was 2 o'clock in the morning and I did not wish to prolong the scene which preceded the writing . . . He said 'write' and I wrote.

It may have been at this stage in cross-examination, when the prosecution was at last appearing to make some progress, that Marshall Hall's mischievous spirit again asserted itself. Robert Churchill, the firearms expert, was still in court, sitting at the exhibits table. While Clarke was putting questions to Marguerite, Marshall Hall left his seat, a conspicuous progress in which he was obliged to disturb several other barristers, and went over to where Churchill was sitting.

As Macdonald Hastings relates in his *The Other Mr Churchill*, Marshall Hall said under his breath, 'Take the pistol to pieces.' Churchill later recalled, 'I did as I was told and then he whispered "What reports have you had about the partridges?" It was early September, the shooting season was just beginning and he was a keen game shot. For the next few minutes we talked about sport; and, all the while, we exchanged the various mechanical parts of the pistol until, at last, Marshall Hall rose to his feet with a solemn "Thank you."

'At first, I imagined he was resting his mind by talking about sport in the middle of a difficult case. Later I recollected that I had never heard a word of the prosecution's case while we were together. I have little doubt now that his conversation . . . was a diversion to distract the attention of the jury at a point in his case when he was anxious that they shouldn't listen too carefully to the other side. Instead, they were watching us.'

Marshall Hall would not have felt the need for distraction when Clarke came to question Marguerite about the sexual side of her marriage. Madame Fahmy coped very well with what was probably a fairly discreetly worded inquiry into the allegations she had made about her husband's amorous inclinations. Tears could be seen in her eyes as she declared that her relations with Ali had 'never been quite normal'.

CLARKE: I take it that from the time of his first objectionable suggestion you hated your husband bitterly?
MARGUERITE: I loved my husband and, when he had been so bad, I despaired and I told him I hated him. I did not hate him, but only what he wanted me to do.

Clarke's cross-examination was beginning to nosedive. The trend was accelerated by some very clumsy questioning about knowledge of the pistol's mechanism. It is a golden rule of cross-examination that you should not, if at all possible, reduce a witness to tears. To be fair, Marguerite had tended to the lachrymose from the moment she had stepped into the witness-box, but Clarke went over the previous day's old ground in far too much detail, even to the extent of putting the pistol back in her unwilling hands.

Calmness gave way once more to emotion. 'She wept while speaking, supporting her head with one hand and with the other made gestures deprecatory, emphatic, disdainful . . .', reported the *Evening Standard*, and, when Clarke put to her that she must have known that there were other cartridges in the gun, she cried out, 'I don't know anything of its mechanics. I . . .' before breaking off in distress. She burst into loud sobbing and fell back into her chair.

The effect of Clarke's heavy-handed questioning was to rob many of the prosecution's stronger points of their force. If she had, as she said, fired the first shot out of the window early in the evening, how was it that no one, apart from her maid, had heard it? The thunderstorm was not then raging. 'Did you not fire that first shot to see that the pistol was in working order,' Clarke had asked, but she maintained that she had only been trying to get the bullet out of the gun.

The white evening dress was passed to her, and tears welled up in her eyes as she pointed to the back of the garment, where Ali had torn off some of the small beads in the course of the struggle. She affected to shudder as the dress was handed back to a court usher, but had sufficient composure to parry Clarke's next question.

CLARKE: Did you know that your husband was completely unarmed when you pointed the revolver [sic] at him?
MARGUERITE: I did not know; he often had a pistol in the jacket of his dressing-gown. The thunderstorm was so awful and I was in such a terrible state of nerves I do not know what I thought of it at the time.

Soon afterwards, Clarke came to the end of his cross-examination in a distinctly downbeat way.

CLARKE: Were you not fully aware that when your husband attacked you, you could immediately have rung the bell and got assistance?
MARGUERITE: I could not speak English. What could I say?
CLARKE: Could you not have got your maid to stay with you that night?
MARGUERITE: She had gone to bed and was on the eighth floor. I had no telephone to her.

Marshall Hall's short re-examination was largely taken up with Rigby Swift's 'waste paper', the declaration which Marguerite had written in January 1923, and which she had left, sealed, with her lawyer, Maître Assouad, 'only to be opened in case of her death'. It had, in truth, virtually no evidential value, merely reiterating what Marguerite had been saying in evidence, but, predictably, Marshall Hall was able to maximize its dramatic effect.

Yvonne Alibert gave evidence which broadly supported her sister's case – no surprises here – as did Aimée Pain, the maid, with whom Marguerite had spoken at such length in Bow Street police station just hours after the shooting. Aimée confirmed her mistress's story of the pistol going off between 8.30 and 9.00 on the night of 9 July (an incorrect time, by any reading, as Marguerite was then uncomfortably seated in Daly's Theatre), but had somehow forgotten to mention this to the police, because she was 'so upset'.

Eugène Barbay, Marguerite's faithful chauffeur, came close to over-egging the pudding on his mistress's behalf:

CLARKE: What do you mean when you say she was always crying?
BARBAY: She had her handkerchief to her eyes.

CLARKE: Even at the dressmaker's or dinner or the theatre?
BARBAY: She always had red eyes. She was always trying to stop.
CLARKE: Oh, she did try to stop sometimes?
BARBAY: Yes, but for never more than half an hour at a time.

With descriptions of Marguerite's bruised face in Paris, given by a witness described by the *Daily Telegraph* as 'Madame Hélène Beaudry, a singer', the defence evidence closed. It remained for Marguerite's advocate to make the speech of his lifetime.

20

Bella Donna

Marshall Hall, rising painfully from his seat, began his closing address just before 3.30 in the afternoon, not the best time to start a keynote speech. The jury had already been subjected to nearly four hours of evidence that day and concentration inevitably tends to slip after lunch.

As was his custom, he began quietly. There were only two issues in the case: 'Either this was a deliberate, premeditated and cowardly murder, or it was a shot fired by this woman from a pistol which she believed to be unloaded at a moment when she thought her life to be in danger.' Mindful of the ruins of Clarke's cross-examination, counsel dared to assume that the jury were already well disposed towards his client: 'You must not allow your sympathy for this poor woman to interfere with returning a proper verdict,' he adjured. 'Do not descend to little, minor or petty details, but take a broad view of the facts . . .' That 'broad view' would become, as the speech progressed, a projection of Ali Fahmy as a monster of Eastern depravity and decadence, whose sexual tastes were indicative of an amoral sadism towards his helpless European wife.

'She made one great mistake, the greatest mistake any woman can make: a woman of the West married to an Oriental,' said the Great Defender, turning the jury's attention to the slight figure in the dock, so quietly dressed in black, her chin resting on her hands, calm now after the tears and emotion of her evidence.

'I daresay the Egyptian civilisation is and may be one of the oldest and most wonderful civilisations in the world. I don't say that among the Egyptians there are not many magnificent and splendid men . . .' – here came the sting – 'but if you strip off the external civilisation of the Oriental, you get the real Oriental underneath and it is common knowledge that the Oriental's treatment of women does not fit in with the idea the Western woman has of the proper way she should be treated by her husband . . .'

And that husband was not the 'nervous, retiring young man' of Percival Clarke's instructions (Marshall Hall had given his jejune opponent a clever backhanded compliment to 'the way he had performed a difficult and thankless task'). Not at all: the 'mysterious document' that Marguerite had composed herself in January 1923 showed how afraid she was that some of Fahmy's 'black hirelings' would do her to death.

'In 1923, in the midst of civilised London, it seems odd that such a threat should have had any effect on the woman. But think of Egypt,' he contrasted. 'It is the curse of this case that there is something we can't get at, that is, the Eastern feeling.' The dead man's personal private secretary had possessed that 'Eastern feeling' in abundance. 'One almost smiles when my friend asks "Why did you not get Said Enani to protect you?",' said Marshall Hall, appearing to take the jury into his confidence. 'You have seen Said Enani and have heard something about him. Is he the kind of man you would have as the sole buffer between yourselves and a man like Fahmy? . . . Do you believe anything said by Said Enani that was hostile to this unfortunate woman?' Defence counsel was now in full xenophobic flight, with no sign of a rebuke from the judge. 'I suggest that it is part of the Eastern duplicity that is well known.'

Spicing his argument with gratuitous references to colour, he continued, 'Do not forget Costa, that great black Hercules, who came day after day for orders, and who was ready to do anything. Don't you think she had ground for fear of this great black blackguard who owed his life to Fahmy?'

It had all been an Easterner's plot to lure Marguerite into a kind of white slavery. 'Picture this woman,' he invited the jury, 'inveigled into Egypt by false pretences, by a letter which for adulatory expression could hardly be equalled and which makes one feel sick . . . At first, all is honey and roses. He shows her his beautiful palace, his costly motor-cars, his wonderful motor-boat, his retinue of servants, his lavish luxuries, and cries "Ah, I am Fahmy Bey; I am a Prince." This European woman became more fascinated and attracted to this Oriental extravagance . . .'

As the end of the court day approached, Marshall Hall, knowing that he would be unable to finish his speech in one piece, developed his

'Eastern feeling' theme, giving the jury something to mull over that evening in the close confines of the Manchester Hotel.

'The curse of this case . . . is the Eastern feeling of possession of the woman, the Turk in his harem, this man who was entitled to have four wives if he liked – for chattels, which to we Western people, with our ideas of women, is almost unintelligible, something we cannot quite deal with.'

Overnight, a massive police operation outside the Old Bailey prevented any queues forming, but, as ever, the courtroom was crowded almost beyond capacity when the trial resumed. Even some barristers were content to stand during the proceedings. Public interest in the trial was now intense; it attracted press attention throughout the world and was one of the first major criminal trials to have been the subject of news reports on the radio. British listeners had to wait until 7.00 p.m. each day for their information, a restriction imposed on the BBC to protect the interests of newspaper proprietors.

Most people thought that Friday 14 September would bring the jury's verdict on Marguerite's innocence or guilt of murder and there was a perceptible tension in Number One Court when Marshall Hall resumed his final address to the jury that morning. He soon came to a consideration of Fahmy's character, a central feature of his speech. Ali might have been only twenty-two or twenty-three, but he had 'learned a lot and had many mistresses'. Referring to the time Marguerite had come home with Mukhta Bey, after the visit to a Cairo cinema, Sir Edward's voice rang with indignation as he told of the blow in the face given to Madame by Fahmy before an Egyptian friend to whom he laughed and joked after having shown his mastership of this Western woman', reported the *Daily Telegraph*.

This brutal behaviour extended into the bedroom. Fahmy was 'a great, hulking muscular fellow' who was able to force his will upon his wife. Before launching into his attack on Ali's depravity, Marshall Hall eyed the public gallery. 'If women choose to come here to hear this case, they must take the consequences. It is a matter of public duty that I must perform.' In the event, none of the women spectators left court while defence counsel wrestled with the vexed question of sodomy.

'The whole sex question is one of mystery,' announced Marshall Hall, in a curiously worded passage. '. . . Nature gave us the power to get morphia from the seed of the poppy, gave us alcohol, and cocaine from the seed of the coca plant in Peru. Probably there are no better things than these in their proper places. Probably thousands in the War had cause to bless them. Just as they are the greatest boon to men and women, so probably these three things taken together are three of the greatest curses that are in the world at the present moment. It is not their legitimate use; it is the abuses of morphia, alcohol and sex that give all the dreadful trouble in the world.' Fahmy, declared counsel, had 'developed abnormal tendencies and he never treated Madame normally'.

There had been no direct evidence before the court to prove that Ali had taken drugs, but these references to morphia and cocaine were most probably designed to create the image of Ali as a drug-crazed sex fiend. The more sensational newspapers regularly printed stories about the 'drug menace', a threat commonly imputed to the activities of black people.

In July, thirty-seven-year-old Edgar Manning, described by the *World's Pictorial News* as a 'vile black man', was sentenced to three years in prison for trafficking in 'dope' and opium, which he supplied to prostitutes, 'women of a certain class'. 'NEGRO ON ''SNOW'' CHARGE' headlined the *Sunday Pictorial* early in August 1923, reporting the case of Jack Kelson, who later received a similar term for possessing cocaine. In a sensationally worded passage, *Lloyd's Sunday News* had declared that 'many of the blacks are engaged in the drug traffic and nearly all are armed. Razors are their favourite weapons and all-night orgies their recreation . . .'

The thrust of Marshall Hall's untidy, emotionally charged argument was that Ali Fahmy, an 'Oriental', effectively a black man in the eyes of the all-white jury, had disqualified himself from their consideration, mainly by reason of his race and his sexuality. Employing a popular canard, Marshall Hall implied that, because Ali had been bisexual, he would invariably practise sodomy as his preferred mode of intercourse with women.

Viewed dispassionately, Marguerite's defence was less than coherent. Did she shoot Ali in the hotel corridor because she thought he was going to kill her or because she feared that he would force himself sexually upon her again? How did this fit in with the virtually unchallenged evidence of John Beattie? The Great Defender would simply pass that by.

Rational argument went out of the window. Marshall Hall would choose to rely on rough patriotism and homely sentiment. '. . . Maybe she thought she would be safer in London than in Paris. There are people who even in 1923 . . . have a high opinion of English safety and English law. She may have thought that it would be a little more dangerous for these black emissaries to work their fell purpose at the bidding of their master.' Tugging hard at the jury's heartstrings, he added, 'I wonder how many mothers have braved a great many dangers to see the child they loved. Because her child was illegitimate, maybe Madame Fahmy loved it all the more.'

Visibly sweating now and in great pain, Marshall Hall turned up the dramatic pressure as he came to the night of the shooting and the great thunderstorm. 'You know the effect of such a storm when your nerves are normal. Imagine its effect on a woman of nervous temperament who had been living such a life as she had lived for the past six months – terrified, outraged, abused, beaten, degraded – a human wreck . . . Imagine the incessant flashes of lightning, almost hissing, as you remember, it seemed so close . . . She saw her husband outlined by a vivid flash in the doorway and there to her hand on the valise she saw the pistol – harmless, she thought . . .'

Then came one of the great moments of Old Bailey mythology. 'They struggle in the corridor. She kicks him and he takes her by the throat. Do you doubt it? The marks are spoken of in the prison doctor's report.' From his seat in counsel's benches, Marshall Hall physically imitated how, according to the defence, Ali had 'crouched like an animal, crouched like an Oriental and then it was that the pistol went off'.

He had picked up the gun, the very gun Marguerite had used to kill her husband, and pointed it at the jury as he made submissions about its mechanism, with a view to establishing, contrary to the facts, that very little pressure on the trigger would discharge several shots. 'All this time . . . his practised finger manipulating it, so that the jury could not keep their eyes off it . . .', recounts Bowker. To represent the fatal shots, he gave three loud raps on the wooden shelving in front of him. 'Once, twice, thrice, I care not, the whole thing was spasmodic,' he cried and, Bowker tells us, 'as though to symbolise the falling of the wounded Fahmy, he let the pistol fall with a clatter on to the floor . . .'* causing some people in court to shout out in surprise.

There followed a moment of silence, maximizing the dramatic effect, before Marshall Hall reminded the jury that Marguerite had said (her words), *'Mon chéri, ce n'est rien, réponds-moi'* ('Sweetheart, it is nothing, speak to me'), as Ali lay dying. 'What a place,' he said, 'for a deliberate planned murder – the corridor where the lift was going up and down and people were moving about. Would she choose the Savoy Hotel for such an act? Would she have left at the hotel the address of the nursing

---

* Marshall Hall always maintained that the pistol slipped from his fingers, but this seems an unlikely accident to have happened to a man so expert in firearms: see A. E. Bowker's *Behind the Bar*.

home to which she was going? Would she have wired to Paris, saying she was going there the next day? . . .'

Then he did something very naughty indeed. Percival Clarke's conduct of the prosecution's case had been a drab and uninspiring affair, in marked contrast to the triumphant abilities of his father, Sir Edward Clarke, in 1923 still alive in retirement. Marshall Hall, with some cruelty, played on this unhappy comparison. 'To use the words of my learned friend's great father many years ago at the Old Bailey in the [Adelaide] Bartlett case, "I do not ask you for a verdict; I demand a verdict at your hands."'

This would have been a good moment on which to have finished, but there was the still the last advantage to be wrung from the 'Eastern feeling'. As with the fictional Mahmoud Baroudi, so it had been with Ali Fahmy. 'Eastern men, as I have said, are courteous, civilised and elegant, but underneath lies the Eastern temperament and the Eastern idea of how a woman should be treated. In some cases, a Western wife is a triumph for an Eastern man to possess; Eastern men are proud of such a possession, but they are not prepared to sacrifice their right of domination.'

Then came the peroration, delivered as shafts of September sunlight intermittently penetrated through the glass roof of the court:

> You will remember, all of you, that great work of fiction, written by Robert Hichens, *Bella Donna*. Some of you may have seen the masterly performance given of it at one of our theatres. If you have, you will remember the final scene, where this woman goes out of the gates of the garden into the dark night of the desert. Members of the jury, I want you to open the gates where the Western woman can go out, not into the dark night of the desert, but back to her friends, who love her in spite of her weaknesses; back to her friends, who will be glad to receive her; back to her child, who will be waiting for her with open arms. You will open the gate and let this Western woman go back into the light of God's great Western sun.

At the final words of his speech, delivered almost in a whisper, Marshall Hall looked up and pointed at the glass ceiling of the courtroom, 'where', Marjoribanks writes, 'the bright English September sun was streaming in and suffusing the packed court with its warmth and brightness', after which, manifestly exhausted, he sank back into his place.

21

Verdict

Marshall Hall's was an almost impossible act to follow, but, for once, prosecuting counsel's arid delivery made some impact, as Percival Clarke struggled to bring the debate back into the realms of reason. 'You have had the advantage,' he told the jury in a quiet monotone, 'of listening to two dramatic speeches from one of the most powerful advocates at the Bar. I shall try and take you from the theatrical atmosphere which has prevailed in this court for three or four days . . .' Clarke's final speech, for all its dryness, began promisingly. In the theatre, for example, the 'Blood and Thunder' school was no longer as fashionable as it had been before the war, and, it might be supposed, some jury members now possessed a relatively sophisticated approach to life's problems.

The last words of that mighty defence effort had been paraphrased from the pulp fiction of *Bella Donna*. Introducing themes from that Edwardian sensation was risky, as Clarke was quick to point out, and a less impulsive advocate than Marshall Hall would have reflected at length before making use of such material. Clarke referred to *Bella Donna* as a 'play' (Mrs Patrick Campbell had felt herself miscast as Ruby Chepstow in a 1911 West End production), 'a strangely unfortunate play, I think, to recall to your mind. You will remember that the woman who went out into the desert, out into the dark, was the woman who had planned, and very nearly succeeded in murdering her husband. In that respect, it may be that the simile between the play and this case is somewhat alike [sic].'

Additionally, there were unspoken dangers in the indiscriminate use of *Bella Donna* by the defence. Around midnight on 3 October 1922, Percy Thompson, a thirty-two-year-old shipping clerk, had been stabbed to death in an Ilford street while walking home with his wife from the local railway station. His assailant, twelve years younger, was Frederick Bywaters, who had been the lover of Thompson's wife, Edith, for over a year before the murder. Edith had destroyed the letters he had written to her; Bywaters, for reasons of his own, had kept her correspondence.

Edith Thompson and Frederick Bywaters were tried for murder at the Old Bailey in December 1922. Much of the prosecution's case against Edith derived from those love-letters. There was no direct evidence that she had known beforehand of Bywaters's plan to murder her husband, but the letters could be interpreted as showing, if nothing else, that thoughts of murder had been in the lovers' mutual contemplation for some considerable time. There were references to powdered glass, to poisons, and to *Bella Donna*, a particularly unfortunate choice of book for Edith Thompson. She was eight years older than Bywaters and was presented by the Crown as a 'corrupt, malign sorceress', very much in the mould of the fictional Mrs Chepstow.

No traces either of powdered glass or of identifiable poison were found in Percy Thompson's body, but prosecuting counsel (the Solicitor-General, Sir Thomas Inskip KC) made much of the *Bella Donna* theme: 'She refers constantly to this book and the lesson it is to teach them as a possible method of taking her husband's life.' Edith Thompson had fancied herself a self-taught literary critic. *Bella Donna* had featured as only one of a host of novels in which she tried, with conspicuous lack of success, to interest her resolutely non-intellectual lover, who worked as a ship's steward. Hichens's potboiler helped seal Edith Thompson's fate, even though she had described the character of Ruby Chepstow as 'abnormal – a monster utterly selfish and self-living'.

Marguerite Fahmy, an experienced woman and a decade older than her husband, was a far more suitable candidate for the role of *Bella Donna* than Edith Thompson, who had been no more than a bored, day-dreaming Ilford housewife. Mrs Thompson had gone to the gallows accompanied by remarkably little public sympathy. Would Marguerite's jury, astuter perhaps than their Victorian counterparts, take a cooler, more sceptical view of the evidence than that suggested by the emotional flummery of Marshall Hall?

It was easy, said Percival Clarke, 'to speak ill of those who are dead'. Marshall Hall had tried to introduce prejudice against Fahmy, so that the jury would think that he, a brute, had deserved to die. 'I have no brief for the dead man,' Clarke told his listeners, reminding them of Marguerite's early lapse from the path of virtue: 'From the age of sixteen upwards, this woman had had experience of men and the world.' Just like *Bella Donna*.

So far, so good. But Clarke could not keep up the pace. He ought not to have reminded the jury of his hideously inept question about the occupation of Marguerite's father, lamely attempting to justify the unjustifiable by explaining that it was asked 'merely to show the ambition of the woman'.

No doubt he pointed out the discrepancies in Marguerite's story: the pistol, first said to have been fired shortly before Fahmy had attacked her, later said to have gone off before the visit to the theatre; the scene of the struggle – was it in her bedroom, as she had originally said, or his, where the small pearls torn from her dress had been found? And those improbabilities: would such a woman, a pistol owner for some nine years, not know how to use it? And there was her shaky account, of how the action had been transferred from the suite into the hotel corridor.

Clarke had begun his speech just after midday and it was now after 3.00 p.m. Marguerite had listened to both speeches without the services of an interpreter and was having to use her imagination to divine what these strangely dressed English lawyers had been talking about for so long. As Clarke's wearisome arguments ploddingly unfolded, a dreariness unbroken by the sort of dramatic gestures that were Marshall Hall's stock-in-trade, Marguerite began to think that all was lost. The *Evening Standard* noted that 'She sat with her head hanging limply forward and her black gloved right hand supporting her forehead. Now and again . . . her eyes were closed and . . . tears were trickling down her cheeks.' In the closing moments of Clarke's address, she also seemed unable to keep still. 'Her head moved from side to side and she twisted and untwisted her handkerchief round her fingers,' reported the *Daily Telegraph*.

The jury could be forgiven, with the day's speechmaking now well into its fourth hour, for not absorbing the Crown's better points. There was, for example, the fact of Marguerite and Said Enani dancing together to the music of the Savoy Havana Band in the hotel ballroom that fateful night. Marguerite had said that she had danced just a couple of steps in an atmosphere of crisis. 'I care not how many steps it was,' said Clarke, 'whether one step or two steps, or whether it was to the door or round the room. Was this desperate woman in a painful condition dragged off to dance . . . Whatever evidence is there at all except that she went of her own free will?'

At last, he encapsulated the Crown's case. Fahmy, as the evidence of

John Beattie and the post-mortem had proved, was shot from behind while bending down, playing with a dog. 'What really happened,' he suggested, 'was that the accused, angry, cross, quarrelling, went back, lost her temper and her head, seized the pistol which she knew was in working order and fired it at her husband.' All very well, but the prosecution had never fully explored the true reasons for so violent an outburst of temper on Marguerite's part. The jury would have to do what they could with the material before them.

That material now came to be reviewed by Mr Justice Rigby Swift in his summing-up, which, as a punctilious reporter noted, began at 3.27 that Friday afternoon. Rigby Swift, aged forty-nine, had been appointed a High Court judge three years earlier, by the almost equally youthful Lord Chancellor Birkenhead, formerly Sir F. E. Smith KC. Both men had roots in the Liverpool area and both were enthusiastic Conservatives: Swift had been Tory MP for St Helens for eight years until 1918. (Present-day judicial appointees are usually more discreet about their politics.) But their intellectual qualities were poles apart. F. E. Smith had enjoyed meteoric success after his First in Jurisprudence at Oxford and was the youngest Lord Chancellor to be appointed in modern times. Rigby Swift, his junior by two years, was never an Oxbridge man and practised in Liverpool for a decade and a half before testing the water in London. 'Wherever I am,' he once said proudly, 'can be summed up in one word – Liverpool.'

The eighth child of a solicitor (his mother's family name was Daft), Swift's practice was nurtured by local legal connections and his bluff, no-nonsense manner brought him a great deal of work. Legal biographies and obituaries tend to the hagiographic, but, reading between the lines, it appears that Rigby Swift's chubby features and ruddy complexion were, in part at least, due to a fondness for drink, a failing not exactly unknown in the legal profession. 'In later years,' wrote a later Lord Chancellor, Lord Sankey, 'he became a sick man and was not always able to control his strong opinions.'

Madame Fahmy's trial was among Rigby Swift's earlier cases and irritability only occasionally surfaced, usually in the afternoons, when the soporific effects of the traditional Sheriff's luncheon were beginning to wear off. His unashamedly provincial manner was exemplified by 'a deliberate Lancashire drawl', which caused him to be known in the courts, half-humorously, as 'Rigbah'. He thought of himself, with some justification, as a 'plain man' and believed in 'the wholesome deterrent of flogging'.

A keen churchman, Swift was for many years a churchwarden and possessed all the inbuilt puritanism of the English middle class. 'The judge's code,' wrote E. S. Fay, 'was of the strictest. "I am, above all things, an early Victorian" . . . The Bible was his favourite reading . . .' The Fahmy case must have nudged the judicial eyebrows ever higher as revelation followed revelation about international high life in the early 1920s.

Rigby Swift's summing-up began in a way which suggested that he was hostile to the accused, an impression reinforced by the judge's particularly grave tone of voice. 'Unless you find something to your satisfaction, something which has been brought home to your minds, that the killing of Ali Fahmy by this woman was not murder, you are bound to return a verdict of wilful murder. This is not a case of giving the accused the benefit of the doubt . . .' In other words, the old presumption that all homicide was murder, unless the contrary could be proved, might yet serve to hang Marguerite Fahmy.

The judge's compliment to Marshall Hall ('a brilliantly eloquent speech made by one of the foremost advocates at the Bar') was followed by a disparagement, as is often the case with plaudits from the Bench. 'You have heard a great deal about the bad character of the dead man, but . . . the prisoner is not to be acquitted because you believe that [he] was a bad, and, indeed, a detestable character. It is no . . . excuse for homicide that the person killed was . . . a weak, depraved or despicable person . . .'

And yet that character assassination of Ali Fahmy had left its mark, a seed planted by the defence in the fertile soil of English prejudice. 'I have had many years' experience, but I am shocked and sickened at some of the things which it has been our duty to listen to in the course of this case . . .' In a clear reference to the eager curiosity in the trial shown by a large number of women, the judge continued: 'These things are horrible; they are disgusting. How anyone could listen to these things who is not bound to listen to them passes comprehension.'

Turning to the evidence, the judge resumed a stance seemingly antipathetic to the defence. If Beattie's testimony was right, then the killing was unjustified, unexplained and amounted to murder. The jury had to examine Marguerite's story: if they decided that it was untrue, there was no answer to the charge. Was there, asked the judge, corroboration of her version of events? According to Rigby Swift, there was and the tide of the summing-up began to flow in Marguerite's favour. What she had told Dr Gordon early on the morning of 10 July at Bow Street police station was 'substantially the same story' as her evidence in court and was 'not a tale that has been concocted by the legal advisers'.*

Furthermore, said the judge, 'the letter written to Dr Gordon about her leaving for Paris was strong corroboration of her story' and the finding of the bullet in the accused's room and of the beads in Fahmy's room was 'really remarkable corroboration' of her story. With respect to the judge, it is difficult to see how any of these elements could corroborate Marguerite's account of the central issue in the case: how she had come to fire three shots at her unarmed husband in a hotel corridor.

If the judge really was changing tack, Marguerite knew none of it. Late in the afternoon, Rigby Swift asked the jury if they would like a short break for tea or to adjourn till the next day. A majority was in favour of going on, but, noticing the lack of unanimity, the judge decided to resume the case on Saturday morning. Mlle Simon whispered to Marguerite that the case would not, after all, finish that day. Marguerite, who had sobbed spasmodically throughout the judge's address, prompted by his frequent references to 'murder', covered her face with her hands at the news of postponement, stood up, swayed, then collapsed into the arms of her two wardresses, who needed the assistance of a male colleague to carry the defendant bodily downstairs from the dock.

Almost as soon as the court had risen that Friday afternoon, women and men started to loiter around the public entrance to the Old Bailey. As Marguerite's prison taxi pulled away from the rear of the building, someone shouted 'Good Luck, Fahmy!' That cloudy, cold and windy night, the City of London Police were in energetic mood and kept the crowd on the move, but as fast as they cleared people away from the door, another group took their place.

Marguerite spent a restless night in the hospital wing at Holloway, despite the usual sedative. Just before she left for court, a well-wisher gave her a sprig of white heather. By 8.00 a.m., an enormous crowd had gathered outside the grim courthouse and, half an hour before the trial resumed, Number One Court was jammed to the walls. In a helter-skelter rush to get the best places in the public gallery, several women tried to climb over the rows of seats, tearing their stockings as they attempted to get the best vantage point.

Rigby Swift posed three possible verdicts. Guilty of murder; Guilty

---

* Compare Dr Gordon's record of Marguerite's words on 10 July (see page 121) with her evidence in court (see Chapter 19). Rigby Swift appears to have overlooked major differences between her two accounts.

of manslaughter; and Not Guilty altogether. Accepting Marshall Hall's argument, the judge effectively dismissed the issue of manslaughter. The element that would reduce murder to manslaughter was provocation, 'some physical act . . . so annoying or aggravating as was likely to destroy the self-control of an ordinary reasonable person'. The judge observed that there did not seem to have been anything in the nature of provocation at the moment of the shooting. Marguerite had alleged that Fahmy had spat at her, but that was barely sufficient by itself and had occurred too long before the shooting.

If, however, the jury accepted that Fahmy had seized Marguerite by the throat, that could lay the foundation for a defence of justifiable homicide and a verdict of Not Guilty. The jury should pay close attention to evidence of the Fahmys' marital life. 'You are not to say,' warned Rigby Swift, 'here is an Oriental man, married to a Frenchwoman and therefore things were likely to be so and so . . .' The judge's seemingly moderate approach to the consideration of that stormiest of marriages soon vanished. Swift had been deeply swayed by Marshall Hall's speech and now began to dwell on the theme of 'abnormality', adopting, in less inflammatory language, the agenda of race and sexuality set down by the Great Defender.

'If the evidence shows you that these two people were not ordinary normal people, as you and I understand people, and . . . that their relationship was not the ordinary, normal relationship of husband and wife, you might the more readily believe [the defendant's] story of what happened . . .' Said Enani's important evidence was dismissively treated. 'He was, and is, in a difficult position and it is for you to decide whether all that has been said about him is justified . . . You must remember he was the dead man's friend. They were inseparable.' On the other hand the so-called 'secret document' of 22 January 1923, once referred to by Swift as so much 'waste paper', was now to be regarded as throwing 'a good deal of light upon the relationship of these parties . . .' and as confirming Marguerite's contention that Ali had often threatened to kill her.

The judge had been particularly shocked by another peculiar document in Marguerite's hand, the one in which Ali was meant to have condoned her adultery. 'It is a disgraceful and disgusting document,' sermonized the judge, taking the paper at its face value, 'which shows to us that the relationship between these two people was not the ordinary relationship of man and wife to which we are accustomed in this country.' That relationship was 'something abnormal, something extraordinary', as were the events which took place at the Savoy Hotel on the night of the tragedy. Marguerite's evidence about Ali's alleged sexual tastes was 'shocking, sickening and disgusting . . . If her husband tried to do what she says, in spite of her protests, it was a cruel, it was an abominable act . . .'

The contrast between West and East, so much a feature of Marshall Hall's two speeches, was endorsed by the judge. 'We in this country put our women on a pedestal: in Egypt they have not the same views . . . When you hear of this woman being followed about by a black servant, you . . . must not allow your indignation to run away with your judgment.'

When the judge came to review the evidence of the witnesses in the trial, one eye-witness, who would have seen almost everything of relevance to the killing of Fahmy Bey, was not mentioned. This witness had never been called to give evidence in any of the legal proceedings, though he had been in and around the Fahmys' suite throughout the material time. He was the Nubian valet, the diminutive, eighteen-year-old youth who, according to his late master, did not matter and was nothing. The police did not bother to take a statement from him. Even his name is unknown.

Rigby Swift's summing-up ended with a simple question: 'Has Madame Fahmy made out to your satisfaction that she used that weapon to protect her own life?' After the bailiffs had been sworn to keep them in 'some private and convenient place', the jury filed out of court at 12.24 p.m. Marshall Hall spoke a few sentences of comfort in French to Marguerite, and Maître Asso.uad shook her by the hand in encouragement, before, smiling wanly and looking very pale, she returned to the cells to await the verdict. Number One Court emptied and people tried to snatch a brief lunch.

Almost exactly an hour later, an usher returned to court, indicating that a verdict had been reached. Marshall Hall and his corpulent sidekick, Curtis-Bennett, hurried back into court, closely followed by the Clerk of Arraigns. Three sharp knocks again rang out to mark Rigby Swift's return to his place on the Bench.

Marguerite, 'very composed', dressed still in deep mourning, with a black, low-brimmed hat and veil, moved slowly into the dock, where she sat awaiting her fate, her head resting on her hands. Asked to stand, she stared straight ahead at the judge, not venturing to look at the jury as they returned. Some women sitting behind the dock stood up, 'trembling visibly', noted the *Evening Standard*, as the Clerk inquired: 'Members of the jury, are you agreed upon your verdict?' 'We are,' said the foreman.

'Do you find Marguerite Fahmy guilty or not guilty of the murder of Ali Kamel Fahmy Bey?'

The official court interpreter, Ashton-Wolfe, was surely not the only spectator to have waited, with thumping heart, during the momentary but profound silence.

'Not guilty,' replied the foreman. A woman shrieked and the court erupted into cheering, stamping feet and tumultuous applause. Marguerite, giving what the *Daily Mail* described as 'a little gurgling cry', collapsed into her seat and wept, black-gloved fingers pressed against her face. Her two wardresses fought back the tears; both women on the jury were visibly moved and one, Mrs Austin, broke down completely, covering her face with her handkerchief as she sobbed aloud.

'Clear the court,' shouted Rigby Swift above the pandemonium. It took nearly five minutes before order could be restored and the jury asked if they found Marguerite guilty or not guilty of manslaughter. The foreman's reply was the same as it had been to the previous question and Rigby Swift, beckoning to Ashton-Wolfe, said brusquely, 'Tell her that the jury have found her not guilty and that she is discharged. Let her go.' Marguerite was helped downstairs, to be seen by the prison doctor, while the young and vivacious Mlle Simon was thanked by the judge for her assistance and the jury were discharged from further service, if they so wished, for ten years.

Marshall Hall, as an old campaigner, would have known the likely verdict from tell-tale signs as the jury returned. Generally speaking, if juries are going to convict, they appear solemn and do not look towards the dock. The evident expressions of relief on the faces of some of the male jurors, even, here and there, a slight smile, showed that this was to be yet another notch on Marshall Hall's forensic gun.

His triumph, however, was tarnished by physical distress and pain. Feeling too ill to see Marguerite, he was helped to the robing-room by Bowker, his clerk, and said that he felt 'all in'. He had committed more than his usual share of nervous energy to the Fahmy case and, drenched in perspiration, was given a good towelling down and change of clothes by his clerk, before slipping out of a side door to avoid the waiting crowds.

People who had been cleared from the court milled around in the Main Hall on the first floor of the Old Bailey, waiting vainly for Madame Fahmy to appear. But she remained below and the crowd mistook Yvonne Alibert for her sister as she emerged, weeping tears of joy, after a brief embrace with Marguerite in the room underneath the dock. A foolish woman, smartly dressed, who pushed her way over to Yvonne, kissed her on the cheek and breezily exclaimed, 'Bravo, I'm so glad you're free as I've often been to Paris', was rightly awarded first prize in the *Daily Sketch*'s 'Imbecility Stakes'.

Helped by Maître Assouad, Yvonne made her way with difficulty down the broad marble staircase, smiling through her tears and exclaiming, according to the English press, '*Mon dieu! Mon dieu! C'est magnifique; c'est terrible.*' Outside, a solicitor's young clerk had broken the news to the waiting throng, shouting 'She's acquitted!' As Yvonne reached the steps leading into the street from the Old Bailey's main entrance, the crowd rushed forward, shouting 'Bravo the Madame', and Yvonne, now relishing the impersonation, responded with her arms outspread in triumphant gesture. Hats were thrown into the air and weeping women clutched at her body, in the mistaken belief that this was indeed the sensational Madame Fahmy.

Yvonne managed to scramble into a waiting car, where she joined some of Marguerite's Parisian friends. After police had cleared a path, Yvonne leant out of the car window, blowing kisses to the crowd and shouting '*Les anglais sont très bien*', as people climbed on to the cars and taxis trapped in the crush, waving handkerchiefs, walking-sticks and umbrellas.

Marguerite, now a free woman, remained in the Old Bailey for three-quarters of an hour, as anxious as her defender had been to avoid the ordeal of recognition. Police obligingly lined up outside the barristers' entrance in Newgate Street, successfully diverting the crowd. Marguerite gave a last hug to one of her wardresses before finally quitting the scene of her trial. Almost unnoticed, she left by the Lord Mayor's entrance at the rear of the building, her small, limp form lying motionless against the back seat of a cab.

22

What the Papers Said

Travelling with the weary Marguerite in the back of the taxi was Maître Odette Simon, who had rapidly advanced from being volunteer interpreter to the status of friend and confidante. A suite had been reserved for Madame Fahmy, not at the Savoy, with its tragic associations, but at the more discreet Princes' Hotel, which then stood at 190–96 Piccadilly.*

Waiting for her arrival were her lawyer, Maître Assouad, her sister Yvonne, Dr Gordon, and numerous French well-wishers. Steps were taken at once to secure the maximum commercial advantage from Marguerite's notoriety. The press thronged the hotel lobby, desperate for the chance to interview Madame. Representatives came from all over the world: one large syndicate of American newspapers sent an open cheque. Despite the fact that the *Weekly Dispatch* and the *Evening News* claimed to have had an exclusive right of interview, accounts of Marguerite's first words in freedom appeared in several other papers, though the *Sunday Pictorial*, obliged to disappoint its readers, made out that Madame Fahmy had been 'forbidden to pose or interview by her medical advisers'.

Dr Gordon was on hand to supervise his patient's welfare and almost her first action on reaching the hotel, after wiring the good news to Raymonde, safely in Paris, was to telephone Dr Morton, the prison doctor, with whom she seems to have struck up a close friendship. While the newshounds crowded around her (no doubt after suitable financial

---

* Another probable reason for Marguerite's choice of Princes' Hotel was to avoid a confrontation with Ali Fahmy's family, who were staying at the Savoy.

arrangements had been made with Maître Assouad on his client's behalf),
she sat quietly in her Egyptian-style armchair, occasionally sipping a
small glass of Benedictine and smoking cigarettes, which, from time to
time, she generously pressed upon the reporters. Still dressed in black,
she wore a single row of pearls, and bracelets on each wrist. It was
noticed that Marguerite, hatless for the first time since her trial began,
was wearing her hair 'caught up with side curls', not bobbed as she had
been in July. She looked wan and drawn.

'*Je n'ai aucun plan pour l'avenir*' ('I have no plan for the future'), she
began, tactfully adding, '. . . *je dois rendre hommage à la justice anglaise*'
('I must pay my respects to English justice'). She still felt dazed and
'*abroutie*' (stupefied) from the effects of the sedative injection she had
received in prison. '*Laissez-moi ajouter que j'ai souffert atrocement durant
les débats de ne rien pouvoir comprendre de ce qui se disait autour de moi, alors
que ma vie était un jeu . . .*' ('Let me add that I suffered terribly during
the trial from not being able to understand what was said about me,
when my life was a game').

'Maggie Meller' was starting to recover her spirit. Unable to follow
much of the evidence, her thoughts had wandered, causing her to muse
on the jury, 'what we French call "bourgeois" – people who had left
quiet lives in quiet homes, their simple pleasures and their businesses,
to sit in judgment . . . What did they think of Marguerite Fahmy, I
wonder, and the life so different from their own? Were they shocked at
. . . the simple, brutal truth?' She also remembered how Percival Clarke
had fidgeted with his gown, how his wig had gone awry, and how he had
punctuated those bloodless questions with a nervous cough.

From time to time, she had understood a word or a phrase. The
judge's use of 'murder' had scared her terribly, but she was downright
annoyed when she heard prosecuting counsel scornfully describe her as,
'that woman of thirty-two'. '*Voyons, messieurs,*' said Marguerite tartly, 'a
woman of thirty-two is not old!' She was also unhappy at the contrast
drawn between her age and that of her young husband. 'Surely his youth
did not excuse his violence, his wickedness and, shall I say, his terrible
abnormalities?'

It was those very 'abnormalities' and the controversial issue of inter-
racial marriage that was the subject of much of the homegrown press
comment on the Fahmy case in the next few days, now that the papers
were free from reporting constraints operative during the trial. The
Evening Standard censured 'the readiness with which the French inter-
marry with coloured people . . . with whom we hardly mix at all' and, in

the same edition, 'A Barrister' warned that '. . . white women take serious risks in marrying outside their own race and religion . . .', mooting the possibility of forbidding 'mixed marriages' altogether. 'Where a white woman weds a coloured man,' adjured the sleazy *Reynolds's News*, '. . . she does so at her peril.' The *Weekly Dispatch* thought that such marriages 'always [had] the danger of tragedy . . . the moral of the very disagreeable Fahmy case'.

The *Sunday Pictorial* warned parents of young English girls about the dangers lurking in Continental resorts such as Deauville, where 'a considerable proportion of the holidaymakers live East of Suez . . . the men are often handsome, frequently rich and entertaining . . .' (It was obviously safer to stay in Bognor.) 'A woman who marries a man not of her own race is taking a step that leads . . . to disaster . . . As a slave she has been taken and as a slave she will be held.' The *Daily Mirror*, too, emphasized 'the undesirability of marriages which unite Oriental husbands to European wives' and, without naming E. M. Hull and her school, roundly condemned 'women novelists, apparently under the spell of the East, [who] have encouraged the belief that there is something especially romantic in such unions. They are not romantic. They are ridiculous and unseemly.'

The *Pall Mall Gazette*, under the heading 'CRIMES OF PASSION – A VERDICT THAT MUST NOT BE MISUNDERSTOOD' likened the Fahmy trial to 'the coloured wrappers of a "shilling shocker"'. Ali and Marguerite were castigated as being 'most distinctly "un-English"'. 'Nothing could be more repulsive than the utterly worthless pleasure-hunting type of life unfolded to the court.' Mining the rich vein of English puritanism, the *Gazette* loftily proposed that 'if the "Prince" had been sent to the plough and his wife to the wash-tub, they might have done the world substantial, if humble, service . . .', but they were no more than a pair of 'exotic and uncongenial creatures' and the verdict should not be thought of as importing the dangerous foreign notion of a 'crime of passion' on to English soil. At the other end of the political spectrum, a similarly censorious approach was shared by the worthy, excruciatingly dull *Daily Herald*. 'This Egyptian "Prince",' it wrote, 'was one of those weeds who flourish in gardens where no-one works honestly with spade or fork . . .'

Concern was expressed about the interest taken in the case by members of the public, especially women, who had loitered about or queued for hours for the chance of a seat in the public gallery. To the *Manchester Guardian*, the 'blend of squalor and cheap glamour of great wealth provides exactly the mixture which stimulates a Central Criminal Court crowd. The sightseers seem to be equally divided between the seedy hangers-on who specialise in murder trials and fashionable women in furs . . .'

The *Law Journal*, noting that many of these richer women had secured their seats with the help of connections in the City of London, wondered if the Corporation 'might consider whether the most important criminal court in the country ought to be reduced to the level of a playhouse . . .'

The allegations made in respect of Ali Fahmy's sexual behaviour could only be hinted at, but, even with the prudery of the time, hints could be broad ones. The *Illustrated Sunday Herald* informed its readership that Fahmy was 'master from boyhood of satiating his eastern voluptuousness . . .', while *Reynolds's News* produced a 'SECRET HISTORY OF THE TRIAL – WHERE THE NEWSPAPER REPORTS STOPPED SHORT', written by 'One Who Was There'. The text did not live up to its titillating title. 'Nobody who was not present [sic] at the trial can have any idea of the horror . . . too dreadful even to be hinted at . . . the abnormal and extraordinary relationship between man and wife . . .' This sort of behaviour was foreign to our shores, as the *Daily Chronicle* soothingly confirmed: '[Fahmy's] particular vices are commoner in the East than here.'

In *John Bull* the usual mixture of racism and sexual prurience was laid on with a trowel, raising 'the ugly but inevitable question of colour. Is it right, is it proper, is it even without danger for a Western girl to associate with a man of the East?' Fahmy had used his father's money 'to indulge in pleasure of a most perverted kind . . . [and had] brought into his nest more white victims than it is possible to compute. From the desire for many wives and for women of a certain class he now developed a . . . sexual perversion which should have unfitted him for human friendship.' Homosexuality was not directly mentioned, but Fahmy was supposed to have become 'completely unsexed . . . all became as nothing to him beside the one mad desire to live unnaturally'.

Perhaps the most telling commentary, certainly the most self-righteous, came from a *Sunday Express* editorial headed 'THE CHRISTIAN ETHOS'. 'It must not be imagined that this just verdict opens the door to the perilous anarchy of sentimental pity and maudlin compassion in cases of murder by a wife of her husband . . . on the contrary, it closes the door upon it. If Ali Fahmy had been a normal husband, the jury would not have acquitted his wife.' Forty years later, the writer Macdonald Hastings put the argument more crudely: 'The reason why Madame

Fahmy shot her . . . husband . . . was because he was a sodomite.'

The *Sunday Express* called for a 'a renascence of the sense of sin . . . a revival of abhorrence for moral turpitude and depravity' and came close to mentioning the unmentionable. 'Ali Fahmy is incredible, but . . . he existed. He is not a fantastic degenerate out of a Russian ballet. He is not a decadent out of Proust's *Sodome et Gomorrhe*. He is not a literary gargoyle invented by Oscar Wilde. He is not an epicene pervert escaped from the noisome verbiage of *Ulysses* . . .' The verdict of the Fahmy trial was 'a vindication of womanhood against the vices that destroyed Rome. It protects womanhood against the horrors which brought down fire from heaven upon the cities of the plain . . .'*

Although, along with Sir Edward Marshall Hall and Mr Justice Swift, the *Sunday Express* was convinced that 'the status of women in our Western civilisation is immeasurably higher than it is in the Orient', one contemporary snippet of news, reported in the *Daily Chronicle*, was overlooked by the sanctimonious commentators. Rose Little was a young woman who had been married in February 1923. Three days later, her husband had knocked her down. Thereafter, he did so every Sunday, without fail. These were 'little tiffs', the man told Sittingbourne magistrates, who ordered him to pay his wife maintenance at the rate of just £1 per week.

A feeling that there was more than a whiff of humbug in English reactions to moral issues raised in the Fahmy trial was fanned into a blaze in Egypt, already in political ferment after the return from exile on 17 September 1923 of the veteran nationalist leader Zaghlul. The British had packed him off to the Seychelles two years earlier and his homecoming was, inevitably, a triumph, coming a month before the first elections of the semi-independent Egyptian state.

Nationalist sentiments were especially prickly at this time: the Foreign Office gravely minuted that the Fahmy trial was being used to stir up anti-British feeling in, of all places, Switzerland. Reports of Marshall Hall's comments and the judge's summing-up, which appeared to endorse what defence counsel had said, were received with indignation in Cairo and Alexandria.

The Bâtonnier of the Egyptian Bar sent a long cable to the British Attorney-General, Sir Douglas Hogg, complaining that Marshall Hall had allowed himself 'to generalise and to "lash" all Egypt and, indeed, the whole East', and describing his comments as 'unjust and deplorable'.

---

* The author James Douglas was then editor of the *Sunday Express*. In 1928, he would write of Radclyffe Hall's novel of lesbian love *The Well of Loneliness*: 'I would rather put a phial of prussic acid in the hands of a healthy girl or boy than the book in question . . .'

Hogg, who as Attorney-General doubled as head of the English Bar, sent an inadequate and anodyne reply, hoping that the Bâtonnier 'may have been misled by a newspaper summary'.

Marshall Hall's letter to Hogg, written in the light of the Egyptian protest, was a sorry apologia: 'Any attack I made was . . . on the man Ali Fahmy and not on the Egyptians as a nation . . . The only thing I remember saying that might be misunderstood was that it was a mistake for the Western woman to marry this Eastern man . . . If, by any chance, in the heat of advocacy, I was betrayed into saying anything that might be construed as an attack on the Egyptians as a nation, I shall be the first to disclaim any such intention . . .'

Almost alone among the English press, the *Daily Chronicle* saw merit in the Egyptian protest. 'The impression might be gained,' it wrote, 'that English opinion, in condemning the depravities of Ali Fahmy, was led to regard these as characteristics of Egyptian society . . .' Sir Henry M'Mahon, British High Commissioner in Egypt between 1914 and 1916, shared this balanced, unsensational view of the East: 'It is a mistake to imagine . . . that women in Moslem countries are regarded as intellectually negligible. In numerous cases, they have claimed and obtained high positions . . .'

In Egypt, the *Mokattam* spoke for other Arabic newspapers (patronizingly referred to as the 'native press' in the *Egyptian Gazette*). 'The error which was committed by Sir Marshall Hall [sic] and Mr Justice Swift . . . is not, however, the first mistake committed by Westerners . . . as the majority of people in England are ignorant of family life in Egypt . . .' Recalling the Russell divorce case of earlier that year, a juicy saga of aristocratic bedroom fun, the *Mokattam* forcefully pointed out how easy it would be to judge 'the highly civilised English community, relying on the reports of crimes and the cases of divorce which appear daily in the London press'.

Furthermore, Marshall Hall had seriously misrepresented the Egyptian law of divorce. Dr Abdul El-Bialy Bey, who had held a watching brief for Ali's sister Aziza in the trial, wrote to the *Daily Chronicle*, pointing out that Egyptian married women had the absolute right to dispose of their property in any way they liked and that the civil code allowed a wife to divorce her husband for cruelty or on any other justifiable grounds. 'Madame Fahmy,' he averred, 'could easily have divorced her husband through a Moslem court for the causes mentioned by her.'

Ali Fahmy's reputation was a casualty amid all these outpourings of justified wrath. In the light of the unpalatable allegations made at the trial, the Egyptian government felt bound to issue a statement, which claimed that although Ali had enjoyed the reputation of being a 'notable and personal friend of King Fuad . . .', this was incorrect. His only meeting with the monarch had been at the foundation-stone ceremony at the Magagha Hospital. Ali was described, ungenerously and inaccurately, as having been 'of modest extraction and practically uneducated, except for the veneer acquired in the demi-mondaine [sic] . . . a libertine of the cosmopolitan type'. A more measured epitaph came from the newspaper *Al Lataig Al Musarawa*: 'Those who surrounded him . . . called him the Prince of Youth. The public, high and low, was a spectator of his prodigality and they regretted deeply that his great wealth brought such little profit to his . . . countrymen.'

His widow stayed on in London, only venturing out of Princes' Hotel on one occasion, before, heavily veiled, she caught the boat-train at Victoria on 23 September, to travel back to Paris with her sister Yvonne. *Le Figaro* commented wistfully, '*Elle a quitté Londres et ses brouillards où elle a tant souffert*' ('She has left London and its fogs, where she has suffered so much'). In the meantime, she had received shoals of congratulatory telegrams, several offers of marriage (one from an earl, another, 'in perfect French', from a professional man in northern England) and a theatrical agent had tempted her, without success, to appear on the Paris stage.

Before she left, she afforded the *People* a second interview in which, unbelievably, she expressed herself 'too distracted to think of any fortune which her Oriental husband might have left her'. Reflecting on her awkward religious position, 'her wonderful eyes grew dim with tears . . . "I am afraid of what our Church will say"', she murmured.

The French press, preoccupied that summer with recurrent domestic political crises and with Germany's unhappy occupation of the Ruhr, largely ignored Marguerite's fate until the start of her trial. At first, some of the references to her were disparaging, as when *Le Temps* spoke of '*Madame Marguerite Fahmy Bey, mieux connue à Paris sous le nom de Maggie Meller* . . .' ('. . . better known in Paris as . . .'), but the mutual distrust between England and France soon surfaced.

The *Manchester Guardian*'s Paris correspondent reported that 'the execution of Mrs Thompson gave a shock to French public opinion which, even while it is not particularly gallant towards women, yet draws the line at hanging them . . .' Indeed, no woman had been guillotined in France since 1887, whereas in Britain a dozen women had been hanged in the same period.

English juries were described as '*si rigoureux*' ('so harsh') by *L'Intransigeant*; while *L'Illustration* commented, '*En matière d'homicide, on sait que les jurys anglais se montrent toujours impitoyables*' ('With regard to murder, one knows that English juries always show themselves to be merciless').

The schoolboy prurience of the English press was absent in France and the racial element less evident. Ali had been '*un despote maladif*' ('a morbid tyrant'), but the emphasis was on the shattered dreams of this elegant Parisian woman. 'LE MIRAGE DE MAGGIE MELLER' was front-page news in *Le Gaulois*: '*Pauvre petite princesse des mauvaises mille et fois nuits! Tout ce malheur est né d'un mirage . . .*' ('Poor little princess of the unlucky Thousand and One Nights! All her ill-fortune was caused by an illusion'). Marguerite had been '*L'esclave de son mari, le jouet de ses caprices*' ('The slave of her husband; the plaything of his whims').

From being regarded as an ill-fated demi-mondaine, Madame Fahmy was fast becoming a latter-day St Joan, a symbol of French womanhood, on trial for her life before a tribunal of the flint-hearted and sexually repressed English. Percival Clarke's faltering cross-examination was transformed by *Le Temps* into an interrogation '*fourmillant de pièges extrêmement difficiles à éventrer*' ('swarming with traps extremely difficult to break out of'). The presence of Mlle Simon, '*une jeune et jolie Parisienne*' had, in France at least, just the effect that her defender had hoped, '*prêtant son concours à une compatriote malheureuse assise sur le banc des accusés*' ('giving her help to an unfortunate compatriot seated in the dock'). Though Marshall Hall had delivered '*une brillante plaiderie*' ('a sparkling address'), prosecuting counsel had responded with '*une réplique froide et monotone*' ('a cold and monotonous reply').

The perils of dictation over the telephone were exemplified in the reporting of the judge's name; several newspapers referred to him as 'Ribby Swist', whose summing-up was regarded by *Le Figaro* as '*extrêmement sévère pour l'accusée*' ('extremely hard on the accused'). The verdict was a surprise to many. *L'Intransigeant* reported a conversation between two astonished travellers in a Paris commuter train, shortly after the news of Madame Fahmy's acquittal had reached the Paris newsstands at 4.00 p.m. on 15 September. One said '*C'est extraordinaire . . . Jamais je n'avais cru les Anglais capable de cela*' ('It's extraordinary. I never thought the English capable of it'), while the other replied, '*Avec leur rigorisme – C'est inouï!*' ('With their severity, it's unheard of!').

The satirical weekly *Le Canard Enchaîné* took a sideways look at the trial and at Madame herself, about whom its writers nursed no illusions. A spoof interview with Marguerite began, in deadpan style, '*C'est avec*

172

une joie patriotique que la France entière a accueilli l'acquittement de Mme Fahmy . . .' ('The whole of France has greeted the acquittal of Mme Fahmy with patriotic joy . . .') an absurd exaggeration followed by a dig at Madame herself. '*Mme Fahmy, qui quelques confrères appellent Mme Maggie Meller – car elle n'a jamais épousé M. André Meller . . . était Mme Grandjean avant de devenir Mme Fahmy*' ('Mme Fahmy, who some friends call Mme Maggie Meller, because she wasn't married to Mr André Meller . . . was Mme Grandjean before becoming Mme Fahmy').*

Maggie Meller had come to symbolize, wrote *Le Canard*, the virtues of the French race: '*gaieté, esprit de détente (si l'on peut dire), en opposition avec le sérieux hypocrite des Anglais*' (gaiety, spirit of relaxation (so to speak), as opposed to the solemn hypocrisy of the English). '*Détente*' was a play on words: it also means 'trigger'.

Maggie, '*notre illustre compatriote*', confided her plans for the future. She was thinking of going back to the *Folies Bergère*. With waspish humour, *Le Canard* gives her supposed reply: '*Mais, cette fois, sur la scène et non plus au promenoir*' ('But this time on the stage and not walking about again'), a jibe at the days before the Great War when she had plied her trade as a prostitute at the *Folies*.

The article ended on a savagely accurate note. 'Will you be inheriting your husband's fortune?', she is asked. The reply is perfect. '*Grands yeux étonnés, délicieusement ingénus, "Certainement, puis qu'il est mort"*' ('With great astonished eyes, deliciously innocent, "Of course. He's dead, isn't he?"').

---

* The reference to 'Grandjean' may have been to the wealthy Jean d'Astoreca, Marguerite's long-time lover.

23

Loose Ends

After leaving the Old Bailey and the scene of one of the greatest triumphs of his long career, Marshall Hall had gone straight down to his country cottage at Brook in Surrey to rest. The telegraph boy brought the old campaigner a pleasant surprise that Saturday evening, a cable from Madame Fahmy, who had resumed her maiden name for the occasion: '*De tout mon coeur je vous suis profondément reconnaissante – Marguerite Alibert*' ('With all my heart, I am deeply grateful to you').

The next day was Marshall Hall's sixty-fifth birthday, which he marked by replying gallantly and at some length to Marguerite's wire. Paying tribute to her testimony, '*bravement donnée*' ('bravely given'), he apologized for not having personally congratulated her after the verdict, excusing himself on the ground of her manifest exhaustion. '*J'espère que l'avenir vous donnera beaucoup de moments heureux pour remplacer les misères passées. C'est encore une fois que "la vérité est triomphante"* . . .' ('I hope that the future will give you many happy times to replace the sad occasions. "Truth is triumphant" once again').

Marguerite's telegram was soon followed by a letter, elegantly expressed and written from Princes' Hotel:

> Septembre 15me 1923
>
> *CHER MAÎTRE – J'arrive et dans cette ambiance de bonheur un regret m'attriste, celui de n'avoir pu vous prendre la main et de vous dire merci. Mon émotion était si grande que vous me pardonnerez d'avoir fermé les yeux et de m'être laisser emmener. – Votre profondément reconnaissante M. FAHMY.*

174

('DEAR MASTER – I arrive and in this happy atmosphere one regret saddens me, that of not being able to take your hand and thank you. My emotion was so great that you will forgive me for having closed my eyes and for allowing myself to take my leave – your profoundly grateful M. FAHMY')

On 21 September, Marguerite, a client with whom Marshall Hall was having a most unusual post-trial relationship, visited him at his chambers in 3 Temple Gardens. She saw his comfortably furnished room, original Victorian caricatures decorating the walls, within which the Great Defender sat at his Chippendale desk with its red morocco inset. Marguerite was shown in by Edgar Bowker, who recalled in *A Lifetime Within the Law*, 'Marshall Hall . . . sitting with his back to the window, his face in shadow. As Madame Fahmy entered, the sun shone full on her, lighting her vivacious features and gilding her dress . . . I see her standing there and smiling, and Marshall Hall rising from his chair to welcome her in French. She stayed for tea, and from time to time I heard laughter in the room and her rather shrill voice mingling with Marshall Hall's vibrating and measured tones . . .'

Marshall Hall had a serious purpose beyond personally receiving the thanks of his attractive client. He dearly wanted to add her .32 Browning semi-automatic to his already extensive collection of firearms. Normally, acquitted people are given back any of their possessions which have been used as exhibits at their trial, but the pistol had been imported illegally. Marshall Hall's first step was to get Marguerite's disclaimer and he wrote out a note, in English, addressed to 'The Chief of Police, Scotland Yard', asking that the Browning automatic pistol, 'Exhibit No. 2 in the trial of Rex v Fahmy', might be handed to him. Marguerite obligingly appended her signature to the document.

Shortly before she returned to France, Marguerite wrote yet another billet-doux to her saviour, saying that she had been enraptured to see him and how pleased she was that at last the English newspapers were telling the truth about her. Maître Assouad had penned a neat demolition job on Ali Fahmy for the *World's Pictorial News* of 23 September and the first instalment of her own hastily cobbled together memoirs, was published the following day in the *Illustrated Sunday Herald*, and also appeared in the *New York World* and *Le Petit Parisien*.

Marshall Hall, determined to get hold of the pistol, began his campaign by sending Marguerite's disclaimer to Divisional Detective Inspector Grosse. 'I shd very much like to keep the pistol as a memento,' he wrote, pointing out that he had a valid permit for a weapon of that calibre and ending his letter on a note of barefaced flattery: 'May I take this opportunity to thank you for the great fairness you deployed towards my client in the difficult case you handled so skilfully.'

Grosse, evidently won over, minuted that there seemed to be no objection to Marshall Hall's request, but, higher up the chain of police command, doubts were lurking. 'I do not know of a precedent,' wrote a Chief Inspector. '. . . It is usual for the police to keep such weapons and, if of sufficient interest to retain and store in [the Black] Museum.' His superior considered that 'a dangerous precedent would be created,' adding, 'I doubt if we should give it up.' The legal advice was to similar effect, accompanied by a curious reason for not prosecuting Marguerite for unlawful possession of a firearm: '. . . that, of course would be impossible under the present circumstances, even if she were in the country and amenable to our jurisdiction, because we should be accused of persecution . . .'

The matter was resolved in an extraordinary way. Sir Wyndham Childs minuted, 'I think we should refuse to hand it over on Madame Fahmy's request. It would be another matter entirely if we handed it over to Sir E. Marshall Hall as a small memento of a case in which he made such a thrilling speech.' Two letters were sent from Scotland Yard to Marshall Hall on 11 October 1923. The first was an officially worded refusal of his request, on the grounds that Madame Fahmy had been in unlawful possession of the pistol and the Commissioner therefore could not recognize her authority to hand it over. The other, also signed by Wyndham Childs, was a personal note which made a confidential invitation: '. . . if you would like to send somebody round to see me in about a month's time, [the Commissioner of Police] will be happy to send you the souvenir . . . which you desire. My only regret is that the lady did not get a "right and left". . . '

Marshall Hall's delighted reply confirmed an 'old pals' act' of sizeable proportions. Long-ago shooting expeditions to the moors of Forfar were recalled: 'I often think of our happy times at Hunt Hill and our journey down together on that awful night . . .' and 'Fido' Childs's phrase, 'right and left' (presumably a suggestion that Ali Fahmy's genitalia should have been blasted away), was enthusiastically echoed: 'PS I think I know where the left barrel ought to have proved effective and I agree.'

'Fido's' private opinion of Madame Fahmy was not much more generous than his attitude to her husband. The first instalment of

Marguerite's memoirs had provided a colourfully embroidered account of her arrest and detention at Bow Street police station. 'Naturally, one does not believe all the statements made by this hysterical woman,' he minuted crustily, 'but I would like to know what "E" Division have to say . . . about it.'

If Marshall Hall could rest content with a hard case fought and won, his colleague, Sir Henry Curtis-Bennett KC, was left with less happy memories of a trial in which he had done little other than collect his substantial brief fee. It must have been a frustrating experience for someone in his already eminent position to be upstaged by Marshall Hall, whose courtroom technique differed radically from that of his suave younger contemporary, who, despite his looming presence (by 1930, he weighed nearly twenty stone), rarely made a scene or mishandled a witness and was almost invariably the soul of politeness.

Driving with his wife through Chelmsford, on his way home to Boreham in Essex, on the last day of the Fahmy trial, Curtis-Bennett had to contend with a wet and greasy road. As he overtook a stationary bus, a woman suddenly walked out into his path; he swerved to avoid her and nearly did so, but she was struck by the car's large mudguard and killed. Luckily for Curtis-Bennett, he had been travelling comparatively slowly and had driven for over twenty years without incident. A verdict of accidental death was recorded by a Coroner's jury.

Officialdom was anxious to tidy away the troublesome Fahmy case as soon as possible after the verdict and Madame's very welcome return to the land of her birth, but the vexed issue of how both Ali and Marguerite had been able to get into the country, each carrying guns and ammunition, continued to worry the Home Office until well into December. One harassed official fruitlessly canvassed a faint possibility: '. . . I suppose these two had not applied for an import licence?', but there was no doubt that the guns had been illegally imported. 'Customs must not search persons without reasonable cause for contraband . . .', responded the redfaced Customs and Excise. 'Obviously it would not be right . . . to subject every person landing to a personal search . . .'

The Savoy's management must also have harboured the wish that a very tiresome episode in its history would soon be over and forgotten. Towards the end of September, a development in the hotel's entertainment policy provided a welcome distraction from the sordid revelations of the Fahmy trial. Wilfred de Mornys, Musical Director at the Savoy, announced the introduction of a second resident band, the Orpheans, which would join the already highly successful Savoy Havana Band.

The *Evening Standard* saluted the Orpheans' début under the title, 'LONDON'S BRIGHTER EVENINGS'. 'Last night, I heard the Savoy Orpheans play in the splendidly re-decorated Savoy Hotel ballroom . . .', wrote a correspondent. 'They play beautifully with a swing and rhythm that set the feet stepping and tapping almost unconsciously . . .'

The hotel's publicity machine was in top gear, emphasizing that the band contained a number of top American musicians and had, reported the *Referee*, a '£900 piano with its double keyboard [which] is making some interesting experiments with the fox-trot rhythm . . .' The *Radio Times* promised listeners that the Savoy Orpheans would be a feature of the winter's entertainment. 'They will play at the Savoy Hotel, whence the music will be transmitted to a land wire to 2LO, and so, through the ether to your receiving sets.'

In England, amid such gentle diversions, memories of the antics of that unwelcome pair of foreigners, Ali and Marguerite Fahmy, began to fade from the public mind.

24

Guilty as Charged?

Madame Fahmy had been triumphantly acquitted in a wave of popular sympathy. Nine months and a day before Marguerite stepped into the dock of the Old Bailey's Number One Court, Edith Thompson had been executed at Holloway Prison. The Home Secretary's refusal to recommend a reprieve was endorsed by, among others, the poet T. S. Eliot and, with rather less intellectual clout, by the *Sunday Pictorial*, which wrote, with probable accuracy, 'We believe that the Home Secretary's decision . . . is in accordance with the weight of public feeling.' The *Daily Express*'s leader on the Fahmy trial stated firmly that 'the case differed at every turn from the Thompson murder and Madame Fahmy is entitled to her freedom'.

Inevitably, the two criminal trials had quite different factual backgrounds. In Madame Fahmy's case, there was no doubt that she had fired the fatal shot from her own gun; Percy Thompson, on the other hand, had been stabbed to death by a third party, Mrs Thompson's lover. The Crown had introduced a series of letters written by Edith Thompson to Frederick Bywaters in a successful attempt to show that she had been a party to the murderous act, even if, in the opinion of her defence counsel, Sir Henry Curtis-Bennett, the truth was that she was hanged for immorality.

There was also nothing in common between the characters of the dead men. Mr Thompson was a dull, unimaginative hypochondriac; Ali Fahmy, depending on one's view, was a neurotic and at times selfish playboy or, as the defence would have the jury believe, a monster of Eastern decadence and depravity, an 'unnatural brute'. It is idle, but nevertheless tempting, to speculate about the result if Edith Thompson's husband had been black and if her letters had contained allegations of the sort that Marguerite Fahmy would make in the course of her own trial.

The link between the two cases is the deadly factor of immorality, to which the English have always attached excessive importance. There is a deep-rooted national tendency to judge people on their sexual mores, when logic demands that such behaviour has little or nothing to do with the matter in hand. In the days of capital punishment, the life of a condemned person could depend upon just such extraneous factors. Ruth Ellis, hanged in 1955 for shooting her lover outside a Hampstead public house, had struck courtroom observers as a 'brassy tart', whose background, the twilight world of Fifties drinking clubs, somehow got into the argument about her reprieve. Post-war standards were slipping, a stand had to be made, and all the hackneyed arguments were wheeled out to justify the actions of the state in putting a woman to death.

Although in retrospect it is not surprising that Madame Fahmy walked free from the Old Bailey, it should be remembered how gloomily her defending advocate had once viewed her chances of acquittal. Marshall Hall was only too aware that his client's past life could very possibly put a noose about her neck. By keeping the exposure of her real character to a minimum and by imputing to her husband sexual behaviour of the very basest sort (thus shifting the moral spotlight away from the wife), Marshall Hall went a long way towards securing a favourable verdict. The sexual dimension, coupled with a crude racism, served Marguerite Fahmy well, although it would be churlish to underestimate the considerable histrionic talents she demonstrated in her own defence.

One of the major weaknesses of English trials is the adversarial system, where two advocates battle it out before a judge (who supposedly holds the ring), playing a sort of game in which all too often counsel seem preoccupied with keeping as much information as possible away from the jury. In Madame Fahmy's case, several vital elements were either ignored or dealt with in an unsatisfactory way. Most of the blame for this lies at the door of prosecuting counsel, aided and abetted by a judge of inferior intellectual ability.

Thanks to the judge's ruling, which wholly ignored the suggestions of venal conduct and of homosexuality that Marshall Hall had put to Said Enani, Marguerite's own background escaped searching inquiry. Percival Clarke's ill-judged question about the cabdriver father had backfired on the prosecution and the jury were left with the impression that Marguerite was a divorcee who had enjoyed a number of affairs and whose love child had been legitimized by marriage to Charles Laurent. The jury were not to know the truth: that Marguerite had worked as a very ordinary prostitute until 1914, when she became 'Madame Maggie Meller', the high-class courtesan of the sixteenth *arrondissement*.

Another important element and one which, as far as can be known, never came to the jury's attention, was Ali Fahmy's mysterious journey from the Savoy to the Piccadilly area, made at the height of that tremendous thunderstorm. At least three newspapers reported how Ali had been seen in the hotel foyer, still wearing evening dress, at about 1.00 a.m. and the *Daily Express* specifically mentioned Piccadilly as the general direction.

Although this sort of reportage is always questionable, such late-night excursions had been very much a feature of Ali's life both in Cairo and in Paris. That sweltering Monday in London must have been a time of intense emotional pressure, accompanied by a desire for relief, away from his increasingly bad-tempered wife. The relationship with Marguerite was at an all-time low: he had long doubted her fidelity, and with reason; she was now openly talking about divorce, accusing him of cruelty both physical and sexual; and, come hell or high water, she was going back to Paris the next day, leaving him to spend his Season in London alone and shamed.

The available evidence suggests a sexual motive for leaving the hotel. He was away for perhaps an hour, ample time for a liaison or a visit to a club, and Ali was quite rich enough to have paid his cabdriver to wait until he decided to return to the Savoy. Ali's exact destination remains a mystery. It could have been any one of a number of late-night clubs in the West End, many operating illegally.

If he had merely wanted an after-hours drink, away from the Savoy, he could have tried 'Ma Meyrick's' at 43 Gerrard Street, Soho. Mrs Kate Meyrick, known as the 'Queen of the Night Clubs', had fallen foul of the licensing law on numerous occasions and, in autumn 1923, the famous '43' had been re-styled 'Proctor's Club' after a police raid. The club, entry to which was obtained through a series of locked doors, was on the first floor and drinks were dispensed to waiters from a small portable bar with a lid like a roll-top desk, which could be closed at a moment's notice. Dancing took place from 10 p.m. until 6.00 a.m. in what was described by *John Bull* as a 'miniature palace of revelry' whose patrons talked and flirted 'with vulgar abandon'.

Cocaine, at a street price of £56 an ounce, and 'hashish' (cannabis) could be found without too much bother. A lively description of London's gambling and drug scene appeared in the *Sunday Pictorial* later that summer: 'At 11.00 p.m. when restaurants and buffets are obliged to stop the sale of [liquor], one may see small parties of gay men and women crowding into taxicabs . . . At the back of Piccadilly Circus and Piccadilly, there are quiet streets of large houses which appear . . . dead.'

Admission could be secured by a distinctive knock or password. Even when the outer door was wide open, no light could be seen and, at the end of a dark passage, behind a heavy curtain, lay 'a luxurious room, crowded with men and women in evening dress'. No attempt was made to hide 'dope' in these 'swagger gambling dens', where 'girls with unnaturally brilliant eyes sit sniffing cocaine . . .'

Street prostitution, both male and female, was very much in evidence around Soho. Transvestite male prostitutes had a favourite café 'in one of the back streets off Shaftesbury Avenue, where the people who pose as women gather together and take counsel . . . to decide where victims are to be found . . .', according to *John Bull*. This was possibly the Black Cat Café in Old Compton Street, since made famous by the writing of Quentin Crisp.

Most likely, Ali would have sought his pleasure indoors, at a brothel or in one of the seedier clubs. If Ali was in a mood for sex with a man, it could explain why Said Enani, normally his regular companion, was left behind. This and other evidence suggests that Said, whatever Marshall Hall thought about him, was heterosexual.

Whatever happened, it could very possibly have acted as a spur to the bitter row which raged in the suite immediately before Ali was killed. It appears that the police took no steps to identify and interview the cabdriver who had taken Ali from the Savoy and who had probably driven him back there. In one sense, there was no reason for them to have done so: it was clear that Ali had died by his wife's hand and, once that was established, it was up to her to clear her name. Clarke did not ask Marguerite about her reaction to Ali's absence that morning, and for her part she was hardly likely to have wanted to introduce this sort of evidence into the case. So the jury, unless they could remember July's newspaper reports, never knew about that rain-sodden journey.

Said Enani made no mention of the trip. In his statement to police, made on the day of the shooting, he wrote of talking to Ali after Marguerite had gone to her room and of seeing him enter the lift, en route for the suite, at 'about 2.00 a.m.'. His deposition, made at the coroner's court on 12 July, reads, 'Deceased then went upstairs at 1.45 and I went to my room.'

Perhaps the loyal secretary, not for the first time, was covering up for his master's indiscretion, out of regard for his surviving family. It is possible to read Marguerite's evidence as indicating that her husband had left the suite, if not the hotel itself, not long before the fatality occurred, though she seems to have put Ali's absence at only about half an hour.

A further matter which was never canvassed was whether Marguerite had known the content of the three telegrams, each worded 'NOTHING TO BE DELIVERED TO MY WIFE ON MY ACCOUNT DURING MY ABSENCE. FAHMY', sent off during the interval of *The Merry Widow*. Marguerite had made an unsuccessful attempt to collect one of the expensive Vuitton handbags while Ali was away in Stuttgart in June. Her reaction to the discovery that Ali was pre-empting any attempt to clear those plush Paris stores of all the expensive goods held on his account was likely to have been a violent one. Clarke appears not to have made any use of these telegrams in his cross-examination of Marguerite, leaving the jury unaware of their existence.

Marguerite also escaped searching inquiry about her financial circumstances. Shortly before the fatality, she had written to Dr Gordon in terms that suggested that she was dependent on her husband to pay the cost of her operation. She also made out that Ali had taunted her with banknotes, money for her travelling expenses to Paris. There is no doubt that Marguerite was already a wealthy woman by the standards of the day, when she married Ali. The evidence suggests that she could easily have afforded to pay for both the operation and the journey back to Paris, where, the previous month, she had bought another horse for her already considerable stable.

A more delicate topic, and one handled inadequately by the prosecution, was the vexed question of Madame's piles. Just how long had she been suffering from this painful complaint? Ali Fahmy might indeed have preferred one mode of intercourse to another, a predilection which caused the condition to develop, but it appears that native English embarrassment at discussing anything to do with that part of the anatomy prevented a proper inquiry into Marguerite's claims. Neither Percival Clarke, let alone the prudish, provincial-minded judge, ever explained to the jury that prostitutes had practised anal intercourse from time immemorial as the surest way of avoiding conception.

The post-mortem on Ali Fahmy's body should have provided the prosecution with its deadliest ammunition. It was conducted by Dr Maurice Newfield, House Physician at Charing Cross Hospital, on the day after the shooting. Examination of Ali's body (his djellaba was quaintly described as looking 'rather like a tennis shirt') revealed seven different wounds collectively representing the tracks of the three bullets fired from Marguerite's gun.

One bullet had entered through the left side of Ali's back, about two inches from the spine and roughly in the 'mid dorsal region'. 'A probe was [inserted] and the direction [of the bullet] was found to be upwards and outwards towards the left arm', at the top of which, in the region of the armpit, three wounds could be seen. Another had struck the left neck, two and a half inches behind and three quarters of an inch below the left earlobe, with only a short track (about three quarters of an inch), running downwards and forwards.

The third, fatal, bullet had entered Ali's head through the left temple, tracking right across the brain to an exit point two inches behind the right earlobe. Marguerite had shot Ali Fahmy straight through the head.

Dr Newfield's first statement to police was made on the day of the shooting, before the post-mortem had taken place. 'From the absence of singeing or burning,' he wrote, 'I concluded that the firing had most probably occurred at some small distance from the victim.' Generally speaking, singeing and burning become more prominent the closer the gun is to the victim when it is fired. At the post-mortem it was discovered that, in the case of the fatal head wound, 'there was slight blackening of the skin and for an area of one square inch a number of small black spatterings . . .'

The forensic evidence seems to support Beattie's account of seeing Ali, seconds before he was shot, bending down and whistling to Marguerite's errant lapdog. The first bullet in the back brought him down, a second, wilder, shot passed through the left side of the neck, and the *coup de grâce*, delivered neatly through the left temple, was fired by Marguerite from a closer range, as suggested by the slight blackening around the entrance wound.

No doubt some of these points were made to the jury, but surviving accounts of the trial suggest that, somehow or other, the effect of the post-mortem findings got 'lost in the wash', as lawyers say when important facts become overwhelmed in a mass of other evidence.

What did happen on that stormy night in the summer of 1923? Marguerite's story of the crouching Oriental, ready to leap on her in a hotel corridor where, even at that late hour, people were passing and repassing, seems intrinsically ridiculous, as does her melodramatic account of Fahmy demanding his favourite sexual activity, accompanied by the waving of banknotes before his wife's helpless eyes. Much of the rest of Marguerite's narrative was culled from material compiled with an eye to an expensive divorce settlement.

From what is known of Marguerite's tough, combative character, the reality must surely have been that, with domestic affairs in crisis and suffering the torments of haemorrhoids doubtless aggravated by the hot, sticky night, she lost her temper, went back to her room, and picked up her pistol, which was already loaded, as was her custom.* Having fired once out of the window to check that it was working, she ran back into the corridor and shot her husband dead. The idea that Marguerite, a pistol-packer for nine years, did not know how the firearm worked is laughable.

But this was a classic *crime passionnel*. By a splendid paradox, the stolid English jury rightly acquitted Marguerite Fahmy of murder, though their reasons for doing so were, without doubt, profoundly wrong, strongly influenced by Marshall Hall's shameless use of xenophobia, racism, popular hostility to homosexual men and a pervasive ignorance about sexual matters in general.

To some extent, the crime of passion is now recognized in English law. The Homicide Act of 1957, passed in response to concern at the execution of Ruth Ellis (who had been badly treated by her lover, suffering a miscarriage shortly before the shooting), enables a verdict of manslaughter to be recorded in appropriate circumstances. And, of course, the death penalty for murder has been abolished.

Madame Fahmy was a lucky winner in a great lottery, the English system of criminal justice. Less fortunate people, charged with a crime for which our narrow, chilly society could find no excuse, lie entombed in prison quicklime.

---

* The capacity of the pistol's magazine was eight rounds, contained in a clip loaded into the butt of the gun. Only six bullets were ever accounted for, which raises the possibility that Marguerite had fired the gun on other occasions, possibly in France or in Egypt.

185

POSTSCRIPT: THE AFFAIR OF THE SYRIAN CARPET MERCHANT

Though her lawyer, Maître Assouad, had told journalists in London that she would never return to Egypt, Marguerite boarded the SS *Esperia* at Naples on 20 October 1923, bound for Alexandria, where she arrived two days later. Once his client was safely in Cairo, the Maître announced to an astonished world that Marguerite was pregnant by her late husband, the happy event to occur the following April.

This was not the only piece of extraordinary news that month. Marguerite's sixteen-year-old daughter, Raymonde Laurent, wrote a well-publicized letter to a friend in Cairo, informing one and all of her intention to embrace Islam. She had privately sworn to become a Muslim if her mother were acquitted of the murder charge and regarded the verdict as no less than 'a miracle of the Moslem faith'.

The reason for these bizarre developments is not hard to divine. There had been much gossip in the newspapers about the diminution of Ali's fortune by reason of his gross extravagance, but once the dust had settled it had become apparent that he had left an estate valued at some £2.5 million and no will. Marguerite's chances of inheriting all or part of this vast sum were considerably hindered by the fact that it was she who had killed him. A Muslim court would demand more than a 'Not Guilty' verdict: she would have to satisfy them of her complete innocence in the matter. Failing that, the estate would be divided, half between Ali's three surviving sisters and the other half to his closest male relative, a paternal uncle, who worked in Ali's office at Cairo and used to complain that he was badly paid.

186

POSTSCRIPT

Much to Marguerite's chagrin, the administrator appointed to superintend Ali's estate was his brother-in-law, Dr Assim Said, who was not well disposed towards her. Marguerite's lawyer began an action in the Egyptian probate court, the *Meglis Hesbi*, to have Dr Said replaced as administrator by someone less hostile to her interests. The case drifted on into the New Year, was twice adjourned in January and again the following month, when Marguerite, now back in Paris, was invited to appear before them. Events in Paris were to overshadow the decision of the Egyptian court.

In the meantime, another startling development was reported by a French newspaper, which claimed during November that Marguerite was to be married to Said Enani. Said issued an angry denial to the London correspondent of *Al Ahram*, saying that he was minded to consult his lawyers about the rumour. He did not have very much time in which to do so: early in January 1924, he died of pneumonia in Paris.

Marguerite's campaign to win her share of Ali's fortune proceeded apace, but in April her plans came to an abrupt halt, in circumstances that bear a distinct resemblance to a Feydeau farce. Hiding behind a tapestry in the entrance hall of a clinic at 82 rue Dareau (only some three hundred yards from Marguerite's birthplace), on the evening of 9 April 1923, was Commissioner Michet of the Paris police, normally stationed across the Seine in La Muette, a district of the sixteenth *arrondissement*.

Marguerite had called him in to hear a short conversation between herself and a marvellously shady character, Yusuf Cassab Bey, a Syrian moneylender and carpet merchant, normally resident in Cairo. Stepping from his place of concealment, the Commissioner arrested Cassab on charges of attempted fraud and hauled him off to prison.

Cassab, who, in the past, had sold some of his carpets to Ali Fahmy, told his story to the *Juge d'Instruction* (investigating magistrate) three days later. The whole matter revolved round finding an '*enfant du miracle*' ('miraculous child') for Marguerite, who was not pregnant, and never had been. Under Muslim law, a posthumous son could inherit a proportion of his father's estate, variously stated as a quarter or a half. A generous two-year period, it seems, was allowed for any such claim to be made. If evidence could be produced to show that Marguerite had borne a son, she would become, indirectly, a substantial beneficiary. The problem, of course, was that she was not pregnant. So the child would have to be a fiction, recorded in the documents as having died shortly after its birth.

Enter Cassab Bey. On 15 October 1923, Cassab met Maître Assouad, surely not by chance, in the Café de la Paix in Paris. Cassab agreed that Marguerite's chances of getting her hands on the money were slim. The wily merchant told Assouad that he had an idea that would annoy the Fahmy family, and had a meeting with Marguerite to discuss his plan. Shortly afterwards, she left Paris for Cairo, where the pregnancy was announced, much to the discomfiture of Ali's family, who immediately stated that they would contest her claim.

Cassab, too, returned to Egypt, where he approached a friend with medical connections in Paris, one Dr Kamel. On 11 January 1924, Cassab telegraphed to Marguerite: '*Je m'embarque. Je serai le mercredi 27 à Paris. J'ai des sérieuses propositions à vous présenter*' ('I'm on my way. I shall be in Paris on Wednesday the 27th. I have some important proposals to put to you'). On arriving in Paris, he went to see her. Marguerite had moved from her apartment in the avenue Henri-Martin, possibly to escape the attentions of the press, and was now living at an equally plush address in the rue Georges-Ville. According to Cassab, Marguerite told him that she had cleared his plan with her lawyers, but that she had not so far been able to find a doctor willing to certify the birth of a phantom child.

Cassab introduced Marguerite some weeks later to Dr Kamel at Claridge's Hotel. Kamel had found someone willing to provide a false certificate for 200,000 francs (£2500), half payable on signing the contract, the balance when the birth certificate was handed over. Before this meeting, however, Cassab had received a disturbing letter from his son in Cairo, telling of a visit from a member of the Fahmy family, who were already deeply suspicious about Marguerite's 'pregnancy' and the 'shameful things' going on in Paris.

The family had evidence which damned Marguerite on three counts. First, a certificate which showed that she had undergone an ovariotomy; second, a declaration from Holloway that she was not pregnant during her imprisonment there; and, third, testimony about her private life in Paris. If, said the family representative, Marguerite was willing to withdraw her declaration of pregnancy, the family would pay her £15,000 in settlement of her claim against the estate.

When Cassab showed Marguerite his son's letter, her temper got the better of her, not for the first time. She had never had an ovariotomy, she declared angrily, merely an operation to remove her appendix. Headstrong as ever, Marguerite brushed aside the settlement offer and told Cassab that she was going into the clinic the following Friday, probably 4 April. In court, Cassab tried to make out that he had no idea where the clinic was and had paid a M. Finance, a '*marchand de coton hydrophile*' (cotton-wool salesman) some 250 francs for the information. The clinic at 82 rue Dareau was run by Madame Champeau, a professional midwife, married to a doctor.

At 11.05 a.m. on 9 April, the curtain rose on the last act of this long-running comedy. A domestic servant, employed at the clinic, called at the Registry of Births at the town hall of the fourteenth *arrondissement*, to announce that a boy had been born at the clinic on the 7th. Probably to the knowledge of Madame Champeau, the doctor officially appointed to verify births had already left with the day's list and the pink form that was an essential document of record. In his absence, the registrar's clerk made an informal note of the claim.

Forty minutes later, a Mme Renée Masdurand, midwife at the Champeau clinic, hurried into the town hall, claiming that, as a matter of great urgency, the birth of the child should be formally recorded, because it had taken place on the 9th, not the 7th. 'We don't have the official doctor available,' she was told. 'Give me the pink form,' insisted the midwife, 'Madame Champeau . . . is going to see the doctor. She'll show him the child and return the form.'

The clerk reluctantly handed one of the precious forms to Mme Masdurand, telling her to return it before the office closed that afternoon. 'I'll bring it back at 5 o'clock,' promised the midwife, but it was not returned and, in the event, was never signed by the doctor. The reported birth was a hoax. Plainly, an attempt had been made to hoodwink the Registry, a plot which came to nothing, as *Le Canard Enchaîné* suggested, because Marguerite, who had suddenly realized that she was in danger of being found out, and thus risked prosecution, decided to shop Cassab that very evening.

The hearing of Marguerite's allegation of attempted fraud against Cassab ran to some five days. He claimed that he had been entrapped by Marguerite, who had originated the plot and was in it up to her ears. Marguerite, on the other hand, said that Cassab was himself part of a campaign by the Fahmy family to persecute her: this does not explain how her lawyer came to announce a bogus pregnancy the previous October and Marguerite, of all people, had most to gain from the subterfuge. Putting on a brave face, she attended the hearing swathed in mink and generously exonerated Mme Champeau, wife and mother, from complicity in the affair. 'That woman has five children,' said Marguerite, 'and is most certainly a victim of the machinations of Cassab Bey . . .'

When Madame Champeau came to give evidence, she told of being pestered, almost threatened, by Cassab to take part in the deception, but she had refused any involvement. She admitted sending her staff to the town hall, but it was merely to report the births of two other children, a month earlier, on 5 and 10 March. She had never asked 30,000 francs (£575) for the false certificate, as Cassab had claimed.

It was all quite absurd. The Paris press gleefully recounted the attempts of the principal conspirators, Cassab, Marguerite, and the 'doctoresse', Mme Champeau, to extricate themselves from the mess. 'L'AFFAIRE CASSAB BEY OU LES MÉLI-MÉLOS DE LA RUE DAREAU' ('THE CASSAB BEY AFFAIR OR THE MIX-UPS IN THE RUE DAREAU') headlined Le Figaro, while Le Canard Enchaîné, under the heading 'NOUVELLE INNOCENCE DE MADAME FAHMY' ('NEW INNOCENCE OF MADAME FAHMY'), mercilessly sent up Marguerite for a second time: 'Everybody remembers Madame Fahmy Bey, who, for simply having killed her husband, had to undergo all sorts of unpleasant things in London.'

Le Canard wittily suggested that Marguerite had realized that the scheme was 'une infâhmie', before turning in the unfortunate Cassab to the police. 'She's willing to kill as many husbands as you want, but to tell a fib – never!'

M. Barnaud, the investigating magistrate, decided that there was insufficient evidence against Cassab, who was released at the end of April and immediately returned to Cairo, undertaking not to communicate with Marguerite again.

The Cassab Bey affair seems to have put paid to Marguerite's attempt to recover a slice of Ali's money in Egypt, as well as to her very considerable social ambitions at home. She had been shown up as a less than honest participant in a ludicrous plot and, by declaring a pregnancy, albeit a false one, she had also undermined the allegations about Ali's sexual preference made so robustly by her defence at the trial. Marguerite, once the envy of the demi-monde, was now the butt of jokes. All Paris was laughing.

Wisely, Marguerite decided to leave town for a while and early July found her enjoying the summer season in Carlsbad (Karlovy Vary), Czechoslovakia. Described as 'The Queen of Bohemian Watering Places' in the New York Herald, the resort was overflowing with rich foreigners, Marguerite's favourite quarry. President Masaryk was there, along with an assortment of the Austrian aristocracy and the American super-rich, a Rothschild or two, Viscount Cowdray, and the renowned violinist Fritz

Kreisler. Marguerite, now approaching thirty-four, appears to have been determined to make the very best use of fleeting time.

Despite the probable failure of her assault on Ali's fortune, Marguerite was not poor and, with her usual self-possession, was evidently enjoying life. Hearing that Marshall Hall had taken a rare prosecution brief in the murder trial of Jean-Pierre Vacquier, a Frenchman, she wrote from Carlsbad: '. . . *Je savais par les journaux que vous étiez contre l'accusé et de ce fait je me plaignais – mais oui!!! . . .*') (I've found out from the papers that you are against the accused and I'm complaining about that fact – yes indeed!!!) She visited Marshall Hall in London, the Great Survivor saluting the Great Defender, on several occasions before his death in February 1927.

On 13 January 1971, *Le Figaro* carried a short announcement in the Bereavements column: '*On nous prie d'annoncer le décès de la princesse FAHMY–BEY survenu le 2 janvier. Le service religieux et l'inhumation ont eu lieu dans la plus stricte intimité*' ('We are asked to announce that the death of the princess FAHMY-BEY took place on 2 January. The religious service and the burial have taken place in the strictest privacy'). She had died, at the age of eighty, in the fashionable Paris suburb of Neuilly.

Long before, Marguerite had written of her wayward young husband, 'While he loved me, I was happy.' She never remarried.

NOTE ON SOURCES

As a result of the verdict, no official transcript exists of the trial. The press reported trials much more extensively in 1923 than is the case today, with the exception of sexual matters, and newspaper accounts form the basis of the reconstruction of court proceedings. Among the fuller reports are those in the *Daily Telegraph* and the *Evening Standard*.

Marguerite Fahmy's own account of the case appeared in the *Illustrated Sunday Herald* in five weekly instalments between 23 September and 21 October 1923.

SELECT BIBLIOGRAPHY

H. ASHTON-WOLFE *The Underworld* (Hurst & Blackett, 1925)

A. BENNETT *Imperial Palace* (Cassell, 1930)

J. BERQUE *Egypt: Imperialism and Revolution* (Faber, 1972)

A. E. BOWKER *Behind the Bar* (Staples Press, 1947)

A. E. BOWKER *A Lifetime Within the Law* (W. H. Allen, 1961)

E. S. FAY *The Life of Mr Justice Rigby Swift* (Methuen, 1939)

E. GRICE *Great Cases of Sir Henry Curtis-Bennett KC* (Hutchinson, 1937)

M. HASTINGS *The Other Mr Churchill* (George G. Harrap, 1963)

J. HENRY *Detective-Inspector Henry's Famous Cases* (Hutchinson, 1942)

R. HICHENS *Bella Donna* (Heinemann, 1909)

E. M. HULL *The Sheik* (George Newnes, 1921)

S. JACKSON *The Savoy* (Stanley Jackson, 1964)

E. MARJORIBANKS *The Life of Sir Edward Marshal Hall KC* (Gollancz, 1929)

N. WARNER-HOOKE and G. THOMAS *Marshall Hall* (Arthur Barker, 1966)

R. WILD and D. CURTIS-BENNETT *Curtis: The Life of Sir Henry Curtis-Bennett KC* (Cassell, 1937)

DOCUMENTARY SOURCES IN PUBLIC RECORD OFFICE

(i) CRIM 1/244:   Inquest depositions, with list of exhibits and sketch plan. See also CCC Court Book for 10–15 September 1923. (Committal depositions no longer extant.) Indictment and list of witnesses.

(ii) MEPO 3/1589:   Metropolitan Police file, open to public inspection since 19 January 1989. Special Branch papers referred to in the docket have apparently been destroyed.

(iii) HO 45/14618:   Correspondence regarding Mr Justice Swift's observations on pistol control and request for information to HM Customs & Excise.

(iv) FO 371/8989:   Correspondence with British authorities in Cairo.

NEWSPAPER AND PERIODICAL SOURCES

NEWSPAPERS

Daily Chronicle
Daily Express
Daily Graphic
Daily Herald
Daily Mail
Daily Mirror
Daily News
Daily Sketch
Daily Telegraph
Morning Post
The Times
Evening Standard
Evening News
Pall Mall Gazette

Star
World's Pictorial News
Illustrated Sunday
　　Herald
Lloyd's Sunday News
News of the World
Observer
The People
The Referee
Reynolds's News
Sunday Illustrated
Sunday Pictorial
Sunday Times
Weekly Dispatch

Sunday Express
Aberdeen Press
　　& Journal
Manchester Guardian
New York Herald
(European edn)
New York Times
Le Figaro
Le Gaulois
L'Intransigeant
L'Illustration
Le Temps
Egyptian Gazette

PERIODICALS

Illustrated London
　　News

John Bull
London Mail

Tatler
Le Canard Enchaîné

INDEX